THE FILMS OF
MARTIN SCORSESE

THE FILMS OF MARTIN SCORSESE

Eric San Juan

ROWMAN & LITTLEFIELD
Lanham • Boulder • New York • London

Published by Rowman & Littlefield
An imprint of The Rowman & Littlefield Publishing Group, Inc.
4501 Forbes Boulevard, Suite 200, Lanham, Maryland 20706
www.rowman.com

6 Tinworth Street, London, SE11 5AL, United Kingdom

British Library Cataloguing in Publication Information Available

Library of Congress Cataloging-in-Publication Data

Names: San Juan, Eric, 1973– author.
Title: The films of Martin Scorsese : gangsters, greed, and guilt / Eric San Juan.
Description: Lanham : Rowman & Littlefield, [2020] | Includes bibliographical references and index. | Summary: "This volume looks at the 24 features directed by Martin Scorsese in chronological order, providing an overview with some historical context, followed by a brief synopsis, and other details per film. Eric San Juan provides an accessible analysis diving deep into the themes, techniques, and innovations of each movie."—Provided by publisher.
Identifiers: LCCN 2019059449 (print) | LCCN 2019059450 (ebook) | ISBN 9781538127650 (cloth) | ISBN 9781538127667 (epub)
Subjects: LCSH: Scorsese, Martin—Criticism and interpretation.
Classification: LCC PN1998.3.S39 S26 2020 (print) | LCC PN1998.3.S39 (ebook) | DDC 791.43023/3092—dc23
LC record available at https://lccn.loc.gov/2019059449
LC ebook record available at https://lccn.loc.gov/2019059450

CONTENTS

ACKNOWLEDGMENTS

No book is written in a vacuum. My thanks to Stephen Ryan, whose enthusiasm for the project lit a fire under me. This book would not exist had he not lobbied for it. I am also in debt to Jim McDevitt, whose frank feedback and thorough reading helped me improve every single page. His work was tireless and his friendship unerring, and for that I am grateful.

Thanks also to Cary Christopher, whose eagle eyes were a big help in correcting the text, and to Eric Preston and John Zarate, whose early feedback helped me refine the chapter on *Raging Bull*. And thanks to Robert San Juan for taking a road trip with me to see *The Irishman*.

Immense gratitude is also given to the giants on whose shoulders I stand. The journalism and film criticism of Roger Ebert, Richard Schickel, Amy Taubin, and many others not only proved a valuable resource in researching this book, but it also helped guide the way for all who have followed in their footsteps.

And finally, thanks to Martin Scorsese for creating the masterpieces this book examines. They have been engaging, enlightening, and endlessly entertaining.

INTRODUCTION

Few mainstream filmmakers have as pronounced a disregard for the supposed rules of filmmaking as Martin Scorsese. His inventiveness displays a reaction against the "right" way to make a movie, frequently eschewing traditional cinematic language in favor of something flashy and unexpected and contrary to the way "proper" films are done. Yet despite copious voice-over, freeze-frames, fast cuts, and dizzying editing, he's become one of the most influential directors of the last fifty years, a critical darling (though rarely a box office titan), and a fan favorite. That makes his body of work ripe fodder for a broad, movie-by-movie analysis.

Scorsese is perhaps the most unpredictable auteur of the last fifty years. His best-loved work tends toward violence and kinetic energy and innovative use of popular songs, but he's much more than mobsters and mayhem and music. He constantly surprises. From charming children's fables to somber meditations on the nature of faith, period pieces, sprawling biopics, music documentaries, and (of course) gritty crime dramas, few directors with as singular a vision as his can boast such varied work. He's even an award-winning documentary filmmaker, with more than a dozen documentary films to his name (though this work is beyond the purview of this book).

Yet he *does* have a singular vision. Dig deep, and you find a connective tissue that ties his work together, a distinct sensibility that, despite its eclectic nature, makes his movies uniquely *Martin Scorsese*. In the pages ahead, I explore that connective tissue, pick apart the themes that tie it all together, and celebrate the work of one of cinema's greatest directors. I look at the con men, the criminals, the gangsters, the moguls, and the nobodies of his filmography. I examine the techniques that have made him stand out as one of the most innovative directors in history: the needle-drop soundtracks, the outbursts of violence, the daring camera work, and more. And I look at the themes that are ultimately the engine driving all of this: themes of self-sabotage, of alienation, of faith, and of guilt.

To fully understand the well from which Martin Scorsese's work is drawn, it's first important to understand Scorsese himself because the best of the director's work is often deeply personal. Born in 1942 in Queens, New York, his family moved to the Little Italy section of the city when he was still young. His parents, Charles and Catherine, were both working-class children of Italian immigrants who labored in the city's garment district. Due to severe asthma as a child, young Marty (as his friends still call him) did not play sports or have much physical fun. Instead, he observed life on the streets from his apartment window. Watching from above gave Scorsese a bird's-eye view of the people who populated his neighborhood: how they interacted, the subtle power dynamics at play, and more. Going to the movies with his father was his primary exposure to the wider world outside the city. And it was a *lot* of movies. If it hit the screen, they saw it, and he soaked it all in. These two formative experiences helped him think visually when it came to expressing his observations to others. "My movie camera really goes right back to when I was raised on the Lower East Side. Because of asthma and other reasons . . . I had to sometimes distance myself. The objectivity was almost like using a movie camera," he once said.[1]

You can't separate Martin Scorsese from his Little Italy upbringing, either. The two are inextricably intertwined. Those he observed from that apartment window were working-class people, often poor, and street crime was a normal part of what he saw. As he entered his teen years, he became part of that world, albeit from a distance. In his neighborhood, trading words on the street with someone could result in a fight or worse. Scorsese himself was never a full-blown street crook, but he ran with some hell-raisers in his youth, as depicted in semi-autobiographical films like *Who's That Knocking at My Door?* and *Mean Streets*. Witnessing those street conflicts, verbal or otherwise, became an essential building block of his work.

For all the music and violence and style of his films, Scorsese's work is very much about *people*: what drives them; what consumes them; what obsesses them; and perhaps most important of all, what fills them with guilt. Of all the human traits that run through his work, self-destructive tendencies and the guilt that comes with them are arguably the most notable. It may be a stereotype to associate this with the director's Catholicism, but Scorsese himself sees the two as being linked, and indeed, as the oft-repeated story goes, as a teen he once considered becoming a priest. Though he long ago abandoned that potential career path, Catholicism never left him. Faith and all the contradictions that come with it have always been a vital part of his worldview:

> It's always in you. My search for faith has never really ended from when I became aware that there was such a thing as faith and started to look at how it's acted out in your daily life. It's in *Mean Streets* and it's in *Taxi Driver* and it's in *Raging Bull*, ultimately. And then *The Last Temptation of Christ* was a major step for me in trying to come to terms with these themes, these ideas of the Incarnation of Christ—what does it really mean?[2]

That his faith has been an important part of his life is unsurprising, given his upbringing in Little Italy of the 1940s, '50s, and '60s. Today, the neighborhood is just a small tourist trap with a smattering of restaurants and shops spread over a few blocks of New York City's Mulberry Street, but at one time it was a thriving community filled with Italian immigrants. Celebrations of faith were part of the lifeblood of the community. Religious iconography was everywhere. Going to church was just an expected part of life. Overall, the neighborhood and its people molded and shaped him, helping develop the sensibility that would make him a cinematic innovator who has always felt a little askew from the traditional Hollywood he loved. But eventually, he'd move on.

In the 1960s, he attended New York University, earning a bachelor's in English and his master of fine arts degree in film. There he made several short films, including an infamous anti–Vietnam War short called *The Big Shave* (1967) that featured a man shaving his way to self-mutilation. In 1967, he directed his first feature-length film, *I Call First*, which stars Harvey Keitel and was edited by Thelma Schoonmaker, both of whom would become integral to his work. *I Call First* would later get additional footage and be retitled *Who's That Knocking at My Door?* becoming his first theatrical release. The picture received a glowing review from a young film critic called Roger Ebert. As Scorsese and Ebert grew in stature in their respective fields, Ebert would become perhaps the most notable Scorsese booster on the planet, dubbing him our greatest living director.

And so a career was born. By now the rest of the details are familiar to most. A long-running creative collaboration with Robert De Niro resulted in a string of classics, including *Taxi Driver*, *Raging Bull*, and *GoodFellas*, regarded by many as the best in their respective decades. The director built a reputation on kinetic violence and invented the needle-drop popular music movie soundtrack style that today is an essential part of what makes movies by filmmakers like Quentin Tarantino, James Gunn, and others so exciting. After years as an outsider, he's now hailed as one of the greatest directors of all time, joining the ranks of the very luminaries he used to idolize—all from a skinny Italian kid in a little apartment in New York City.

So what makes Martin Scorsese movies tick? What can we learn from them about cinema and, more specifically, about Martin Scorsese himself? In the arts, a common area of debate is whether we can separate the art from the artist, but a more apt question is, *should* we separate the art from the artist? The answer to the former is an unequivocal yes. You can watch *GoodFellas* with no real idea who Martin Scorsese is, why he is important, and how his experience informed the movie, and it's still going to be a dynamic picture, visceral and truthful and a flight of pure, dark, supremely entertaining fantasy. How the art on-screen makes you feel requires no knowledge of its creator. It succeeds because it's a brilliant piece of work that operates on multiple levels, with surface-level style and the depth of gripping character exploration. So yes, you can separate the art from the artist.

But *should* we? That's a larger question. Context is important. Understanding where a work comes from allows us a more profound understanding of what that work *is*. It provides a framework from which to gain further insights into what a movie is trying to say. Scorsese's films can be appreciated without knowing anything about him, yes, but when put in the context of who he is and what he has experienced—his upbringing, his neuroses, his obsessions, his fascinations, his formative years, the highs and lows of his life, his influences, his insecurities, the music he loves, the books he reads—one gains a richer understanding of exactly what makes these movies tick. The sense of anger, isolation, and rebellion in early works like *Taxi Driver*; *New York, New York*; and *Raging Bull* are reflections of Scorsese at that time in his life. The exploration of film history and the desire to leave behind a legacy in *Hugo* or dwelling on the past in *The Irishman* is all the richer when seen with an understanding of who Scorsese was when he made them. *The Last Temptation of Christ*'s quest to understand its titular character is more potent when you recognize the director's own personal journey of faith, not to mention the long struggles he had trying to make the picture, and so on.

Most important in all this is that Martin Scorsese is a man brimming with *questions*: questions about who we are, what compels us to act the way we do, how we could be corrupted, or how we can corrupt ourselves. Scorsese pictures are typified by many things—creative camera work, antihero characters, swift violence, and copious profanity, among other traits already mentioned—but at their heart, what Scorsese pictures are really about are exploring the human condition, particularly the darker parts of ourselves that lead us toward self-destruction. It's a theme seen repeatedly in his work: Men who have everything fall apart around them as a result of their own actions. "I like to chart a character like that," Scorsese said, "see how far they go before they self-destruct."[3] It's seen over and over, from *Raging Bull* to *GoodFellas*, *Casino*, *The Wolf of Wall Street*, and more.

Scorsese's characters are richer, more believable, and more *alive* in no small part because he is an actor's director. He is unusual among the ranks of auteurs in that his process is so collaborative in nature. Actors love working with him, not merely for the prestige, but also because he affords them so much creative freedom. "Of all the directors I've worked with, Marty is the best at providing an atmosphere where actors can do their best work. He trusts actors and involves them," Ellen Burstyn once said.[4] Many of his best-known scenes were created through improvisation, either on camera or during rehearsal sessions, that are then fine-tuned for the camera. Joe Pesci's "funny" scene from *Good-Fellas*, De Niro's famous "You talking to me?" monologue in *Taxi Driver*, Pesci and De Niro's final argument in *Raging Bull*, Matthew McConaughey's strange chants in *The Wolf of Wall Street*, and many others sprang from the creative freedom he affords his actors. "Marty loves that on the set, when an actor does something that's not expected, or something that just *happened* to happen. He loves that, he capitalizes on it. He says, 'Oh, that's great. Let's go further with that,'" Schoonmaker said of him. "Accidents are very important."[5]

He lets the characters speak for themselves, too, in a technique often frowned upon in screenwriting classes but that he uses throughout his filmography: voice-over. Narration is the exception in Hollywood, not the norm, but in Scorsese's hands it becomes just another tool in his vast arsenal. "There's something interesting about voiceover," he said. "It lets you in on the secret thoughts of the characters, or secret observations by an omniscient viewer. And for me it has a wonderful comforting tone of someone telling you a story."[6]

To some extent, there is a narrative tying these pictures together that reflects on the sweep of Scorsese's life and career. Each chapter ahead suggests angles from which to see any given film and sometimes aids in seeing each movie in the context of Scorsese's life and career. This is *not* a biography. Little time is spent on the intimate details of the director's life. Nonetheless, the broad beats often come up when they pertain to his art, whether it's his early life in Little Italy, his struggles with drugs in the 1970s, his self-doubts in the 1980s, his series of rocky marriages and relationships, or his examinations of the idea of legacy in the latter parts of his career. When these topics come up, it's because they're important to a specific film, they provide key context to understanding a creative period of his life, or they help us understand an essential theme in his work.

There are a handful of ideas that come up repeatedly because they are themes that permeate the director's entire body of work. Some are obvious, as they've been touched on in pretty much every Scorsese analysis ever written. His use of music and the raw way in which he depicts violence are two obvious examples, though I do not linger on either. The subject of guilt is near unavoidable when taking a deep dive into the director's catalog, fueled by his devoutly Catholic upbringing and the self-doubt he grappled with as a young filmmaker. Greed, sour relationships, and operating on the wrong side of the law are also common themes. So, too, are protagonists who are the architects of their own downfalls, a topic I return to repeatedly. Scorsese has long been fascinated with rise-and-fall stories, tales of people who seem to have it all and then lose it. *Raging Bull*, *GoodFellas*, *The Wolf of Wall Street*, and others all deal with this, but a more telling element is not merely the rise and fall aspect of these stories; it's how the fall is usually the protagonist's own fault.

My goal is to get to the beating heart of his work. More than for the sake of organization, this is why I discuss his films in chronological order. That's how I have done previous works on the movies of Akira Kurosawa and (with author Jim McDevitt) Alfred Hitchcock, and that trend continues here.

There is value in viewing and analyzing the films of a single director in chronological order. Certainly, any picture can be appreciated and examined on its own, but when seen in the context in which it was made, when fit snugly between the film that came before and the one that came after, we get not just a greater appreciation of the circumstances that led to the finished work being what it is but also a clearer picture of why certain artistic choices may have been made. Movies are not created in a vacuum, after all. *The Last Temptation of Christ*, for example, is not the sparse, ragged picture it is because Scorsese intended it to be. It was an artistic decision made of necessity, driven by budget limitations and the long struggle to get it made in the first place. The preceding picture, *The Color of Money*, was made in large part to prove to Hollywood executives that he could still make them money after a series of box-office failures. *The Age of Innocence* would likely look much different without the director's previous experiment in making a mainstream thriller (*Cape Fear*). *The Aviator* happened in part because he liked working with Leonardo DiCaprio so much on *Gangs of New York*, and so on.

In assessing a film's critical success, I often cite the Academy Award nominations it received. To be clear, this is not an indication that a movie's worth is measured by Oscars. The Oscars have only as much value as an individual places in them. As a metric they are no more or less worthy than any other. Still, in Hollywood the Academy Awards are *the* award, the most prestigious of all the major award ceremonies and the one most followed by the industry and public alike. Further, much like legends Alfred Hitchcock and Stanley Kubrick, Scorsese's history with the Oscars was at times a rocky one. Until winning for 2006's *The Departed*, Scorsese had been nominated for Best Director five times and was denied five times (for *Raging Bull*, *The Last Temptation of Christ*, *GoodFellas*, *Gangs of New York*, and *The Aviator*). He'd subsequently go on to be nominated for *Hugo* and *The Wolf of Wall Street*, and the buzz as of this writing is that a nomination for *The Irishman* is likely. Prior to that, it seemed he would receive the same epic snub as Hitchcock and Kubrick, who were nominated five and four times, respectively, but never won. I cite his award nominations at various times in this book, But this should not be read as a suggestion that the Academy Awards hold any significance beyond an industry and cultural one. They do not speak to artistic worth as much as they speak to industry recognition—and because Scorsese has always thought of himself as an outsider working within the Hollywood system, it's an angle worth touching on. And for what it's worth, he agrees: "I wish I could be like some of the other guys and say, 'No, I don't care about it.' But for me, a kid growing up on the Lower East Side watching from the first telecast of the Oscars, and being obsessed by movies, there's a certain magic that's there."[7]

Similarly, I often mention a movie's budget and box-office take. This isn't because either say much about a picture's worth as a piece of art—they don't—but rather because the hunt for funding has so often played a major role in the creative choices he was able to make. *Raging Bull* would not have happened if *New York, New York* did not flop, for example. *Cape Fear* was a commercial obligation that, once successful, allowed him to do *Kundun*. His final epic, *The Irishman*, would not have happened without Netflix stepping in with funding, and so on.

In the pages ahead, each chapter opens with an overview that provides some historical context for the movie, a brief synopsis, and other details. The meat of each chapter is the analysis. Usually focused on a central thesis related to the film, each takes a deep dive into the themes, techniques, and innovations of the movie in question, noting what sets them apart and what makes them worthy of study. Finally, a conclusion looks briefly at the impact, if any, of the film and how it sets the stage for Scorsese's next work.

There is a lot to delve into here. On the surface, Scorsese's work is typified by shocking violence and rampant profanity. These are often loud, brash films that appear to glorify the worst kinds of people. He makes heroes of mobsters, thugs, con men, and murderers. Yet dig deeper, and you find the true beating heart of his oeuvre: guilt, collapse, self-destruction, spiritual turmoil, and the complicated hypocrisies of faith, among other themes that are a constant in his work. What is Martin Scorsese trying to tell us? Or rather, what is it bubbling out of his subconscious that gives rise to these ideas in gangster movies, historical epics, biopics, and more? Perhaps it's his devoutly Catholic upbringing. Perhaps it's that he came of age in the turbulent tenements of mid-twentieth-century New York City. Perhaps it's an expression of his own often-insecure place in the Hollywood hierarchy, where, for all his critical success, he's often been seen as a financial risk for studio heads. Or perhaps he just wants to tell us that, despite surface-level stereotypes, human beings are far more complex than they first appear. This book offers no definitive answers, but hopefully it offers you fodder for your own discussions, dissections, and debates. And that's probably exactly as Martin Scorsese would want it.

1

WHO'S THAT KNOCKING AT MY DOOR? (1967)

FILM DETAILS

RELEASE DATE: November 15, 1967

WRITTEN BY: Martin Scorsese

STARRING: Harvey Keitel, Zina Bethune

RUNNING TIME: 90 minutes

ADDITIONAL NOTES: Initially made in 1965 as a student short film called *Bring on the Dancing Girls*, it was expanded in 1967 to a full-length film titled *I Call First*. It was also released in 1970 as *J. R.*

ABOUT THE FILM

It would be neither an insult nor inaccurate to call Martin Scorsese's debut picture a glorified student film. As a student at New York University's Tisch School of the Arts, Scorsese produced several shorts, and not long after his 1966 graduation, he made *The Big Shave* (1967), a six-minute short notorious for its graphic (for its time) self-mutilation. Shortly thereafter, he finished his first feature-length, *I Call First*. It stars fellow film student Harvey Keitel in a role loosely based on Scorsese himself. He also enlisted the help of another film student, Thelma Schoonmaker, to edit the picture. In a brief filmmaking class, Schoonmaker had previously assisted the director with one of his shorts, *What's a Nice Girl Like You Doing in a Place Like This?* so he drafted her to edit his first full feature. Neither realized at the time they would be forming one of the most fruitful creative partnerships in cinema history. That feature-length work would eventually become *Who's That Knocking at My Door?*—an independent and deeply personal debut that, though rough around the edges, helped establish many of the core ideas, themes, and techniques that would come to define Martin Scorsese's career.

Who's That Knocking follows the story of J. R. (Keitel), a young man living an aimless life of drinking with friends, engaging in petty crime, and subconsciously sabotaging relationships. The picture was an evolving piece of work from the start, beginning in 1965 as a short film called *Bring on the Dancing Girls*. That version centered on nothing more than J. R. and his friends partying. Scorsese continued to revise and expand. By 1967, a female character called the Girl was introduced—played by Zina Bethune, the character is never given a name—and J. R.'s struggles with romance became the story's focal point. With the new title *I Call First*, this is the version Roger Ebert saw and praised at the Chicago International Film Festival, the first wider attention Scorsese received as a director. But despite Ebert's praise, his film was still mired in obscurity.

In 1968, his shot at getting a distribution deal finally arrived, but in order to secure the deal, he was asked to add more sex to the movie. He complied, and the film became *Who's That Knocking at My Door?* (Even that wasn't the final title. For a 1970 reissue, the picture was renamed *J. R.*, though the name would not stick.) The result was a picture that immediately laid out many of the techniques and themes that would come to define Martin Scorsese's work.

ANALYSIS

Who's That Knocking at My Door? does not set out to deliver a tight narrative. In fact, the plot is thin to nonexistent. J. R. lives a raucous lifestyle, partying (often dangerously) with friends. He meets the Girl and falls for her. She reveals she had previously been raped, and upset that she isn't a virgin, J. R. ends the relationship. He comes to regret it, but by then it's too late. That's the entire movie.

Like so many student films, this is an experimental and personal movie, a small window into the mind of the director but distorted here and there to make it fiction. Many of the hallmarks of Scorsese's work appear for the first time, already fully formed: the use of popular music to punctuate a scene, freeze-frames, an uncompromising look at life on the wrong side of the law, uneasy relationships with women, internalized guilt, and a subconscious penchant for self-destructive behavior.

Even at this early stage, it's easy to recognize Scorsese's unique touch. His use of music is a big tell. The film opens on an Italian mother in the kitchen, her poor family in an apartment with crumbling walls. A pulsing, repetitive beat clangs in the background like some precursor to modern industrial music, a genre characterized by harsh, mechanical percussion and abrasive instrumentation. This out-of-left-field choice tells us we're in a working-class neighborhood where men break their backs for a living while women toil away for their families in cramped apartments. The contrast between the Italian home life and the percussive soundtrack seems to suggest there is something fighting to break free from the shackles of family life. When the soundtrack switches moments later to "Jenny Take a Ride," a bouncy 1966 rock-and-roll track by the nearly forgotten Mitch Ryder and the Detroit Wheels, the danceable tune is paired with young men knocking one another around for no discernible reason. The music is free-wheeling. Carefree. *Fun.* But the imagery is not. The violence is senseless. This contrast, this idea of making a party scene out of brutality, somehow makes the violence seem all the more primal. It's a technique Scorsese would go on to use masterfully over the next fifty years.

At the same time, Scorsese's choices as far as narrative and continuity are concerned have an art-school looseness about them, shifting from thought to thought and mood to mood in exactly the way you'd expect from a film cobbled together over the course of three years. Though it frequently teeters on the edge of falling apart, he'd later learn to rein in these sudden mood swings and harness them for greatness. When the story of Jake LaMotta's life swings from a whisper in an apartment to a roar in the ring, when Henry Hill's veers from cool gangster hustle to frantic paranoia, Scorsese taps into an approach he first explored in his very first feature film. He does this with sound as often as he does with visuals and editing, too, if not more so. Early on we see J. R. take notice of the Girl. There is a quick cut to a shot of them in conversation, but the shot is silent. It's not immediately evident if this is a memory, a flash-forward, or J. R. daydreaming about what kind of smooth talk he'd deliver in order to pick her up. This manipulation of sound to suggest a warped state of mind, to suggest desire, interest, even obsession, is used again to great effect in *Raging Bull*, where LaMotta often seems out of sync with the world around him when he's observing his wife, Vickie. (And that's just one example.) It's just one of many techniques seen here in embryonic form and later used to greater effect in better movies.

Who's That Knocking can be dizzying, leaping back and forth in time, jumping from scene to scene in ways that sometimes make you question whether you're seeing reality or something in J. R.'s imagination. Is he imagining talking to the Girl, or is this a real conversation? The answer is not always clear. At one point the film shifts from date night at a movie to a series of druggy sexual liaisons with unnamed women, then back to the date again, the sex scene coming midconversation while J. R. waxes philosophical about the difference between women and "broads." You only fool around with some women, he tells the Girl. "You don't marry a broad." Scorsese's utter disregard for clear continuity borders on the extreme here, a boldness that demands trust from the audience. But these are all affectations, techniques the director would come to use more effectively in later pictures. More important than his stylistic choices is what he chooses to *say* with this film.

Scorsese has called *Who's That Knocking at My Door?* semiautobiographical, at least insomuch as it depicts a time, place, and way of thinking. At the very least, there is no doubt that the director sometimes speaks through J. R. The character discusses film in obsessive and often insightful detail, name-drops *The Searchers*, discusses Lee Marvin as a villain, and generally shows a fascination with what makes film work. (A later montage celebrates John Wayne's *Rio Bravo*.) Can there be any question that this is Scorsese showing through the character? That the film itself is rooted in the director's real-life upbringing, immersing us in the grit of New York's Italian neighborhoods of the era, lends further credibility to the idea that much of Keitel's character is a reflection of Scorsese himself. And indeed, "That's me," he told film critic Richard Schickel.[1] Much of it is, yes, though given the attitudes on display late in the film one wonders if Scorsese would want to lay claim to *all* of J. R.'s character traits.

That Bethune's character is simply named "The Girl" is telling. Though she is vital to the film's (sparse) narrative and its exploration of J. R.'s emotional maturity or lack thereof, her existence as an individual *doesn't matter*. Or more accurately, it doesn't matter to J. R. She could be anyone. Her individual wants, her individual needs and experiences, the things that make her a person rather than a puzzle piece to fill a void in his life—none of these things are important to him. (It's important to note that Scorsese himself does not agree with this interpretation of J. R.'s character.)

J. R.'s deeper character flaws are not evident at first. He is charming and likeable. Sure, the people he hangs around with are rough, often criminally so, but he's young and handsome and charismatic, and he loves to talk. In an early meeting between him and the Girl, the camera slowly moves back and forth between them, luxuriating in their long conversation, allowing us to be as charmed by him as she is. If there is darkness within him, we don't see it. *He* does, though. He sees his own darkness. He recognizes his own flaws, or perhaps more accurately, he's plagued by the notion that he is flawed beyond repair, a deeply internalized guilt that has no root or source. It's just *there*.

In the first feature for both Scorsese and Harvey Keitel, Keitel and Zina Bethune depict the first of many rocky relationships in Scorsese's filmography. *Warner Bros./Photofest*

And so we come to another hallmark of the Scorsese filmography: religion; faith; and most important of all, guilt (usually of the Catholic variety). The religious imagery, tainted spirituality, and Catholic guilt that run through so much of the director's work is fully formed from the outset of his career. J. R. and the Girl first kiss in front of Catholic iconography, falling onto the bed together, with religious imagery decorating the room. There is an aching quality to their passion; it's close and tender and vulnerable, shown in extreme close-ups yet never explicit. It's not *chaste* exactly, but neither is it sexual. It is deeply intimate. Perhaps that's why J. R. pulls away and stops before they make love. "Not now," he tells her. She wonders why. He won't offer her a reason, simply saying that he is old-fashioned: "If you love me, you'll understand what I mean." (During this scene, we see J. R. slip off the bed, then there is a cut, and we see him get off the bed a second time, one of the earliest instances where Scorsese's disregard for continuity shows itself.)

Calling J. R. old-fashioned is generous. His views on women are antiquated. That's not merely by twenty-first-century standards, either. Even in the 1960s, his notion that women are either mothers or whores was falling by the wayside. The so-called sexual revolution was coming into bloom, yet J. R. wants purity from the Girl. He wants to sleep with her but doesn't want her to *want* to sleep with him. If she desires sex in the same way he does, then she is impure. He believes she is a virgin and wants her to stay that way. That he later fantasizes about sleeping with a series of nameless women doesn't make *him* impure, of course. His standards do not apply to men.

(This sex montage, set to the sound of "The End" by the Doors, was shot well after the film was completed and was inserted at the behest of Joseph Brenner, a distributor of exploitation films. He told the director he needed sex to sell the picture, so Scorsese obliged. It remains to this day one of the most gratuitous scenes of the director's career, though as he points out, "That's the only way we could get it distributed."[2])

The views on purity held by Keitel's character are what ultimately lead to his relationship failing and his return to the streets. One evening, the pair talk, and the Girl reveals a terrible secret to him: She had been raped by a former boyfriend. She and her ex went out on a night drive. They parked and made out, and then he violently raped her. It's a secret burden she's been carrying. Rather than react with sympathy or love or comfort, however, J. R. reacts with disgust and disbelief, dismissing the story as false and breaking up with her right after hearing it.

J. R.'s reaction compounds her victimhood, and the sense of mounting disgust we feel is twisted into something even more grotesque by Scorsese's use of music. She tells her story, then we flashback to the incident and see it for ourselves. It's a normal date: a classic scene, a young boyfriend and girlfriend in the car, practically an American cliché. The scene is set to the romantic doo-wop tune "Don't Ask Me to Be Lonely" by the Dubs. But then the boyfriend gets aggressive. He wants to go further than she is willing. The music begins to distort, the song slowing and slurring, folding in on itself as her quiet date does the same. The scene becomes violent and ugly. It would be disturbing even without the music, but few directors in cinema have ever been as gifted at making musical choices as Martin Scorsese, and here the choice lifts the scene from exploitative to masterfully difficult to watch, a stark lesson in contrasts that shows how quickly our sense of peace can be shattered by a bold musical choice.

That the scene is so grotesque makes J. R.'s callous reaction to what she went through all the worse. He is angry at her. He does not believe her. "How can I believe that story? It just doesn't make any sense. How do I know you didn't go through the same story with him?" he asks. "You let him take you out on some goddamn road, and you don't mind it? It just doesn't seem real, does it? It just doesn't make any sense."

She is understandably crushed. That he is upset about her lack of "purity" is an antiquated enough idea, but it's an honest one in its depiction of Italian American mores of that time and place. For the audience, we're not just struck by his insensitivity. We also realize she never truly meant anything to him. How could she, if this is how he reacts? Much like the religious iconography he surrounds himself with, she is a symbol and little more. Her reality is meaningless to him except to the extent that it serves him.

As noted earlier, however, Scorsese doesn't see it this way. He sees J. R. as torn between his Catholic ideas of virtue and genuine love for the Girl. He says the idea is of "being in love with a girl who is an outsider, loving her so much that you respect her and you won't make love to her. Then he finds out she's not a virgin and he can't accept that. It's that whole Italian-American way of thinking, of feeling."[3]

Yet J. R. isn't merely refusing to accept that she isn't a virgin; he's ignoring that she was *raped*. He even goes as far as to suggest the story is fabricated. This is more than a divide based on differing ideas of virtue. Roger Ebert observed, "He is unable to reconcile his image of her purity with the fact she exists in a sinful world, and has been an innocent victim of it."[4] And indeed, that is the crux of J. R.'s tremendous character flaw: The Girl is a victim, and she is being victimized a second time by J. R. himself.

Following their breakup, J. R.'s return to the world of partying and carousing is hollow and empty. He drinks. He and his buddies blast music and roughhouse. They flirt with girls. In one partying scene, Scorsese cuts in quick freeze-frames of the Girl's rape, suggesting that the stark reality of what happened to her isn't something he can truly dismiss. It gets under his skin, but what understanding he comes to have remains a selfish one. His thoughts are with himself, not with the pain she went through.

When he goes to her and apologizes, it's not an apology at all. He says he is sorry but quickly tries to make out with her. "I understand now, and I forgive you," he tells her. "I'm going to marry you anyway." The Girl is as floored by this reaction as the viewer is. What is he forgiving her for, exactly? He's going to marry her "anyway," as if he's being noble by accepting what he sees as damaged goods? The realization that J. R. isn't the man she thought he was is painful. She knows she can't marry him. Her rape will forever shadow them. "You'll always find a way to bring it up," she says.

And she's right. He insists otherwise, but a slip of the tongue proves her point. He accidentally calls her a "broad," a callback to their previous conversation. He tells her, "I feel the way any reasonable guy would feel," but she isn't buying it, so he takes the route of the stereotypical rejected nice guy and starts to call her a whore. There is no future in this relationship, and the blame rests entirely on his shoulders. Like so many Scorsese protagonists, J. R. is the architect of his own self-destruction.

The film wraps with upbeat music—the song is "Who's That Knocking at My Door?" by the Genies—and rapid-fire Catholic imagery: statues and the Virgin Mary and close depictions of Jesus's bleeding wounds. J. R. kisses a statue of Christ on the feet, and J. R.'s mouth bleeds. Images flash of a woman's leg being fondled, then pantyhose being torn and muffled howls of pain. A cut to J. R. and his friend on a city street. "All right, talk to you tomorrow. See you later," they say, and on that nonchalant note, the film ends. It's as if all the emotional trauma had never happened.

There is a great deal of honesty in that ending, the emptiness of it, the suggestions of lingering guilt that J. R. doesn't have the emotional maturity to confront, much less to fully grasp. All his macho bravado is just a wall around him. He seeks penance. He seeks forgiveness. But he's not even sure what he's seeking forgiveness *for*, which makes his efforts all the emptier.

CONCLUSION AND IMPACT

Scorsese is not kind to this film, though that hardly makes him unusual. Artists are often their own harshest critics, and this being his first feature-length movie, it's not surprising that he sees it for what it is: an early but flawed piece of work. "*Who's That Knocking* I never got right, except for the emotional aspects of it—I got that," Scorsese said. "I dislike it. Only because it took me three years to make."[5]

Who's That Knocking at My Door? premiered at the Chicago International Film Festival in November 1967 and quickly won accolades from Roger Ebert, who said it made a "stunning impact" and was a "great moment in American movies."[6] It would be Scorsese's first taste of acclaim. He was just twenty-five.

And though imperfect, it proved to be a clear statement of vision that provided an early sketch of what would inform the next fifty years of Martin Scorsese pictures. He'd return to this familiar territory in 1973 with *Mean Streets*, but before getting there, he'd first get a taste for corporate filmmaking through an unlikely source: exploitation film legend Roger Corman.

2

BOXCAR BERTHA
(1972)

FILM DETAILS

RELEASE DATE: June 14, 1972
WRITTEN BY: Joyce H. Corrington, John William Corrington
STARRING: Barbara Hershey, David Carradine, Barry Primus, Bernie Casey,
John Carradine
RUNNING TIME: 87 minutes

ABOUT THE FILM

When you are a struggling young artist, you have to take any opportunity you can get. Such was the case when Martin Scorsese was hired by legendary exploitation director and producer Roger Corman, who built a legacy filling the screen with bullets, blood, booze, and boobs. Given their wildly differing sensibilities, in retrospect it seems an unlikely pairing.

Corman brought a slew of films to the screen throughout the '50s and '60s, most low-budget affairs and many with gloriously trashy titles like *Night of the Blood Beast* (1956) and *Attack of the Giant Leeches* (1959). He enjoyed some genuine critical and commercial successes during those early years, too, including 1958's gritty noir *Machine-Gun Kelly*, which helped launch Charles Bronson into stardom; *House of Usher* (1960), starring Vincent Price, one of eight Edgar Allan Poe adaptations directed by Corman; and *The Wild Angels*

(1966), which received lukewarm reviews but which prompted star Peter Fonda to make *Easy Rider* (1969), one of the most influential films of the era.

Corman also had a minor hit in 1970 with *Bloody Mama*, a low-budget crime drama featuring Shelley Winters as a mother who organizes her sons into a crime syndicate. (Playing one of her sons in none other than Robert De Niro in one of his earliest roles.) On the heels of its success, Corman decided to make another female-led crime film. He came across *Sister of the Road: The Autobiography of Boxcar Bertha*, a novel by anarchist Ben Rietman about a female criminal called Bertha Thompson. Chock-full of sex, violence, and counterculture politics, the story was ideal fodder for Corman's edgy sensitivities. He'd serve as producer. All he needed was a director.

He found one in Martin Scorsese. *Who's That Knocking at My Door*'s uncompromising grit caught his eye, and Scorsese wanted to work, and so a brief union was born. Filmed in just twenty-four days and starring Barbara Hershey and David Carradine, who were dating at the time, the movie is what you'd expect from a Corman-produced picture—there is no shortage of bullets, blood, booze, or boobs—but with the earnestness of a young Scorsese.

From an artistic standpoint, *Boxcar Bertha* is not an important film in Scorsese's oeuvre, telling us little about his sensibilities as a filmmaker and the themes that would come to dominate his work, but it's at the very least a *fun* picture with a delightfully twisted performance by Hershey and just enough directorial flair to make it worth a visit. It also proved to be an integral step in the director's career, prompting him to have a clearer idea of the kind of films he did and did not want to pursue.

The movie tells the story of "Boxcar" Bertha Thompson (Hershey), a wild young woman with disdain for authority who falls for "Big" Bill Shelley (Carradine), a Robin Hood–like train robber who wants to smash Depression-era railroad barons and uplift workers ground down by life on the rails. The pair become fugitives, tearing their way through the railroad, robbing the wealthy, sparking worker rebellions, and evading the law until they can't run anymore. In a bloody climax, Bill is killed, and Bertha is left alone. So while exploitation is not exactly Scorsese's typical fare, it does concern criminals and violence, two things he would become a master of presenting.

ANALYSIS

Boxcar Bertha opens and closes with a young woman losing a man she loves. Between those two losses, she spends her time stealing and murdering, so in a way, this is a movie about pained rage.

The first shot is a deep close-up of a pair of eyes looking overhead, so close it calls to mind the work of Sergio Leone, whose *The Good, The Bad, and The Ugly* (1966) still influences directors today. Those eyes are looking at a plane flying overhead. It's young Bertha's father, who, pushed to work by his railroad bosses despite unsafe equipment, crashes and dies. The crash is all fast cuts and violent impacts, terribly cheap looking but effective. This is our introduction to Bertha. She is young, and her smile lights up the screen, but she is portrayed with such sweet innocence by Hershey that the titillating way in which she's depicted often feels *wrong* somehow. But that's part of the point. That contrast, that contradiction between her girlish exterior and her ruthless interior, is how Bertha is able to spearhead an anarcho-crime spree, and it's what makes watching her take on the corrupt Depression-era railroad barons so perversely delightful.

This is a Corman production, though, so even scenes of female empowerment are prone to be tainted with exploitation. When Bertha and her love interest, Big Bill Shelley, first get together, he pushes himself on her. She resists at first, but an old cliché rears its ugly head, and she soon finds herself enjoying his aggressive advances. That's how their on-again, off-again romance begins. It never advances much further than that, either.

Sex is a powerful means of controlling or manipulating Scorsese's antiheroes—Vickie (Cathy Moriarty) in *Raging Bull*, Karen (Lorraine Bracco) in *Good-Fellas*, Ginger (Sharon Stone) in *Casino*, to name a few—but his ant-heroes rarely ever *are* women. Whether it's Bertha doing the controlling is questionable, too. Bill and the others largely follow her lead, despite her actions being more than a little unhinged, but if there is an obsessed party in the relationship, it is Bertha herself. Typically, it's Scorsese's men falling over themselves for women. Here, it's the woman who seems driven by a love or obsession (or both) for a man.

After her introduction and encounter with Bill, Bertha goes on the road. She meets up with a Yankee gambler, Rake Brown (Barry Primus), who gets caught cheating at a card game. One of the gamblers rants about "reds," the supposed communist menace, and she kills him. Later, Bill's name comes up in conversation. For the railroad barons and their supporters, he's seen as a villain; a communist sympathizer; and, in their words, a "nigger lover" (one of many times the word is used in the film). Bertha and Rake then bounce around, disrupting the railroad and bringing attention to themselves. A healthy amount of crime and chaos follow.

Interestingly, Big Bill and his allies are not committing crimes for selfish ends; they are doing so with a cause: They are fighting for workers' rights. Bertha, on the other hand, is doing it purely out of sadistic joy. And she ends up the ringleader of this band of outlaws.

Bertha may have an unhealthy obsession with Bill, but her influence over him is undeniable. His enemies note that "he gets his orders from a broad." He's not always comfortable with the direction she points them in, either. At one point he tells her, "I ain't used to this kind of life." Though he is seen as the leader of a growing antiestablishment movement fighting for workers' rights, in truth she is the instigator behind his worst deeds. He follows her lead. They all do. His motivation truly is justice—at one point while robbing a party filled with rich folks, he says, "I don't want your watch. . . . I just want to smash a railroad"— but Bertha cares less for social justice. The thrill of the chaos she causes seems to be what drives her.

The finale is a riot of absurd bloodshed, bullets blazing, men flying through the air. It would be campy if Scorsese didn't treat the material seriously, and even then, it flirts with camp. Bill is badly wounded in the action and is nailed to the side of a boxcar like a crucifixion—that sounds quite *Scorsese*, but it was actually in the script before he came onboard—and the train rolls away as Bertha runs after it, until finally it rumbles off into the distance, leaving her alone. With the only person she ever loved other than her father gone, the credits roll. When Bertha lost her father, she went on an aimless crime spree. With all that pent-up hurt and rage inside her now, one wonders what this second loss will trigger in her.

CONCLUSION AND IMPACT

For all its violence and nods toward social politics, *Boxcar Bertha* is mostly concerned with delivering cheap thrills—and in that it succeeds. The sheer fun Bertha has causing chaos is evident, in no small part because Hershey and the cast enjoyed making the picture. Granted, it's no surprise they had fun. Hollywood legend is that Hershey and Carradine had unsimulated sex during their sex scenes—and that's not mere rumor; it's the actors themselves making that claim.[1] (Even if true, you'd never know by what is captured on film. There are numerous nude scenes, but the sex is tame enough by today's standards that with some judicious editing it could be shown on network TV.) More noteworthy is how fondly the cast look back on the film. Hershey in particular has called it the most fun she ever had making a picture, and it comes across on-screen.

She and Carradine may have gotten lost in the process, so to speak, but Scorsese didn't. The shots are occasionally stylish and creative—a one-shot first-person search for a pair of giggling lovers in an abandoned house stands out, calling forward to the many excellent oners (long single shots) in his career—but the low budget is also evident throughout. This is especially true of the film's look. *Boxcar Bertha* is set during the Great Depression, but it looks like a 1970s film through and through, right down to the hairstyles. There is little to suggest this is the work of a future genius with notorious attention to detail. Overall, the direction is capable but largely unremarkable. It's sometimes hard to believe you're watching Scorsese. The bloodshed isn't bold or shocking or stylish; it's cheap and loud. The sex isn't sensual or suggestive; it's gratuitous. (An opportunity to show off a little of Hershey's legs is never missed, which feels especially tawdry given that she is presented like a sweet, misguided innocent.) All of this is, of course, Corman shining through. Martin Scorsese may have directed it, but it was undoubtedly a Roger Corman film. There is no embryonic version of Scorsese tucked away here, no toying with hidden symbolism, no deep character exploration. This is the work of a talented young man earning a paycheck. And there is nothing wrong with that.

The director credits Corman and this production with teaching him discipline, how to stay on schedule and budget, and how to get work done. The lessons would stay with him. So would some of the crew. The director called *Boxcar Bertha* a "learning experience which gave me the crew for *Mean Streets*. Without it, without having made *Boxcar*, there was no way I could've made *Mean Streets*."[2]

The director also began to refine the way he prepared movies. Early in his career, Scorsese would meticulously storyboard entire films, planning each shot in advance the way Alfred Hitchcock famously did. He told Richard Schickel that, when Corman asked if he had done any prep prior to the film, "I started showing him these pictures. And then explaining, 'This cuts to this, and this goes this way, and this is just normal coverage, but then there's a move this way.' He said, 'Wait a minute. Do you have this for the whole picture?' I said yes. He goes, 'I don't have to see anymore.'"[3]

This film also taught Martin Scorsese what *not* to be. It may seem strange to say that a little-seen, often-forgotten "trash" film made at the dawn of his career was a pivotal work for Martin Scorsese, but it was. Among those who knew the director's potential, *Boxcar* was seen as a near disaster that didn't at all reflect his unique vision. When screened for friends, "It was like a wake. They couldn't disguise their shock," Scorsese said.[4] John Cassavetes, whom Scorsese greatly admired, told him, "You've just spent a whole year of your life making a piece of shit."[5] Cassavetes's advice? Go make something personal. Go make something that means something to you. Go make a statement. Martin Scorsese took it to heart.

His next film would be *Mean Streets*, an uncompromising look at life on the streets of Little Italy during some of New York's roughest years. With it, the Martin Scorsese we know today was truly born.

3

MEAN STREETS
(1973)

FILM DETAILS

RELEASE DATE: October 14, 1973
WRITTEN BY: Martin Scorsese, Mardik Martin
STARRING: Robert De Niro, Harvey Keitel, David Proval, Amy Robinson
RUNNING TIME: 112 minutes

ABOUT THE FILM

Mean Streets is the first fully formed example of the director's vision at work. Countless familiar elements are refined and focused here into a piece that is unmistakably Scorsese. The music. The acting. The dizzying swirl of the camera. The violence. The uneasy way in which it walks the line between glorifying antisocial behavior and recoiling from it. Faith, guilt, sin. And, of course, the way in which its characters bring misfortune on themselves. It's all classic Scorsese. In some ways it feels like an unofficial sequel to his first picture, in which he first dabbled with these ideas, and in fact it almost was. The lead role was written for Harvey Keitel, who was also the lead in *Who's That Knocking*, and in the earliest drafts of the script, it was intended to be the same character. But *Mean Streets* became its own thing.

In a roundabout way, *Mean Streets* would not exist were it not for Roger Corman, famed producer and director of exploitation films. Scorsese directed

Boxcar Bertha for him, a production that taught Marty how a professional film production works but that did not satisfy his need for personal expression. Rather than take another studio job, at the urging of friends he decided to pursue something closer to his heart.

And indeed, *Mean Streets* is the director's most explicitly personal film. Later pictures may offer keener insights into the things that obsess him—"Life Lessons" from *New York Stories*, *The Aviator*, and *The Last Temptation of Christ* are just a few examples of movies that speak more deeply about what makes Scorsese tick—but this film is nakedly personal insomuch as it's a snapshot of the things he saw growing up, populated by the kind of people who hung out on the corner in his neighborhood. If rural kids lived *Stand by Me* and *Old Yeller* and suburban kids lived *The Goonies* and *American Graffiti*, then Scorsese lived *Mean Streets*. It's little wonder that his work so often presents a perverse yet honest look at violence, given the nature of his neighborhood growing up.

The movie nearly went in another direction, and if it had we may have never experienced the Martin Scorsese we all know today. The reason? *Mean Streets* was almost a blaxploitation film. The genre exploded in the early 1970s, featuring tough black characters and an uncompromising, often over-the-top and outlandish look at life on the streets. Best known for landmark pictures like *Sweet Sweetback's Baadasssss Song* (1971), *Shaft* (1971), *Super Fly* (1972), and *Foxy Brown* (1974), blaxploitation films tackle the struggles of black Americans with larger-than-life characters and explosive violence. Much of the swagger you see in the work of directors like Quentin Tarantino is directly lifted from the genre.

With the genre exploding, Corman saw an opportunity to make more money with Scorsese. He read the *Mean Streets* screenplay and liked it but would only agree to finance the film if all the characters were black. Young and still trying to get a foothold in Hollywood, the director almost agreed. It was actor and director John Cassavetes (*Rosemary's Baby*, *The Dirty Dozen*) who talked him out of it, telling him he should instead focus on making something meaningful to him. The result was Martin Scorsese telling the world, here I am, this is what I do. "In my mind it's not really a film, it's kind of a declaration or statement of who I am and how I was living, and those thoughts and conflicts," the director said. It was the "final culmination of everything I was to do and who I am."[1]

ANALYSIS

This was Martin Scorsese's life. *Mean Streets* captures the streets of Little Italy in New York City circa the late 1960s and early 1970s more accurately than any film ever made. It's a slice of Americana that has since disappeared. Little Italy is no more, now just a short strip of Italian restaurants catering to tourists, a once-ethnic neighborhood swallowed by Manhattan. Where once upward of 90 percent of its residents were of Italian origin and Italian was as commonly spoken as English, today only about 8 percent of residents there claim Italian origins, according to the 2000 census.[2]

The last remnants of this cultural island in the middle of New York City are the axle upon which *Mean Streets* turns, focused especially on the Feast of San Gennaro, during which the film is set. Immigrants from Naples started the festival in 1926 on Mulberry Street, the heart of Little Italy. It began as a one-day religious commemoration but soon grew to a sprawling eleven-day affair with huge displays; music; parades; and of course, food, food, and more food. The festival still exists today, but it's organized by people outside the neighborhood and is largely designed for tourists, more of a temporary Italian theme park than an actual religious celebration. In 2007, a member of Community Board 2 in the neighborhood even said, "No one likes San Gennaro who lives here. . . . Residents complained it was better organized when the Mafia ran it."[3]

The Feast of San Gennaro at its height forms a backdrop for the movie, and it's a vital one because it provides the sights, sounds, and colors essential to immersing us in the ethnic richness of Scorsese's old neighborhood. The concept is much the same as setting a movie about small-town America during the county fair, an event so mom-and-apple-pie it provides a clear window into the kind of America such movies aim to depict. The same holds true here. Setting the story during the feast allows Scorsese to dial up the Italian American imagery and fully sink the audience into this unique urban landscape.

All this context may seem extraneous, but to truly dig into what Scorsese was trying to capture, it's vital to understand the time and place in which it is set. There is a reason the opening titles feature a rounded frame with a typewriter-style font. They look like snapshots from the era, pictures from a dusty photo album stored in the drawer underneath the huge family Bible. This was Scorsese's life. Portions of the film were shot at actual places from his youth, actual places he hung out, actual places where people he knew caused trouble. People from the old neighborhood are featured in the movie, friends and neighbors and even his mother, who would famously go on to be in eight Scorsese movies and a documentary. It isn't just about the vibe and aesthetic, either. Some scenes are plucked directly from true happenings in the neighborhood, such as Robert De Niro's character standing on a rooftop firing a gun off just for kicks.

From the moment *Mean Streets* opens, it's clear we are not going to see a sanitized version of life in the city streets. We see someone shooting up drugs in a bathroom, only to be kicked out. Our first look at Johnny Boy (De Niro in his initial pairing with Scorsese) is of him blowing up a mailbox, the mix of mischievousness and violence that defines the character in one short scene. Then we cut to Charlie (Harvey Keitel) in a church, our first view of the Catholic imagery that obliquely hints at the complex but unseen psychology that motivates both the director and the character.

As narratives go, *Mean Streets* is fairly lightweight. Johnny owes some money to the local loan shark, Giovanni Cappa (Cesare Danova), and is irresponsible about paying it back. Charlie runs interference on his behalf, trying to buy his friend some time to do the right thing, but Johnny doesn't have the right thing in him. He's too wild for that. When another loan shark comes around to collect, Johnny pulls a gun on him. He and Charlie try to leave town but are shot by the shark and his henchmen. They survive but are badly wounded. The end.

Yet delving into the intricacies of the plot or the lack thereof misses the point of *Mean Streets*. This is an exploration of a time and place and a way of living, not an attempt to tell an engaging story. Moment after moment is about painting the world more than about advancing plot. And the vivid exploration of this world goes hand in hand with the exploration of Charlie, who Scorsese says includes elements of both himself and his father.

Charlie exists on the fringes of neighborhood crime. He's not a mover and shaker; he's a low-level street guy just getting by any way he can. So are his closest friends. There is solidarity in their collective (and often criminal) behavior that speaks to the tightness of the community, even in the face of violence. When a brawl breaks out at a pool hall and the police arrive, the combatants quickly stop. "We're just friends," they insist. Police are outsiders in the neighborhood, unwanted. The cop takes a bribe, and the fight resumes. This is a New York that was still a city of a thousand tightly packed towns, every few blocks not just a different neighborhood but also a different world.

An integral part of Scorsese's world is music—music blaring from apartment windows; music on a car stereo; and, of course, music in the movies—and here he begins to first show just how powerful popular music can be in the hands of a great director. He has a way of drawing the viewer into a moment in a way suited for music videos, and it's showcased here to great effect. A party scene midway through the film is lengthy and hazy, with long stretches of blaring tunes and dizzying camera work that offers an altered sense of reality. Charlie is drunk, soaring, reeling, stumbling, celebrating, and we're in the moment with him. As he'd later do in films like *Raging Bull* and *Casino*, he indulges in manipulating time, camera speed, angle, and (of course) sound and music to give us a warped sense of perspective. We see Charlie as if from a fishbowl, staggering with him through the club, the lights and sounds seeming to encompass the world. It's these brief moments of daring that make Scorsese pictures what they are.

These scenes are effective in part because he designed them from the start with specific music in mind. He often builds scenes around those music choices rather than the other way around, sometimes going as far as to film with the song playing on set so camera movements can be timed to the song being played. This is not a normal approach. Typically, a movie's soundtrack comes later in the process, after the footage has been shot. For Scorsese, right from the beginning, it's a vital part of the creative process, an approach that has influenced modern directors like Quentin Tarantino (*Reservoir Dogs*), Edgar Wright (*Baby Driver*), and James Gunn (*Guardians of the Galaxy*).

Music in scenes like this is important not merely because it creates a more compelling scene. It also immerses us into the world on-screen. It's an integral part of the lives Charlie and Johnny lead. It's part of the tapestry of their lives, just as it was for Scorsese himself. It's true for all of us. Each of us has a soundtrack that defines us. Our choices in music say something about us; music punctuates key moments in our lives; and for many, specific songs are inextricably linked to specific people, places, and relationships. Therefore, to know Charlie and Johnny, we *must* know their music, too.

It sometimes seems like music is the only tie that binds the two. Some viewers will have an understandable desire to question their friendship. Johnny is a bit of a jerk. Worse than that, actually. He owes people money and *taunts* them about it. He's sarcastic and irresponsible. Even when he's being given chances others wouldn't be given, he shrugs them off. No clear-headed person should trust Johnny. Charlie's loyalty to him might seem baffling, if one doesn't understand the dynamic of neighborhoods like Little Italy, but the concept of loyalty among certain communities of Italian Americans ran (and still runs) strong. Therefore, Charlie has his friend's back. He gets Mike to agree to lower Johnny's debt. If Johnny doesn't pay, then Mike will have his legs broken. (It's a cliché but one rooted in truth.)

When given a job, however, Johnny doesn't show up. It's an insult that later puts both he and Charlie in danger. Charlie sticks by him regardless. Part of this is the value placed on loyalty in the Italian American community, both loyalty to friends and loyalty to your neighborhood. Much of this stems from the way Italians emigrated to the United States and how they settled, especially in urban areas. A great wave of Italian immigration to the United States began around 1880, with four million arriving (usually in New York) by 1924, fully half of them between 1900 and 1910.[4] However, Italian unification in Italy did not fully coalesce until after World War I. That means Italian immigrants often identified more with their home villages and towns rather than with Italy as a whole. This had a direct impact on the makeup of Italian American communities in the United States: "Fellow villagers and people from the same region or province ended up clustering together in self-segregated neighborhoods within the broader Italian settlements."[5] This culture of solidarity lingered for decades in these ethnic communities and was a major part of the director's early life. He explains:

> The Neapolitans, when they came over, somehow they wound up on Mulberry Street. So Mulberry Street became Little Naples. The same thing happened with Elizabeth Street and the Sicilians. But Naples is one city, and Sicily is a lot of little towns, and very often my mother would say, "Oh, yeah, he married so-and-so, but she was a different nationality." A different village, she's talking about.[6]

Even today, aspects of this linger in areas of New York, New Jersey, and the surrounding region. (I am of Italian American heritage, and anecdotally, many Italian Americans still place a great deal of emphasis on the region of Italy their relatives emigrated from.) In short, sticking together is considered a big deal.

But Charlie's loyalty to Johnny isn't merely a manifestation of lingering ethnic solidarity. There is something more at play that reveals itself in part through Johnny's self-destructive behavior and how that behavior affects Charlie. Johnny's antics catch up with them in the end. In a surprise ambush, the pair are attacked while driving through the city. Johnny is shot in the neck. (De Niro will be shot in the neck again a few years later in *Taxi Driver*.) Charlie is shot in the hand. Vibrant, red blood spurts, a blend of the gratuitous violence of the exploitation genre Scorsese had just dabbled in with *Boxcar Bertha* and the real-world grit that peppers his most audacious work. Music blares. The pair crash into a building. They live but are badly wounded and are taken in by authorities. It might be seen as a tragic end had the pair not brought it upon themselves. As is so often the case in Scorsese films, the protagonists are the cause of their own troubles. They're not victims of outside forces; they're actively making choices that upend their own lives.

For Johnny, it's juvenile recklessness and a disregard for authority. He's a young man without much to lose and no sense for his own mortality, a born troublemaker who lives to snub his nose at anyone he feels is trying to control his life, even his own friends. Charlie is different. Charlie's worst choices stem not from an aversion to authority or recklessness or, as is the case with a number of Scorsese antiheroes, greed. They come from guilt. Guilt for *what* is an open question, though perhaps the answer isn't important. The concept of Catholic guilt is a well-known one, so much so that it often becomes a cliché, yet it also

Charlie's Catholic guilt is a silent but potent motivation behind everything he does, a theme that continues throughout the director's work. *Warner Bros. Pictures/Photofest*

seemed inescapable for some Italian American communities. Certainly, for Scorsese, the concepts of faith and sinfulness, prayer and contrition, and Catholicism and guilt are intertwined. Why else would his protagonists so often be surrounded by religious iconography, despite being people of sin?

Scorsese himself suggests that Charlie's motivation in protecting Johnny comes from a desire to seek penance for unaddressed sins. "He's doing it for himself," the director notes. "He's not doing it for Johnny. He's doing it so that he can feel better, so he can have the guilt taken off his shoulders for whatever the hell he's thinking or whatever he did, or what he *thinks* he did."[7] In a sense, Charlie is seeking penance for past wrongs, even if, as Scorsese suggests, he doesn't even know what those wrongs are. He wants to become a good person, and Johnny is his way of proving to himself he can be noble. Perhaps elements of J. R. from *Who's That Knocking* remain in Charlie's character; in some alternate universe where the films are still connected, maybe Charlie would have felt immense guilt over his treatment of the Girl in the first film.

Whether it's even possible for a man to absolve himself of sin in this way is not a question the movie attempts to answer. Here, it's an unanswerable question, especially because Charlie isn't even conscious of what he's trying to do. He doesn't know what drives him to play guardian angel to his uncontrollable friend. He doesn't even think about it. He just does it, driven by something inside himself he's not ready to confront. And perhaps he never will be.

This notion of guilt is one of the hallmarks of Scorsese's filmography, arguably the most important repeated theme in his body of work. Discussions on this have usually revolved around the idea of Catholic guilt, for obvious reasons—it's a deeply rooted part of the Italian American culture in which the director was raised—but as I get further into his career, I delve into guilt as a theme removed from Catholicism. Guilt for previous wrongs torment Sam Bowden in *Cape Fear*, for failing to address a spouse's mental illness in *Shutter Island*, and for an inability to prevent death in *Bringing Out the Dead*.

So here we have a dizzying swirl of almost pathological guilt, street violence so commonplace the characters take it for granted, the thrilling surge of music punctuating key moments of life, not to mention rocky relationships—Charlie's relationship with Teresa Ronchelli (Amy Robinson) is a mess—street-level solidarity; characters who engage in self-destructive behavior; and the ever-looming, often uncomfortable presence of faith in the midst of all this.

When Martin Scorsese calls *Mean Streets* a declaration of statement, it's apparent why. These are thematic hallmarks of virtually every picture he ever made. Many contain most or all of these elements—all of them at least one. This movie *is* Martin Scorsese.

CONCLUSION AND IMPACT

Mean Streets won acclaim by critics—Pauline Kael praised its "unsettling, episodic rhythm"—though it was not a crossover success.[8] Mainstream audiences did not flock to see it. What it did do, however, was attract the attention of Hollywood insiders, who took note of the young director's penchant for uncompromising realism and emotional turbulence. Among them was actor Ellen Burstyn, who saw a screening at the urging of Francis Ford Coppola. As soon as she saw it, she knew this young up-and-comer would be the perfect director for the next picture Warner Bros. executives wanted her to make, a drama called *Alice Doesn't Live Here Anymore*. It would end up being Scorsese's mainstream breakthrough.

4

ALICE DOESN'T LIVE HERE ANYMORE (1974)

FILM DETAILS

RELEASE DATE: December 9, 1974
WRITTEN BY: Robert Getchell
STARRING: Ellen Burstyn, Kris Kristofferson, Diane Ladd, Jodie Foster, Alfred Lutter
RUNNING TIME: 112 minutes
OTHER NOTES: The inspiration for the TV sitcom *Alice*, which ran from 1976 to 1985.

ABOUT THE FILM

A single mother's often humorous journey toward self-actualization does not sound like Martin Scorsese material, yet not only does that describe this Scorsese picture, but it also proved to be his mainstream breakthrough—so mainstream, in fact, that it was spun off into a highly successful sitcom that ran for nine seasons and 202 episodes—this from the man whose next picture would be about a psychopathic introvert obsessed with a teenage prostitute.

Alice Doesn't Live Here Anymore tells the story of Alice Hyatt (Ellen Burstyn), a woman struggling to build a new life for her and her son, Tommy (Alfred Lutter), after being suddenly widowed. The pair travel together, making their way to where she grew up in Monterey, California, with a dream of starting a career as a singer. Life repeatedly sidetracks them, however, until, while work-ing as a waitress, she encounters David (Kris Kristofferson). A rocky romance is sparked, and the pair make a go at a life together.

Originally attached to Shirley MacClaine, Warner Bros. offered the role to Burstyn after MacLaine turned it down.[1] Burstyn was in production on *The Exorcist* (1973) at the time, when Warner Bros. asked whom she'd be inter-ested in working with for the upcoming *Alice*. All she knew was that she wanted someone who would bring a realistic edge to the story. After a call to Francis Ford Coppola, she screened *Mean Streets* by a young director named Martin Scorsese, and that was all it took. She knew this was the guy.

For Scorsese, taking the job was a career move. After making *Mean Streets*, some said he couldn't direct women (a somewhat dubious claim, given *Boxcar Bertha* had just come out, though it is fair to say that Scorsese's filmography is deeply male-centric). Friends advised him to grab an op-portunity to prove otherwise.[2] Meanwhile, Burstyn wanted a director who could bring grit and truth to the story, someone who could subvert the then-stereotypical view of what life for women in America was and should be like. The pairing served both.

ANALYSIS

The women's liberation movement emerged in the late 1960s, but though it was picking up steam by the mid-1970s, there remained cultural norms so ingrained in American society that the idea of a single woman who wasn't dependent on a man was still unusual in 1974. So for Burstyn, *Alice Doesn't Live Here Anymore* was a chance to subvert America's expectations of women, especially single mothers, and Martin Scorsese was the right director to bring it to screen.

The subversion Burstyn was looking for is evident in the very first shots of the film. The opening scenes are bathed in a sunset glow, almost otherworldly, as if plucked from some alternate universe version of *The Wizard of Oz*. It's a pastoral setting, a slice of pure Americana that exists only in fantasies. Charming music plays. We're in Monterey, California. Here we meet Alice as a young girl, but this isn't the dainty, dreamlike America of the golden age of Hollywood. "I can sing better than Alice Faye. I swear to Christ I can," Alice declares, and we hear her mother yelling for her, threatening to "beat the daylights out of her" and saying, if anyone doesn't like it, "they can blow it out their ass." This is not Dorothy. This is not Kansas. This is not the American dream. This is the troubled truth of the working class.

We then flash-forward twenty-five years or so to adulthood. Alice is in a love-less marriage. Her husband, Donald (Billy "Green" Bush), acknowledges her only to complain about her inadequacies as a spouse. At night, she lies next to him in bed and cries. She's funny and vibrant and sarcastic, but he is squeezing the life out of her.

That doesn't mean her life isn't shattered when he is killed in a freak car ac-cident, however, leaving her alone to raise their son, Tommy. Left with nothing, she has to reinvent herself and rediscover who she is—who she *really* is when not under the yoke of a spouse who grinds her down. It's significant that Alice is *forced* into this. It's not a choice or decision she made. Rather, fate dealt her a seemingly bad hand, and she must find the inner strength necessary to deal with what will come. This affords her a kind of growth that would not be pos-sible if she had made a conscious decision to leave Donald. Her need to carve out an identity of her own is a surprise, and as such, that means she is initially unprepared for what she will have to face. She doesn't begin with the strength she needs to make it on her own. She has to *find* it.

Alice's sole partner in facing the difficulties of her new life is Tommy. She has a pair of romantic interests in the film, yes—one goes violently bad, the other

Ellen Burstyn won an Academy Award for Best Actress for her portrayal of Alice, a story of female empowerment by a director most often associated with male-dominated stories. *Warner Brothers*

provides a happy ending—but the one anchor she has is her son, and vice versa. Alice is his one island of stability in a sea of uncertainty. He is the same to her. This mother-son relationship is the heart and soul of the movie. Tommy asks why she married Donald, and her response is a pat "Because he was a great kisser." No reflection on the failed relationship, and indeed, doing so would have undermined the idea that the two of them are now alone in the world. The future is theirs. Their interactions are natural and effortless. They joke and play. At one point they even have a raucous water balloon fight in a rented room, trashing the place and soaking one another to the bone. Alice is not June Cleaver, all prim and proper and preparing apple pie while dressed in a pristine apron. They are not a white-picket-fence family. Tommy talks back to her, though rarely is it due to a lack of respect for her. Alice reciprocates at every turn. This isn't to say Tommy can't be a handful. He can. But it's not until another man enters Alice's life that he becomes truly difficult. The sarcastic exchanges and joking interactions between mother and son underscore the unspoken freedom both feel without the oppressive shadow of Donald looming over them. We don't need to be told that, despite the difficulties Donald's death has thrust upon them, both are happier having started over.

Still, the often-lighthearted nature of the film can turn on a dime, a brutal and realistic reminder of what women faced when entering a world once largely dominated by men. For example, after meeting Ben (Harvey Keitel, in his third role for Scorsese), a forward and charming younger man interested in spending some time with her, Alice begins a fling, which she keeps secret from Tommy. It doesn't last. Alice discovers Ben is married. Ben's wife, Rita (Lane Bradbury), comes to the room Alice rents and reveals the truth. Ben and Rita have a child together. She is tearful and hurt, and Alice is deeply upset at having inadvertently damaged someone's marriage.

But when Ben shows up at the apartment, he is no longer the charmer. He turns violent. He's brutal and controlling, filling Alice with terror. He abuses his wife—"Don't ever tell me what to do. I'll bust your jaw!"—and threatens Alice, telling her in no uncertain terms that their affair will continue. It's a harrowing scene, difficult to watch in its starkness, disturbing because you see how trivial it would be for Ben to hurt Alice, and ultimately, it's a showcase for why Scorsese was hired in the first place. It would have been easy for this film to be sentimental. The obvious choice would be for it to be sweet and uplifting and Hollywood, but despite the music-video glitz he brings to screen, Scorsese isn't particularly Hollywood. There is a deep cynicism about humanity that permeates his work. People are ugly creatures, too often cruel to one another, and the cruelties we inflict often cannot be shrugged off with a swell of John Williams music and some soft lighting. Real toxicity leaves real scars—scars that can't be seen, to be sure, but scars nonetheless.

This is what Ben's intrusion into the story offers. It's the metaphorical slap of reality. It's the reminder that, though liberated, though free to forge her own path and create her own destiny, Alice can still be victimized by those who see her as lesser or subservient. The scene adds an undercurrent of uneasiness to everything that comes after because we see how easy it is for a single woman alone in the world to suddenly find herself in a dangerous situation. When David (Kristofferson) finally comes along, we're not ready to trust him. Not yet. We've already seen where trust can lead us.

In some ways, David is an interloper. He's invading the special relationship Alice and Tommy have. What starts as a quick bond between him and Alice's son becomes one filled with tension. Tommy begins pushing David away. He acts like a punk. He talks back. During a guitar lesson, he puts on loud music simply to disrespect David and his home. In response, David breaks the record Tommy is playing. Tommy hurls profanity at him. David strikes the boy. A fight ensues between David and Alice, and they break up. She's in love with him, yes, but Tommy will always come first. They've struggled together in ways no one else could ever understand.

Regardless, Alice's new relationship puts a strain on her relationship with her son. After the fight with David, Alice and Tommy get into an argument in the car. This, too, gets ugly, uglier than any clash they've previously had. At her breaking point, Alice pulls over and makes Tommy walk back home, but Tommy, frustrated and overwhelmed by the emotional turbulence in his life, doesn't walk back home. Instead, he meets up with his friend, the rebellious free spirit Doris/Audrey (Jodie Foster). The young pair get drunk and are caught shoplifting. Alice has to pick him up at the police station. This whole sequence isn't about Tommy per se, but rather it's about the impact David has on Alice and Tommy's relationship. The kid feels cut out. He feels lost. It's another swell in the turbulent ocean of his life and one he is not equipped to handle.

The one thing the pair cling to is the idea of going to Monterey. We hear about Monterey again and again. This is the final goal, the destination where Alice and Tommy will truly start life anew, a place for a new beginning and a better life. But the truth is, Monterey is just a symbol. It's not a real destination; it's a goal meant to represent having reestablished herself as her own person. It's the greener grass on the other side; it's the "somewhere" over the rainbow, the city of Shangri-La. Here the cliché holds true: The journey is more important than the destination.

A major part of that journey involves Alice struggling to find her place in the world. Her goal is to become a singer, like she was before her marriage to

Donald. She struggles with auditions at seedy little bars run by brazen misogynists—"Look at my face. I don't sing with my ass," she scolds one of them—and here Scorsese's living, probing approach with the camera comes alive. In one audition at a piano bar, the camera is in constant motion, swinging around the scene, people and objects at the fore of the frame like something from an Akira Kurosawa film, giving us a sense of busyness and energy and motion. Much like Alice herself, Scorsese is not shy about breaking the "rules" here, either. Twice Alice looks directly at the camera, fleeting fourth-wall breaks the director would later take to a bold extreme in 1990's *GoodFellas* and 2013's *The Wolf of Wall Street*.

This isn't a standard, uplifting, Hollywood story, either. Alice is not destined to have a miracle breakthrough as a singer. She isn't going to rise to stardom. Instead, she becomes a waitress at a divey eatery. When we finally arrive at Mel's Diner, the direction becomes as cluttered and chaotic as the diner itself, full of noise and people and movement. This is where Alice meets the indomitable Flo (Diane Ladd), a fierce, foul-mouthed waitress who is on the surface crude and uncouth but who underneath has a world-weary wisdom that helps give Alice the fortitude needed to cope with the madness of Mel's. Alice may represent feminist ideals in her struggle for personal fulfillment, but Flo is *already there*. She's been there, done that, bought the T-shirt. She knows exactly who she is and makes no apology for it. After having been beaten down by failure after failure, she is just the sort of person Alice needs in her life, too.

But Flo isn't the end of Alice's journey. It is at Mel's that Alice meets David, and it's David who alters the course of her life. Whether for good or ill depends on your idea of what constitutes a happy ending. They fall for one another, and though there are difficulties, Alice decides to stay in Tucson with him.

In some ways, David (and, with it, domesticity) becomes Alice's new Monterey. She still wishes to go, yes, and David offers to give everything up to go with her, but that's symbolic, too, the result of a somewhat-misguided compromise in the screenwriting. Neither Scorsese nor Burstyn wanted Alice to land with another man, at least not in such a traditional way, but studio pressure forced an approach that would make audiences happy. "We tried to work as truthfully as possible within the conventions of the genre," Scorsese said, "and within the conventions was the studio chief telling me, 'Give it a happy ending!'"[3] This is perhaps the one area that undercuts Alice's agency and is the only major blight on an otherwise potent empowerment narrative. Free of a bad marriage and on her own path to self-discovery, she ultimately finds herself in another relationship. Instead of reaching the place where she could fulfill her dreams, she settles down into another traditional pairing. She even says at one point, "I don't know how to live without a man." It's a slight stain on an otherwise progressive journey.

Not that Scorsese saw it as a progressive journey: "To tell you the truth, the reviews that praise *Alice* as a feminist picture couldn't have surprised me more. I don't like to think of it as a woman's picture, but as a human picture—if that doesn't sound too corny."[4] That *Alice Doesn't Live Here Anymore* seems as progressive as it does is as much a commentary on our own times as it is on the times in which it is set. It came during the height of the 1970s women's movement, when reproductive rights, sexual liberation, the passage of Title IX in 1972, and female entry into the workforce in huge numbers revolutionized American culture. "This idea that we were primary in our own lives, to ourselves, was astonishing," Burstyn said.[5] She had just gone through a divorce and was feeling that uneasy mix of empowerment and uncertainty about the future. The world women inhabited was changing. Expectations were changing. More and more women were taking what were then unconventional paths through life. The idea of single moms as people to be championed was only just beginning to enter the mainstream. Eight years later, the *Washington Post* reported, "The increase in single-parent families is one of the most striking social developments of the past generation."[6] So in its day, *Alice* was a sign of the times.

Fast-forward forty-five years, and the story remains relevant. In 2017, the Brookings Institute noted, "Women's labor force participation has increased substantially in the U.S. over the second half of the 20th century, yet this growth has stagnated and reversed since 2000. Today, large gaps remain between men and women in employment rates, the jobs they hold, the wages they earn, and their overall economic security."[7] Women are still seen as the primary caregivers of children, making the balance between home and career especially difficult for single mothers. As of 2017, domestic violence murders were even on the rise for the first time in four decades.[8]

So *Alice* remains as powerful and relevant a story today as it was in 1974, a story that set out to subvert expectations—and succeeded.

CONCLUSION AND IMPACT

The picture struck a chord with audiences. It was a breakthrough hit, earning a huge box office ($21 million domestically, on a $1.8 million budget) and garnering sweeping critical accolades. Burstyn won the Oscar for Best Actress, while Diane Ladd and Robert Getchell were nominated for Best Supporting Actress and Best Original Screenplay, respectively. The movie also won Best Picture from the British Academy of Film and Television Arts (BAFTA), and Scorsese received a Best Director nod, losing to Stanley Kubrick's work on *Barry Lyndon* (1975), which years later would influence Scorsese's *Age of Innocence* (1993). The director was nominated for the Palme D'Or at the 1975 Cannes Film Festival, too. Perhaps the greatest symbol of the movie's mainstream success, though, is also the most unlikely, when one considers Scorsese's overall body of work: It was adapted into a highly successful television sitcom.

Focusing on the ups and downs of working at Mel's Diner, *Alice* ran from 1976 to 1985, spanning 202 episodes and earning high ratings for most of its run. It was a top-ten show for four of its ten seasons and a top-thirty show for all but two; it also earned an Emmy nomination in 1984. The show had some light callbacks to the movie—Vic Tayback reprised his role from the film as Mel, and Diane Ladd returned to Mel's for two seasons, though playing a different character (for the TV series, Flo was played by Polly Holiday)—but it largely forged its own path. Its most significant contribution to popular culture was introducing the classic "Kiss my grits" catchphrase into the lexicon. Scorsese had nothing to do with the series, but regardless, the idea that such a light piece of TV entertainment sprang from one of his movies is a delightful footnote to his career.

That kind of lightness is not a natural fit for Martin Scorsese, however, and his next film would be a bold example of that. It tells the story of a disturbed taxi driver looking for an excuse to go on a killing spree, and it would make legends of both Scorsese and the supporting actor from *Mean Streets*, a lanky rising star named Robert De Niro. It would also result in one of the most artistically fruitful partnerships in film history.

5

TAXI DRIVER
(1976)

FILM DETAILS

RELEASE DATE: February 8, 1976
WRITTEN BY: Paul Schrader
STARRING: Robert De Niro, Jodie Foster, Albert Brooks, Harvey Keitel,
 Cybill Shepherd
RUNNING TIME: 113 minutes

ABOUT THE FILM

If Martin Scorsese never made another film after *Taxi Driver*, he'd still be regarded as one of the most important directors of the 1970s, and it would still be regarded as one of the most important movies of the era. That's how powerful a statement of vision it is.

Taxi Driver was the brainchild of screenwriter Paul Schrader, who would go on to write *Raging Bull*, *The Last Temptation of Christ*, and *Bringing Out the Dead* for Scorsese. Written during a time when he was struggling with a profound sense of isolation and personal frustration, the script was a deeply personal meditation by Schrader, one that revealed parts of himself most would rather keep hidden from view. Because of this, he was picky about who would helm the film. He found a pair of kindred souls in Scorsese and Robert De Niro, both of whom caught his attention after he saw *Mean Streets*. Working on reduced salaries in order to keep the production within budget, the trio created one of the most compelling depictions of social alienation and the violence that can explode from emotional repression ever put to film. "You've got to understand that the original idea came from him," Scorsese said of Schrader. "And that's something that I think over the years, when they say 'Martin Scorsese's *Taxi Driver*,' that's something that can be very painful to Paul. It's really his."[1]

The film centers on Travis Bickle (De Niro), a Vietnam War veteran who takes a job as a cab driver and in his spare time fumes about a city he believes is immoral. After poisoning a date with a young political campaign worker, Betsy (Cybill Shepherd), by taking her to a porno theater, he becomes obsessed with a teenage prostitute, Iris (Jodie Foster). Under the pretense of rescuing her but in truth satisfying an inner urge to lash out with violence, he shoots up the apartment in which she stays, liberating her from her pimp (Harvey Keitel) and getting painted as a hero by the press as a result. But Bickle's motivations weren't pure, and the film ends with a tease that darkness still lurks within him.

ANALYSIS

Alienation can turn a man into a monster, and once one starts walking down that path, it can often be a one-way journey. Right from the opening titles, *Taxi Driver* immerses the viewer in an ominous cloud of paranoia. It's a dreamlike sequence, an anonymous taxi rolling through dirty city streets and dense wafts of steam, horror-tinged strings providing sinister background music. The hazy music makes a sudden switch to sensual jazz—the *Taxi Driver* theme was among the last pieces written by legendary composer Bernard Herrmann for this, his final score—the soothing sax and images of neon lights suggesting a romance with the city. But it twists again. The music warps. The sinister strings return, and the images become blurred, telling us there is a dark side to the city; telling us that this romance is unclean; and most important of all, planting the seeds for the manic nature of our protagonist, a man who can barely contain the demons eating him from the inside out.

The first face we see is Bickle's. Coming right after the title sequence, the viewer subconsciously associates the gloomy, contradictory tones of the titles with Bickle himself. The music, the images, the sound: They sum him up better than any brief biography ever could. "Thank God for the rain that washes the trash off the sidewalks," he narrates, and we'd almost agree with his assessment of 1970s New York if there wasn't something so disturbing about his tone. "All the animals come out at night. . . . Someday a real rain will come and wash all the scum off the streets."

For viewers of the era, these statements would be especially uneasy to hear, in no small part because they wouldn't have been all that difficult to agree with. New York City in the 1970s was a dangerous, crime-ridden metropolitan area that came to represent the worst aspects of the era's rise in crime. In 1972, there were 1,691 murders in New York.[2] That number would not dip below 1,500 until 1984, peaking at 1,826 in 1981. (The city would beat even that record in 1988, 1989, and again in 1990, when an astonishing 2,245 murders were recorded.) By contrast, there were just 290 murders in New York City in 2017.[3] It's a staggering difference.

The city often *looked* like a wasteland of crime, too. Subway cars were so covered in graffiti they'd create the visual language of the 1979 cult classic *The Warriors*. In the summer of 1974, the Metropolitan Transportation Authority (MTA) shut down the rear cars of its subways due to a wave of violence sweeping the trains. At times, upward of 250 crimes were reported per week on the New York subway system. And Times Square, today a by-comparison pristine tourist trap filled with blazing lights, street performers, and overpriced chain restaurants, was in the 1970s a seedy strip of adult movie theaters, peep shows, street prostitutes, and drug dealers.

This was the very real New York in which *Taxi Driver* was set, so it would be understandable for some viewers to initially sympathize with Bickle's cynical view of the city and the mass of humanity who inhabited it. But there is an *edge* there, a darkness that most people will find alien. It's *uncomfortable* to agree with a man like that, even if we agree that the city was in dire need of cleaning up.

But *Taxi Driver* isn't about the city, as much as it seems to be on the surface. It's a character piece, an exploration of a broken man's psyche, a look at what social isolation can do to a person. Throughout the film, Bickle's detachment from society is repeatedly reinforced for us, usually by Bickle himself. He says he doesn't follow politics, he doesn't follow music, he doesn't follow movies. He's entirely alienated himself from society. With nothing else to drive him and either an inability or lack of desire to connect with people—he has chosen to remain distant from his family for reasons that are never stated—Bickle begins to look outward at those around him, and he feels resentment. He doesn't see it as resentment, though. He recasts those feelings as something else.

Roger Ebert once noted that everyone quotes De Niro's famous "You lookin' at me?" line, but they neglect the one that follows—"Well, I'm the only one here"—when in fact that is the "truest line in the film."[4] It's a small line, but it's key to the character.

Bickle thinks himself a hero in waiting. He craves a purpose; he believes he is somehow important, that he has vision that others lack, and if given a chance, he will do something meaningful for the world. "I don't believe a person should devote their life to morbid self-reflection," he says. He's waging a war no one else realizes he is waging. He's not merely angry at the world; he wants nothing more than an excuse to act out on his violent impulses, justifying them in a veneer of justice and righteousness. If Bickle lived in twenty-first-century Florida under its "stand your ground" laws, Bickle would be following Skittles-bearing teens home from the convenience store, hoping for a confrontation that would give him the opportunity to gun someone down.

Seeing the way Bickle's mind works is especially disturbing when watched in the context of late-2010s social politics. The so-called incel movement (*incel* is short for "involuntarily celibate" and refers to an Internet subculture devoted to frustration with women, sometimes manifesting itself in violent fantasies about rape and retribution), the QAnon movement, with its proponents fantasizing about a bloody revolution sweeping the United States clean of undesirables, among others—these groups all reflect aspects of Bickle's character.

Taxi Driver's violent exploration of a man alienated from society was shocking in the 1970s and remains just as relevant in the Internet age. *Columbia Pictures*

Read online forums and discussion groups focused on these movements, and you find strikingly similar sentiments to those expressed by Bickle. For example, on May 23, 2014, a twenty-two-year-old self-proclaimed incel named Elliot Rodger murdered six people before turning his gun on himself. His goal was to punish women, whom he saw as unclean and beneath him. In a chilling video made shortly before the murders, Rodger said, "I've been forced to endure an existence of loneliness, rejection, and unfulfilled desires all because girls have never been attracted to me. . . . I've had to rot in loneliness. It's not fair."[5] Following the murders, Rodger "has been virtually canonized by some fringe communities online."[6]

Similarly, the QAnon movement has embraced a Bickle-like view of the world, one in which the masses cannot see reality before them, and the only path to enlightenment is, according to some, by cleansing the world through violence. Books embraced by the movement include titles like *QAnon and the Battle of Armageddon: Destroying the New World Order and Taking the Millennial Kingdom by Force* and *QAnon: An Invitation to the Great Awakening*. Believers think we are in the calm before the storm, the "storm" being the belief that President Donald Trump will institute a justified martial law and through imprisonment and execution will cleanse the country of Satanic socialists.[7] Despite these beliefs sounding more like trashy fiction than reality, the movement has prompted several would-be vigilantes to act out, including an armed man who attempted to take control of a cement plant in Arizona, convinced it was a front for a child sex-trafficking ring.[8] (A key plank of the movement's beliefs is that Democrats are secretly abusing and murdering children as part of a Satanic child sex ring.[9])

In that context, Bickle's thoughts are especially chilling because we can see them reflected in the social and political landscape before us. His opening narration reads like a manifesto penned by an unhinged Twitter user, fringe hashtags surrounding extremist memes: "Listen, you fuckers, you screwheads—here is a man who would not take it anymore. A man who stood up to the scum, the cunts, the dogs, the filth, the shit. Here is a man who stood up." Indeed, "There are Travis Bickles out there—only now they are being brought together and radicalised on the internet."[10]

Reflecting this worldview wasn't the intent of the film, of course. To be clear, Bickle is not a right-wing character and isn't meant to represent any kind of specific political leaning. He doesn't have an ideology. In fact, he is apolitical, unaware of the political landscape outside of some sparse surface knowledge. After picking up presidential candidate Charles Palantine (Leonard Harris), Bickle tells him he's a big supporter. When pressed to explain why, Bickle admits, "I don't follow political issues much." When asked what he wants from a presidential candidate, he tells Palantine, "Well, he should clean up this city here. It's full of filth and scum. Scum and filth. It's like an open sewer. I can hardly take it. Some days I go out and smell it, then I get headaches that just stay and never go away. We need a president that would clean up this whole mess, flush it out." So no, Bickle is not political, even if we can see aspects of his state of mind reflected in today's more extreme sociopolitical subcultures. He has no agenda. He has no belief system. He has no real ideology and no real principles beyond being angry at the world. Rather, he is alone, frustrated, and looking for a place to point that frustration. Rather than being about political radicalization, the film is about the self-radicalization that can occur through alienation. It's about the damage that can be done via isolation, the mental and emotional decay of urban loneliness. It's something Schrader knew well. Written during a time when his life was in shambles, alcoholism consuming him and his marriage shattered into pieces, writing the screenplay was an exploration of his own personal demons. Travis Bickle wasn't intended to be a political radical or a template for fringe extremism; it was meant to be Schrader himself. "It's me, without any brains," he told film critic Pauline Kael.[11]

The significance of making Travis Bickle a Vietnam veteran will be lost to some viewers under a certain age, but *Taxi Driver* came in the midst of a time when Vietnam veterans were increasingly depicted in entertainment as disturbed, emotionally scarred loners often prone to violence. The first serious film to use the trope was Peter Bogdanovich's *Targets* (1968), in which a disturbed Vietnam vet murders his family and then goes on a killing spree, though the boob-obsessed Russ Meyer got there first with the decidedly less-serious *Motorpsycho* (1965), a campy exploitation picture in which a deranged vet leads a motorcycle gang in a series of rapes and murders. (*Motorpsycho* is also notable for leading directly to the production of Meyer's best-known cult classic, *Faster, Pussycat! Kill! Kill!* [1965], which is effectively a female-led version of the previous movie.) Such major pictures as *The Deer Hunter* (1978), for which Robert De Niro received an Academy Award nomination for Best Actor, and the action-focused Sylvester Stallone vehicle *First Blood* (1982), helped cement the trope into the public consciousness, though, even at the time of *Taxi Driver*'s release, the perception was there. Making the character a Vietnam veteran, even if only mentioned in passing, would have been a cue to the audience saying, "This guy probably has some issues."

Interestingly, Bickle likely knows in his heart that there is something wrong with him, even if he can't acknowledge it. When he first stalks Betsy outside the campaign headquarters at which she works, he speeds off when approached by her colleague, Tom (Albert Brooks in his first film role). This could simply be a case of not wanting to be caught at the scene, but one can read a degree of guilt in his reaction. In fact, he would have little reason to speed away were it not for a realization, even if subconsciously, that he was beginning to dabble in a dangerous game. He knows in his gut that his growing obsessions are dark and wrong. That's in part what his monologues are all about. He is trying to convince himself of his own righteousness in order to allow himself the freedom to finally act out on his antihero fantasies.

Scorsese presents this brilliantly in a brief scene during which Bickle takes an antacid. He drops the tablet into a glass of water, and the water begins to bubble and fizz. In this context, however, it looks more like the water is boiling. The camera lingers there longer than is comfortable, the popping, roiling water a metaphor for Bickle's very soul, disturbed and unable to be at rest.

Bickle's inability to recognize social norms allows him to be forward and persistent in a way most people wouldn't. When he approaches Betsy for a date, the situation is awkward. He's insistent to an uncomfortable degree, but she sees some kind of charm in him and agrees to meet for coffee. Was it mere curiosity that drew her in, or did she truly see something appealing in Bickle's rambling, intrusive approach? Sheppard's performance portrays her as naïvely intrigued by him on an intellectual level. "I don't believe I've ever met anyone quite like you," she says during their first lunch. Bickle is awkward throughout, offering long, unsolicited opinions on Tom that say more about Bickle than they do about the target of his criticism. Tom doesn't respect you, he tells her. These attempts to drive a wedge between them sharply illustrates Bickle's character, in no small part because they ring so true. Like the classic "your boyfriend doesn't treat you right" nice guy, Bickle sees every other man as a threat and seeks to isolate the object of his affections by eroding their trust in others. Unable to rise without tearing another down, Bickle paints the rest of the world as an enemy and from the very start attempts to imprint that worldview on Betsy. If he can isolate her from society just as he is, then he can control her.

The final manifestation of this desire to control her comes when Bickle takes her to the movies. It's a classic choice, the traditional choice. By the 1970s, going to the movies had been the quintessential American date for decades. That's what makes Schrader's choice to have their bad date involve a pornographic movie so powerful. Once commonplace in New York but now a relic of the 1970s, pornographic theaters used to dot the Manhattan landscape, symbols of seediness and the decay of the city. When Bickle takes Betsy to an adult movie, it's a subversion of what was seen as a pure American pastime—going to the movies—and a decision that injects filth into a cherished part of the cultural landscape. Her discomfort is our own. This is Bickle's attempt to drag her into his world. If she can lower herself to this, if he can urge her to suffer it until she accepts it as normal, then he'll have removed her from society at large and pulled her into his small, insular world.

When the control he seeks eludes him and Betsy leaves the theater in disgust, he uses her reaction to justify his disdain for society. "She is just like the others, cold and distant," he says via narration. It's a pathological way to think, but people like Bickle are perpetual victims. At one point he says he thinks he has stomach cancer. There is no reason for him to think this, but Bickle's belief that the world has been unfair to him manifests itself in every aspect of his life. He can't control the world around him and is overwhelmed by its presence, so he attempts to control others. Betsy is just one of *many* things he is unable to control. Languishing in obscurity—"Loneliness has followed me my whole life," he says in narration—and desperate to *matter*, he looks for another place to salve his psychological wounds. He finds it in Iris, a thirteen-year-old prostitute working for a slimy pimp named Charles, also known as Sport (Harvey Keitel, in his fourth role for Scorsese). Bickle spots Iris several times throughout the film, walking the streets in a wide sun hat, tall boots, and tiny shorts. It was a striking image, shocking even for the 1970s, an era when icons like David Bowie and Jimmy Page carried on affairs with fourteen-year-olds and *Sugar 'n' Spice*, a magazine published by *Playboy*, printed images of a nude, ten-year-old Brooke Shields.[12]

In this context, the choice to make the object of Bickle's impulse to find something important to do—someone to save, some sort of "good" to achieve, some way to matter, some way to seize *control* of his life—the choice for this to be a thirteen-year-old prostitute is an interesting and disturbing one. A man attempts to save a child? That story is universal. A man attempts to save a prostitute? That's still an idea audiences can sympathize with. But combine the two, make the character a child prostitute (and a seemingly willing one at that), dress her like the streetwalkers of the era, and make her the subject of attention from a man who had just taken another woman to a porno theater? Stirred into a cocktail glass and shaken, that concoction is enough to make one gag. The filmmakers certainly understood the territory they were delving into was dicey. "They were very uncomfortable about my character. Nobody knew how to direct me," Foster recalled.[13]

The film's uneasy handling of Foster's character is made all the more disturbing through a largely improvised scene between her and Sport, the brawny pimp who manages her life. In a brief scene inserted just prior to Bickle's shooting spree, he and Iris dance in a dim apartment. Sport holds her close and purrs in her ear as they dance. The monologue he delivers was not in the script. With the idea to do Barry White–inspired lyrics as dialogue, Keitel riffed on a romantic mantra Sport likely delivered to her time and again, keeping her under his control. With the context of knowing Iris is just a child, it makes one's skin crawl:

> When you're close to me like this, I feel so good. I only wish every man could know what it's like to be loved by you. That every woman everywhere had a man that loves her like I love you. God, it's good so close. You know, at times like this, I know I'm a lucky man. Touching a woman who wants me and needs me. Yeah, it's only you that keeps me together.

In any other picture, this scene of an adult grooming and manipulating a child clearly underlines Sport as the villain, yet by now we know better. He *is* a villain, to be sure, but is Bickle any better? Sport is a real pimp abusing real girls, yes, yet we sense that perhaps Bickle could be just like Sport if he took a right instead of a left. They operate in much the same way. They manipulate others through their vulnerabilities and, if necessary, will *create* vulnerabilities in the other person in order to control them. Your coworker doesn't respect you, but I do; guys on the street are predators, but I'm not. They're all just shades of gray under the same oppressive tree. Either man will position himself as the only sanctuary his victim has against a world out to devour them both.

Bickle knows he and Sport are alike, though Bickle can't consciously see it. It's a classic case of projection on his part.[14] He recognizes himself in the pimp. He sees himself projected not through a funhouse mirror that distorts reality but through one that shows his true self in another life. The money given to Bickle by Sport earlier in the film traces this journey. The first meeting between this triad of people comes early on, when Iris jumps into Travis's cab to escape her pimp, and Sport offers Travis some cash to keep things quiet before he takes the girl away. Travis begs off on taking the money at first but in the end relents. He carries that twenty with him, looking at it as if it's significant. And it is. To him, it's representative of his own morals; of whether he believes the things he says about scum, about purity, about women; it's about whether those things are true. Ultimately, they are not, but his handling of that bill convinces him they are. Travis Bickle is not a man of ideals or morals; he is a man who believes he sees the world for what it truly is, then uses that bleak vision of humanity to justify his own flawed moral code. He holds onto the money because to him it represents the dividing line between him and Sport. When finally given the opportunity, he pays Sport with it in order to get into Iris's apartment. It's a small rebellion, a feeble gesture to distance himself from his own impulses. He thinks, by rejecting that twenty-dollar bill, he's also rejecting the thing that separates himself from Sport. But if all that separates the two is a twenty-dollar bill, how pure is Bickle, really?

In his mind, at least, there is a vast gulf between them. It's curious that he becomes obsessed with "saving" Iris only after seeing presidential candidate Senator Charles Palantine on television. Suddenly, Bickle becomes consumed with a mission to do something important. He buys an arsenal of guns for no specific reason. He works out with a religious intensity yet maintains a horrible diet. At first, he toys with the idea of assassinating Palantine, going so far as to show up armed at one of his rallies, but he flees the scene after he is noticed by Secret Service agents. He formulates another plan instead. Betsy saw Palantine as a good man, as a man worthy of admiration, but for Bickle the greatest thing someone could do is to "clean up this whole mess, flush it out." He connects the two in his mind, this idea of being the hero who can clean up the city and being the person Betsy admired, so what better way to clean up the city than to subconsciously cleanse it from men like himself? Travis sought to control Betsy, Sport controls Iris, so the mission becomes to liberate Iris from Sport. It's a twisted form of self-flagellation.

The final orgy of violence presents a deranged kind of heroism that repulses rather than attracts. Bickle's first attack on Sport is cowardly, a surprise gut shot with a pistol at point blank range. He then storms the apartment building where Iris lives. He shoots. He is shot. One man's fingers are blasted off in a grotesque display. Bickle is winged in the neck. Blood splatters and sprays. The screenplay describes the scene as the "psychopath's Second Coming," and it is. Sport returns and is killed. When Bickle reaches Iris's room, she pleads for him to stop, but violence has a forward momentum that is difficult to halt. More killing. And when the killing is done, Bickle turns the gun on himself. Click. No bullets left. His final triumph, his heroic suicide, is denied him. He points his fingers at his own head, his eyes deranged, and motions as if he is shooting himself. It's one of cinema's most lasting images and is a remarkably accurate portrayal of how so many of today's shooting rampages end.

Yet the world inside the film sees Bickle's rampage differently than we see it from outside the film. It's painted in the media as an act of heroism. He saved a young girl from prostitution. The papers are filled with praise for him. When Betsy ends up in his cab, she praises him, too. The world sees Bickle as a brave civilian who did something good. Music begins to play as he drives, a sweet Herrmann melody, but as Bickle cruises on, there is one last sound, a backward musical note, and as that note twists, we see a brief glimpse of his eyes in the rearview mirror. They look wild. There is still a monster inside Travis Bickle.

CONCLUSION AND IMPACT

Taxi Driver's legacy looms large. Made on a sparse budget of just $1.9 million, the picture took in $28.3 million at the box office and was one of the top twenty highest-grossing pictures of the year. It received four Academy Award nominations, including Best Picture and Best Actor; won the Palme d'Or at the 1976 Cannes Film Festival; and was beloved by critics. To this day, the American Film Institute ranks it among the best films ever made, and the Writer's Guild of America hails the script as one of the best.

More importantly, the film brought Scorsese the widespread acclaim that would follow him (on and off) throughout his career. It cemented him as one of the most innovative purveyors of violence and darkness in Hollywood, which is saying a lot, considering it was made during a period when some of the darkest films in Hollywood history were made. And perhaps most important of all, it formalized what would become one of the most fruitful director-actor partnerships in film history.

The first time Scorsese and De Niro worked together, in 1973's *Mean Streets*, De Niro was still an aspiring actor trying to carve out a reputation. In 1974, he played the young Vito Corleone in *The Godfather Part II*, for which he won the Academy Award for Best Supporting Actor. By the time *Taxi Driver* was released, De Niro was on the radar of cinephiles as a rising new talent. The picture cemented his reputation and earned him his first Best Actor nomination. In the decades since, "You talkin' to me?" has become one of the most recognizable movie references in pop culture.

Though De Niro had already appeared in a film for Scorsese, their long-running collaboration had yet to truly germinate until this picture. In the early days of the director's career, Keitel had already cemented a place in the director's cast of regulars, appearing in four of his first five movies, two of them as the lead. It would be *Taxi Driver* that would cause a seismic shift in the director's attentions and create one of the greatest director-actor relationships in cinema. Alfred Hitchcock famously returned to actors like Cary Grant and James Stewart, Tim Burton and Johnny Depp have at times seemed inseparable, and during the '70s Diane Keaton practically defined Woody Allen films. But aside from the relationship between Akira Kurosawa and Toshiro Mifine, which is arguably the most creatively productive collaboration in film history, no one else defines director-actor collaborations better than Scorsese and De Niro. Including 2019's *The Irishman*, they'd make ten films together, one of them a short, and several of them are considered among the greatest films ever made. (An eleventh, *Killers of the Flower Moon*, was in preproduction as this book was written.) The three movies widely considered Scorsese's best, *Taxi Driver*,

Robert De Niro and Martin Scorsese developed a shorthand with one another on *Taxi Driver* that over the decades turned into one of the most creatively fruitful collaborations in cinema history. *Columbia Pictures. Photographer: Josh Weiner*

Raging Bull, and *GoodFellas*, all prominently feature De Niro. Of De Niro's five Academy Award nominations for Best Actor, three of them came via Scorsese films (*Taxi Driver*, *Raging Bull*, and *Cape Fear*). For this alone, *Taxi Driver* casts a long shadow over the cinema of the decades to follow.

The film cast a shadow outside its own medium, too. For example, it indirectly changed the comic-book medium. In 1986 and 1987, DC Comics published *Watchmen*, a twelve-issue miniseries by Alan Moore and Dave Gibbons that changed the face of comics forever, to the point where you can divide comics history into pre-*Watchmen* and post-*Watchmen* eras. Later compiled into a graphic novel and adapted into a 2009 film by Zack Snyder, *Watchmen*'s Rorschach, one of its most iconic characters, is a masked vigilante obsessed with cleaning up the streets with amoral brutality. The story begins with an excerpt from his journal, and it's now one of the most famous passages in comics. A portion of it reads,

> This city is afraid of me. I have seen its true face. The streets are extended gutters and the gutters are full of blood and when the drains finally scab over, all the vermin will drown. The accumulated filth of all their sex and murder will foam up

about their waists and all the whores and politicians will look up and shout "Save us!" And I'll look down, and whisper "no."[15]

It may as well be taken right out of Travis Bickle's personal journal. The parallels are so pronounced that, when DC decided to cash in on *Watchmen*'s legacy with a *Before Watchmen* series of prequel spinoffs, issue 3 of the *Before Watchmen: Rorschach* miniseries features Rorschach taking a cab driven by none other than Bickle himself. Further, when Snyder adapted the graphic novel into a feature film, he and production designer Alex McDowell drew directly from *Taxi Driver*, too. McDowell noted,

> Zack and I talked about the best representation of the reality level of the film and decided to use *Taxi Driver* as the core reference. . . . We took frames from *Taxi Driver*, then painted them with the *Watchmen* colors so the end result is both period-correct, pop-culturally referential and graphic-novel layered. One of the bars on the street came directly from *Taxi Driver*.[16]

Though perhaps the most notable shadow cast by *Taxi Driver* is the one cast onto real life. On March 30, 1981, John Hinckley Jr. attempted to assassinate President Ronald Reagan, shooting him in the chest. Hinckley was directly inspired by *Taxi Driver* and, bizarrely, by the young Jodie Foster. He developed an obsession for the movie and for Foster herself, for a time moving to New Haven, Connecticut, to stalk her. After writing her dozens of letters, he finally vowed to do something spectacular to impress her. For him, that something was to assassinate the president. He followed around President Jimmy Carter for a time but was arrested on gun charges before he could act and so turned his attention to the newly elected Reagan. "Jodie, I would abandon this idea of getting Reagan in a second if I could only win your heart and live out the rest of my life with you, whether it be in total obscurity or whatever," Hinckley wrote in a letter to her just prior to his crime. "By sacrificing my freedom and possibly my life, I hope to change your mind about me. This letter is being written only an hour before I leave for the Hilton Hotel. Jodie, I'm asking you to please look into your heart and at least give me the chance, with this historical deed, to gain your respect and love."[17] Perhaps a less crude and angry Travis Bickle would have written the same to a young campaign worker named Betsy. Hinckley Jr. was released on September 10, 2016, and in 2018 a judge ruled that he is allowed to live on his own.[18] In other words, a real-life Travis Bickle is still driving his cab.

Taxi Driver's success emboldened Scorsese. He decided his next film would be a grand experiment in subverting a beloved Hollywood genre. It would be a spectacular failure but one that would set the stage for his next masterpiece.

6

NEW YORK, NEW YORK (1977)

FILM DETAILS

RELEASE DATE: June 21, 1977
WRITTEN BY: Mardik Martin, Earl Mac Rauch
STARRING: Liza Minnelli, Robert De Niro
RUNNING TIME: 153 minutes (original release), 136 minutes (recut version), 164 minutes (1981 re-release)

ABOUT THE FILM

Following the critical and artistic success of *Taxi Driver*, a brooding meditation on a man teetering on the edge of violence, the last thing you'd expect of Martin Scorsese would be a modern tribute to classic Hollywood musicals, yet that's exactly what he set out to produce with *New York, New York*, an ambitious improvisation of a film that showcased what movies from Hollywood's golden age would look like if presented with 1970s grit.

New York, New York attempts to sully the purity of Hollywood musicals with a heaping helping of docurealism—but *sully* is not quite the right word. Scorsese came to the film with genuine affection for this period of cinema. He didn't want to besmirch it as much as he wanted to recontextualize it, to deconstruct it and look at it from a modern vantage point. This wasn't the first time Scorsese delved into this territory. Part of the aim of *Alice Doesn't Live Here Anymore* was

---

to bring an uncompromising sense of realism to what could have been an overly sweet story about a mother and son moving on from a family tragedy. That same concept is at the heart of this not-quite-a-musical.

Scorsese said he was intent on "making a real Hollywood movie and putting my stamp on it." He wanted to bring to the screen a "love of the old stylization, you know, a love of those films, but then showing what it really is like as close as possible in the foreground. That's, I guess, what they called revisionism and that's why the picture—besides being too damn long, it's sprawling—didn't catch on."[1]

On the surface, it was made to look like a classic musical. He wanted to capture the look of postwar films, with accurate clothing and color and even shots drawn directly from the great musicals of Bing Crosby and others. "The homage to the genre, the love note to the genre, was the way the film should look," he said.[2] But the heart of the movie would be something much different, something modern and dark, with the work of John Cassavetes of particular influence. Musicals of the golden age often featured "heels," protagonists with sharply negative traits, but they were *likeable* heels. The audience rarely minded when they got the girl. But Scorsese wanted to scrub away the glitz and present a heel as he'd truly be.

The story in *New York, New York* is a standard one. A GI home from World War II (Jimmy Doyle, played by Robert De Niro) meets an attractive young woman at a VJ-Day celebration (Francine Evans, played by Liza Minelli). He tries to pick her up, she resists, but there is an obvious attraction between them. A love/hate romance blossoms into a relationship, then a marriage, then parenthood, but professional jealousies driven by Jimmy's insecurities and controlling nature eventually tear them apart. In the end, Francine manages to rise above it and becomes a beloved star.

These are all familiar elements, tropes plucked from a dozen bright, colorful Hollywood musicals. In Scorsese's hands, however, the veneer of perfection, of lightness, of coziness and familiarity, all of it is stripped away, leaving us with a film that exists uneasily in two different worlds.

ANALYSIS

The classic Hollywood heel can often be a jerk, but they are rarely *loathsome.* More importantly, they rarely get in the way of a happy ending. But then, classic Hollywood musicals were not directed by Martin Scorsese.

The first scene between De Niro and Minelli in *New York, New York* sets the stage for their entire relationship yet not in the way viewers expect. In many ways, it's a scene familiar to audiences. A handsome, young GI verbally spars with a beautiful, young woman playing hard to get, the way they make one another bristle telling us they actually fancy one another. There is a juvenile aspect to classic Hollywood courtships, playing up the schoolyard notion that, when a boy likes a girl, he picks on her, and when a girl likes a boy, she treats him badly. That so much golden-age cinema leaned on this cliché points to an American culture that had not yet matured past childish notions of how men and women interact. Scorsese picks up on this idea, riffing on it in a familiar way but doing so knowing full well the rest of the film is going to subvert the classic Hollywood romance that inevitably unfolds following these "will they or won't they" meetings.

See, Jimmy is not a nice guy. His persistence follows well-established silver-screen tropes—in Hollywood, the first few "no's" don't count—so for a little while, it's easy to believe we'll see that same story again. But rather than the snarky charmer with a heart of gold, Jimmy is controlling and often cruel. Rather than the sweet romance popular musicals made their stock-in-trade, this is an abusive relationship doomed to fail.

The moment when the relationship goes from a dalliance to something real is during an audition. Jimmy can't make any headway with the bar owner he's trying to impress. His energetic improvisation isn't the kind of crowd-pleasing dance music the owner wants. But when Francine steps in and leads the band in a rendition of "You Brought a New Kind of Love to Me," a swing band standard of the 1930s, '40s, and '50s, the pair learn they work together well. Or rather, they have the *potential* to work together well because in truth Jimmy resents her talent. He doesn't want her garnering any attention.

This is underscored later when the band gets a good review that specifically cites Francine's vocal talents. This doesn't sit well with Jimmy. She begins to unintentionally take a leading role in the band. They get a headline gig at a fancy hotel, with Francine as the star attraction. Later, while rehearsing with the band, she starts the countdown to a song rather than Jimmy, who typically does it. This infuriates him. He informs her in no uncertain terms what the pecking order of the band is. It's rather appropriate that the song they are about to perform is "Take a Chance on Love" because that's exactly what Francine is doing with Jimmy. He is not interested in having a relationship of equals. If she won't take second billing to him, if she won't be subservient to him, then he wants no part of it. He doesn't respect her art. It's not even clear that he respects *her*.

When Jimmy proposes later in the film, it's not the proposal of a man consumed with love, though it initially appears that way on the surface. Francine reads a poem she wrote about him. Upon hearing it, he immediately calls a cab and takes her to the home of the local justice of the peace. He bangs on the door, waking the occupants, and says he wants to marry her right then and there. It's a spur-of-the-moment choice, as improvised as his music, but Francine isn't swept off her feet by the gesture. Rather, she's crestfallen at how reckless it all seems. "I just thought it was going to be different," she says. There is no romance here, no love, just a man trying to scoop up something he wants. In a moment that should be an important milestone in their lives, Jimmy acts like a jerk, controlling and demanding. Even when he expresses his love for her, it's in terms of ownership. "I don't want anybody else to be with you except me," he says.

These scenarios may sound familiar to those who have taken a deep dive into Scorsese's filmography, and they should. *Life Lessons*, his third of the 1989 anthology film *New York Stories* with Francis Ford Coppola and Woody Allen, also deals with an artist who does not respect the art of his female companion and who boldly declares his love for her, not out of love, but out of a desire to possess her. That they both deal with similar scenarios is no coincidence, as they both draw from the same influence: Russian author Fyodor Dostoevsky's 1867 novella *The Gambler*. The story is ostensibly about a man's struggles with gambling as he attempts to pay off crushing debts, but it's also about the dissolution of a relationship. "There are scenes in *The Gambler* that are quite extraordinary about the relationship, the humiliation and love and battles between the two. So, over the years, I was trying to work out something with that. I found that elements of their relationship found their way into my movies," Scorsese said. "In *New York, New York*, a lot of it! The difficulty in being with each other, the difficulty of loving."[3]

It's hardly surprising the theme would resonate with Scorsese, who has been married five times and had a series of turbulent relationships in the '70s and '80s. (In fairness to Scorsese, he married his fifth wife, Helen Morris, in 1999; they've been married twenty years as of this writing.)

Prior to making the film, the director's vision of what it would be was more hopeful than the completed picture turned out to be. He initially described it as a movie "about the decline of the big bands and a couple . . . who try to make a go of it but they have no money and they break up and then they get back together after they make it."[4] The finished product is far more cynical.

To say that Jimmy has difficulty loving is an understatement. When Francine is pregnant, he offers no support. He's out all the time. He refuses to help her. Worst of all, he's emotionally manipulative. She asks him to help, asks him to change his schedule so he can assist with the baby, but that only makes him angry. He claims, without his music, he's useless to her, but that's just an excuse to skirt his parental responsibilities. Later, when she meets with a record company executive to entertain the possibility of getting signed to a deal, he tries to physically wrest her away from the meeting. When she complains that he is hurting her, Jimmy says, "Well, I'm sorry I'm hurting you. If you came with me, I wouldn't have to hurt you."

This is an abusive relationship by any measure. He gets drunk. He gets angry. He's finally kicked out of the club, violently. Why would he act this way? Because he doesn't want her to succeed, certainly not in a way that overshadows him, but in his heart, he knows it's inevitable.

This film's bleak take on the musical may seem cynical, but perhaps seeing cynicism in it is itself a cynical view. Rather, the movie betrays a sadness at the passing of a way of life, or at least a way of life Americans once dreamed of having. Those postwar years were looked back on with great fondness (and in many ways they still are), but reality was quite different than our Technicolor daydreams. The 1970s were a grim decade for cinema, not in terms of quality—it's widely regarded as a high point for the American auteur—but in terms of tearing away the image we once had of the perfect American life. We saw what was beneath the white picket fences and apple pies, and what we found was often ugly. Scorsese had already done this with *Alice* and examined it further in *Taxi Driver*. Many of the same themes are present here; they are merely recast as a traditional musical.

Jimmy would be a lovable scamp in most other movies, but here he is anything but. He's cruel and self-centered. As a result, we get one of the most common narrative arcs in the Scorsese library: the rise and fall. And like so many Scorsese protagonists who fall short of happiness (or success or wealth or freedom or whatever else they seek to attain), Jimmy's downfall is ultimately his own fault. The coming ruination of his relationship with Francine lies at his own feet. He met a charming and talented woman with whom he could share a love for music. They could even build careers together as they built a family together. Francine is certainly willing. But Jimmy's rebellious nature, his refusal to conform to what is expected of him, this is more than just rebellious ideology. It's insecurity manifesting itself in attacks on the people closest to him.

Jimmy's reaction to her success and the way he handles her talent tends toward the petty. At one point late in the film, he and his band are playing in a club after she has been signed to a record deal. She's in the audience. The band begins playing one of her songs, so she approaches the stage to join them, but Jimmy immediately launches the band into a bop number instead. It's unsingable. Dejected, she leaves. The pair get into a big fight in the car. He yells at her.

He yells about the baby. He says she has it easy, she has everything, and he has nothing. His resentment leads him to an outburst of violence—and there ends their relationship. This is not the expected Hollywood ending.

But Scorsese subverts his own subversion by inserting a standard Hollywood ending anyway, finishing *New York, New York* with a huge stage production that could have been lifted right out of the great musicals of the 1950s and 1960s. It's huge. It's stylish. It's extravagant. If there was any doubt that casting Minelli was the right choice—and to be sure, her charm provides a much-needed contrast to De Niro's sulky, angry performance—it's washed away here, when her natural talent for owning the stage is finally allowed to shine in its full glory. She sings the title track, "New York, New York," written especially for the film by composers John Kander and Fred Ebb, who also wrote the musicals *Cabaret* and *Chicago*. It's a huge production set in the same nightclub where the pair first met years prior. (It's worth noting that this lush ending was not in the original release. It was added in a 1981 re-release, along with close to thirty minutes of additional footage. It's that 164-minute re-release that is now the version most commonly seen.)

We do get a brief epilogue. After a rousing rendition of *New York, New York*, Francine and her son run into Jimmy backstage. For a fleeting moment, he seems at peace. More importantly, he appears to be genuinely proud of her success. They part, and all seems well—melancholy, but well. So perhaps Scorsese did give us a classic Hollywood ending after all—but only a taste of one.

CONCLUSION AND IMPACT

New York, New York was a grand experiment by a young filmmaker determined to merge the old and new. He took great pains to emulate the look and feel of golden-age musicals, in part in order to keep audiences off balance. He wanted to evoke those familiar images from a technical standpoint but then subvert them via story and character. Emboldened by the confidence that comes with being young and coming off a critical success, much of this was done by the seat of his pants. Scorsese has a well-deserved reputation for letting his performers improvise, though that reputation can be misleading. In most cases his actors aren't just riffing on set. It's a controlled process. They improvise in rehearsals, then material that Scorsese likes is worked into the script. For the most part, this has been one of his great strengths, leading to such legendary scenes as De Niro's "You talkin' to me?" in *Taxi Driver* and Joe Pesci's "funny" scene in *GoodFellas*.

Here, however, the improvisation was allowed to dominate the movie. Much of the dialogue was developed in improvisation, and it shows. At times the approach veers into self-indulgence. Many early scenes drag on past their welcome, as De Niro and Minelli banter beyond a scene's needs. Their opening introduction stretches on for twenty minutes. A kiss in the rain goes on long enough to be funny, then just keeps going and going. In a scene showing the couple checking into a hotel, witty banter with the guy at the front desk continues long after most directors would have yelled "cut!" And there are many other examples. Perhaps *New York, New York* would have benefited from Thelma Schoonmaker's touch. (In fact, this would be the last feature film Scorsese would direct that *wouldn't* be edited by Schoonmaker.) The director himself acknowledges this shortcoming of the film, admitting in a DVD commentary that he'd have liked to have made the improvised scenes leaner and tighter, but time constraints made it impossible.[5]

In that regard, *New York, New York* proved to be a testing ground for new approaches and techniques. Not all of them worked—he'd perfect how he used improvisation in later films—but in other cases it helped him refine techniques he had already been playing with. He shot music scenes *to* his desired music, for example, rather than assemble them in editing, setting up his shots to match bars of music. He'd later do the same in movies like *GoodFellas* to powerful effect. The scene from that film in which we tour the bodies left in Jimmy Conway's wake, all of it set to the piano outro of "Layla" by Derek and the Dominos, is a prime example of that approach. Each shot was painstakingly designed with the song in mind, with Scorsese going so far as to play the music on-set to ensure they got the timing right. In some respects, parts of *New York, New York* is proof of a concept for techniques of that nature.

But audiences don't go to the movies for experiments, and they certainly don't go to see their favorite genres turned inside out. Clocking in at over two and a half hours upon release (thanks to additional footage, today's home releases are closer to three) and featuring little of what Americans love about musicals, *New York, New York* was a box-office failure and a critical dud, the *New York Times* calling it "elaborate, ponderous" and "nervy and smug."[6] It barely made back its hefty production budget. Oddly, one of the things preventing it from being a total loss for the studio, United Artists, was the success of *Rocky* the year prior. The two pictures got made under an agreement to intertwine their profits—the idea was that *New York, New York*'s expected success would help fund the underdog picture *Rocky*—and as a result, "*Rocky* wound up paying for whatever losses we had on *New York, New York*," according to Mike Medavoy, senior VP of production at United Artists.[7]

The picture's failure sent Scorsese spiraling into depression and drug abuse, sinking him into one of the darkest periods of his life.[8] He had no other pictures to make. He thought he was done. The only thing on the horizon was a story he felt no connection, a book De Niro had been insisting he read since the production of *Alice Doesn't Live Here Anymore*. It was ostensibly about boxing, and it would become what some consider his greatest work.

7

RAGING BULL (1980)

FILM DETAILS

RELEASE DATE: November 14, 1980
WRITTEN BY: Paul Schrader, Mardik Martin
STARRING: Robert De Niro, Joe Pesci, Cathy Moriarty
RUNNING TIME: 129 minutes

ABOUT THE FILM

Following the critical success of 1976's *Taxi Driver*, which garnered four Academy Award nominations, including one for Best Picture, Scorsese found himself at a difficult crossroads. His previous film, the musical *New York, New York* (1977), was a box-office failure, sending the director into a spiral of drugs and depression.[1] His concert film *The Last Waltz* (1978) was an acclaimed work but did little to attract the attention of Hollywood money. Fueled in part by substance abuse, he began to despair, wondering if he'd ever again make a great film.

Robert De Niro had been pitching him an idea for years, however, a biopic based on boxer Jake LaMotta's autobiography *Raging Bull: My Story*. The director was at first reluctant to tackle a movie on a subject he knew little about and cared for even less—boxing—but De Niro was persistent, pushing the film on him even when Scorsese was in the hospital ailing from a bad interaction of drugs and medication. There in the hospital, despite some misgivings, Scorsese eventually relented.[2] The screenplay was developed by Mardik Martin and was heavily revised by Paul Schrader (with input by De Niro, who felt strongly about the material) and focused less on LaMotta's career as a boxer and more on his obsession with second wife, Vickie LaMotta.

Once convinced to make it, Scorsese cast aside his disdain for sports and meticulously crafted a series of intense boxing scenes around which this domestic narrative was wrapped. The resulting work is a technical marvel, thanks in no small part to editor Thelma Schoonmaker, who began her long collaboration with Scorsese with *Who's Knocking at My Door?* For *Raging Bull*, she won her first of three Academy Awards, the other two also for Scorsese pictures (*The Aviator* and *The Departed*). In fact, she would edit every Scorsese movie from this one forward.

In *Raging Bull*, a young LaMotta (De Niro) balances his budding success in the ring against a volatile marriage and the intrusion of local gangsters on his career. He encounters Vickie (Cathy Moriarty), a fifteen-year-old who catches his eye at a public swimming pool. His brother Joey (Joe Pesci) introduces them, and a whirlwind courtship begins. Meanwhile, LaMotta continues his rise through the boxing ranks, briefly winning the world middleweight championship. A long rivalry with the legendary Sugar Ray Robinson also ensues. But LaMotta's obsessive and controlling behavior toward Vickie proves to be emotionally crippling. He takes a brutal beating at Robinson's hands, then destroys his relationship with both Vickie and Joey in a violent, paranoid outburst. We then flash-forward to an older LaMotta running a seedy nightclub, trying to regain his past glory, and grappling with criminal charges stemming from allowing minors in his club. Rather than end on a triumphant note, the film's ending is downbeat.

Though it barely made waves upon release, *Raging Bull* went on to be a critical darling and is now widely considered not only one of the director's best works but also one of the greatest films of all time.

ANALYSIS

No man is a hero. At least, not in Martin Scorsese's world. Nominated for eight Academy Awards and hailed by many as the best film of the '80s, Scorsese's meditation on how violence and personal failure are intertwined, *Raging Bull*, is in many ways the perfect encapsulation of the classic Scorsese protagonist. Ironic, considering the director initially felt little connection to the material and largely made it at the urging of Robert De Niro.

Raging Bull tells the story of real-life boxer Jake LaMotta (1922–2017), a rough, Bronx-bred fighter who rose to world middleweight champion in 1949 and sustained a six-fight rivalry with fellow hall-of-fame boxer Sugar Ray Robinson. But despite all the focus on boxing matches, despite the directorial bravado on display, despite the remarkable technical flair in Scorsese's meticulously crafted fight scenes, *Raging Bull* is not a boxing film. Rather, it's a film about failure. It's about how imperfect people ruin the good things they have in life: their successes, their relationships, their reputation, and their very dignity. In that respect, it's a film very much in keeping with Scorsese's oeuvre.

As a general rule, films are about triumph or success or overcoming obstacles, especially sports films. Our protagonists face difficulties and, after some trials and tribulations, come through in the end. This is frequently not the case with Scorsese's work. His movies are less often about a man's rise and more often about his fall. Travis Bickle (*Taxi Driver*) rescues a child from abuse and prostitution but suffers a complete mental breakdown. Henry Hill (*GoodFellas*) thrives in the criminal underworld but ends up in witness protection. Jordan Belfort (*The Wolf of Wall Street*) becomes extremely wealthy and has everything a man could desire, and he loses it all to greed and corruption. Howard Hughes (*The Aviator*) becomes one of the world's most famous and influential men but implodes into mental illness, and so on.

LaMotta's story is much the same. He rises from the streets of the Bronx, a rough and tenacious fighter; becomes champion; but is ultimately consumed by paranoia and his own violent tendencies. Fat, lonely, forgotten, the Bronx Bull ends up a shadow of his former self, stumbling through clumsy monologues in an effort to evoke the power of his glory days.

The link in all these stories is that these men are the architects of their own downfall. They are not toppled by a corrupt system or an unlucky roll of the dice. Outside forces do not bring them to ruin and humiliation. Their own actions do. As we see more clearly in *Raging Bull* than in any of his other work, Scorsese is concerned with personal failure. This failure is often driven by hubris, just as often by greed, and occasionally by mental illness. Regardless of the root causes of that failure, what's noteworthy is that it's virtually always internal.

For a film so concerned with violence, both physical and emotional, *Raging Bull* opens with stark beauty. A stirring string section plays the intermezzo from *Cavalleria rusticana* by Italian composer Pietro Mascagni, while LaMotta shifts and moves in slow motion, framed simply through the boxing ring's three ropes, displaying an effortless grace we'll never see from him again. It is the opening of a ballet, really. Gentle. Poetic. Beautiful.

The heart of *Raging Bull* is not in its fight scenes but in the relationship between La-Motta and his loved ones. It would also be the first of four times Joe Pesci, Robert De Niro, and Martin Scorsese would work together. *United Artists*

Yet the beauty also tells us something important. Here, as a major bout is about to begin, LaMotta is alone. He is in an arena full of cheering fans, and he is utterly *alone*. No other human beings are visible. The crowd is obscured in darkness. We know they are there only thanks to the occasional pop of flashbulbs. There are no trainers with him. No ringside assistants. No announcers or referees or even opponents. It's just LaMotta relishing a moment of isolated greatness.

This repeats throughout the film, though he is never as great as he is in that opening shot. LaMotta is at his proudest, his most self-assured, his most confident either when he is alone (usually delivering a stumbling monologue to a mirror) or when he is violently pummeling an opponent. The rest of the time, he's a brutish oaf, awkward around people, lacking social graces, sexist even by the era's standards, insecure, and paranoid.

Raging Bull's trajectory is one of steady rise followed by sudden fall, again and again and again. After the title sequence, we see a quick glimpse of an older LaMotta circa 1964, overweight, a lumbering giant waxing poetic about his better days. We then move to those better days, seeing him as a young up-and-comer in 1941, then undefeated, in the first of many bouts we'll see. In a last-minute rally, he batters his opponent. It's not enough. The judges hand LaMotta his first defeat. He refuses to leave the ring, though. A riot breaks out, the arena descending into an orgy of violence around him.

After the fight, he laments to his brother and manager Joey LaMotta that his hands are too small. Because of his small hands, he can never be a heavyweight. He'll never have a chance to fight the best. He presses Joey into punching him, repeatedly, to show that he can take the punishment. Joey does but doesn't understand why his brother wants him to do this. "What are you trying to prove? What's it prove?" he asks.

Jake LaMotta doesn't respond, but the answer becomes apparent. This is a man who refuses to give up. The only thing he knows is how to take (and deliver) a beating. This is underscored most heavily during his final bout against Robinson. Here, LaMotta is in a bad position. He's against the ropes and reeling. The action pauses. LaMotta smiles, the crowd fading into the background, and taunts his opponent. The Bronx Bull knows the fight is lost, but he has something to prove. The camera lingers on Robinson. The sound drops out except for the soft breathing of an animal. Shadows envelop the screen. Then the sound roars back in, Robinson attacks, and LaMotta is given as brutal a beating as is seen in the film. Blood splatters. It runs down his legs. LaMotta's second wife, Vickie, turns her head down in dismay. Robinson wins, and LaMotta's face is left a puffy, swollen mess of blood and flesh.

Yet he never goes down. After the bell, he wobbles to his opponent's corner: "You never got me down, Ray. Never got me down." It's difficult to know if we are supposed to be impressed or disgusted. When we see this, we better understand the bloated, fat LaMotta we see later in the film, lurching around like a drunken king in his club, holding court from the stage. From a distance, we're embarrassed for him. We cringe at him. The whole act is sad and pathetic, the flailing of a man who fails to see that he is washed up, still trying at fame despite the one thing he has to offer the world—his skill in the ring—being well behind him. But look again, and we see who he really is: a man who doesn't even realize when he's beaten.

In an effort to showcase this aspect of LaMotta's personality, Scorsese was forced to be inventive. "I just don't know how to shoot two guys in a boxing ring. I just don't," he once remarked.[3] He was not a sports fan. When De Niro first pitched him the idea of the film, he had no idea how he'd present boxing and had little interest in doing so. Even after he had been convinced, the director made little effort to depict the actual ebb and flow of a real boxing match.

Instead, *Raging Bull* is as impressionistic as any film by Robert Wiene (*The Cabinet of Dr. Caligari*) or Fritz Lang (*Metropolis*):

> Making (the documentaries) *Italianamerican* and *American Boy* showed me how to do *Raging Bull*. I just kept one word in mind: "Clarity," to get to the issue. It seemed to free me. What I liked to do in documentaries when people were telling stories was, rather than dissolving from one image to another so as to soften the cuts, to jump around until I was free of the form. A lot of that impulse wound up in *Raging Bull*.[4]

The bouts don't present action as much as they present the *impression* of action. Most are distinctive and boast their own identity. In the one Robinson fight LaMotta won, they battle, the camera spins 360 degrees, then takes an abrupt push forward as Robinson is felled between the ropes. Things lurch into slow motion, then eases back to normal speed before an instant cut to black, then a microphone descending from the top of the frame. It's a victory depicted by a dizzying whirlwind.

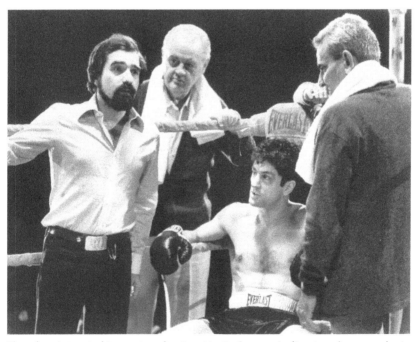

Though uninterested in sports or boxing, Martin Scorsese's dizzying choreography in *Raging Bull*'s fight sequences resulted in the most visceral boxing scenes ever put to film. *United Artists/Photofest*

LaMotta's third fight against Robinson is perhaps the best known of the film. As punches are thrown, animal calls are blended into the sound mix courtesy of sound designer Frank Warner (who, it should be noted, made these creative decisions on his own).[5] The whole bout is filmed as if the arena is on fire, the frame smothered in smoke and heat, and indeed, Scorsese had real flames burning just beneath the frame in order to give the proceedings a shimmering, smoldering effect.

The technical bravado continues through both ferocious and familial scenes. In a memorable montage sequence, Scorsese intercuts LaMotta home movies (shot in color and emulating actual LaMotta home movies) with quick glimpses of LaMotta fights. We see LaMotta versus Zivic in just a few still frames, then cut to home movies with Jake and Vickie. Another fight, then the faded color of Jake and Vickie getting married in court. Fight, then fleeting glimpses of a happy home life. A fight in two quick stills. Joey gets married in bleached-out film. A fight, one swing in stills, black-and-white. Jack and Vickie at a new house, with kids. Four years in time gone in moments, set to music, flashing between potent single frames and shaky home-movie footage. Montage is nothing new. It's a staple of cinema. Many movies have montages fraught with suggestion, and while this one does, as well, Scorsese is content to let the images speak for themselves, these fleeting pictures telling the story of an increasingly violent man and an increasingly unhappy family dynamic.

When we revisit the LaMottas after this sequence, they are doting on their children, with Joey and his wife present, a seemingly normal family. But they're not. Jake's desire to control Vickie is growing stronger. The brothers discuss an upcoming fight. Joey outlines why it's win-win for Jake. Vickie agrees, casually suggesting the other fighter is good-looking while doing so (though only echoing her brother-in-law as she does). Here is where we see a Jake LaMotta who is not merely insecure but also insecure to the point of paranoia.

And paranoia is, more so than violence, Jake LaMotta's defining characteristic. Or perhaps it's insecurity or a blend of both. Vickie's comment is an off-handed one, but it triggers something in her husband. Jake presses her, asking if she has an interest in this other boxer. She denies it. He then demands that Joey keep an eye on her, ensuring she stay loyal. "You start trouble for nothing," Joey says, but it doesn't matter. Jake won't listen. When he fights the boxer in question, Jake brutalizes him, destroying his once-handsome face. And when he wins, he gloats.

Paranoia and insecurity runs rampant throughout the film, and Scorsese's work underscores that whenever possible. It drives the Bronx Bull. This is never more evident than in his relationship with Vickie, his second wife and the one opponent Jake cannot master. Vickie is young, just fifteen when they meet (an uncomfortable fact the director does not dwell on), but she has an air of confidence about her that suggests she is in command of her life. They meet at a public swimming pool after Jake asks Joey to introduce them. Their initial conversation is gentle and awkward, largely improvised by De Niro and Moriarty, Vickie shot through a wire fence between them that serves as a metaphor for their relationship. They can touch, they connect, but there will always be something between them, a steel veil of sorts, the wire mesh of the fence not unlike the ropes of the boxing ring, except here Jake is outside the ring, and Vickie is on the inside.

On their first date together, LaMotta is softly controlling, gentle, but offering a hint at what is to come. He demands she sit closer to him in the car so he can put his arm around her. She's compliant (though one senses that it's not due to weakness on her part). At his apartment, they sit across the tiny kitchen table from one another, but he insists she sit closer. He draws her to his lap. Again, she gives in. As he takes her through the apartment and leads her to his bed, we see the walls and shelves are filled with religious iconography: paintings, statues, rosary beads. Scorsese's Catholic upbringing is evident throughout his work, including here. (Scorsese's icons generally fall from grace, and what could be more Catholic than that?) As LaMotta attempts to seduce this teenager in the very apartment where he sleeps with his wife, holy icons surround them. His first kisses are awkward. There is no sensuality to them. They are the kisses of a child. Intimacy is not something LaMotta knows or understands. But somehow, he makes an impression on her, and they become a couple.

It's interesting to note that, from here forward, Jake's first wife is dropped from the film entirely and is no longer acknowledged. That decision is telling. Scorsese frequently breaks the rules of traditional filmmaking, but he is rarely clumsy. *Raging Bull* is told from LaMotta's perspective; it's a film *about* his perceptions, so from this simple man's point of view, his previous wife effectively just disappears.

Though Jake is controlling, in many ways it's Vickie who controls him, though not intentionally. He is consumed by her. When outside the ring, she is all he is focused on. In demonstrating this, Scorsese employs his most impressive directorial techniques. His technical work in the ring is rightfully praised, but as a result, the equally remarkable material outside the ring is often overlooked. Any Scorsese film will have some degree of directorial showmanship, of course, and *Raging Bull* is no exception. In fact, aside perhaps from *GoodFellas*, no Scorsese picture serves as a better example of his rule-bending, norm-shattering, expectation-defying approach to filmmaking than this one. That it's a black-and-white film made in 1980, in the post–*Star Wars* era, seems notable, yet that's only a surface-level indication of the degree to which this film bucks the norm. Under Scorsese's direction, camera speeds shift at a whim. Audio syncing sometimes seems optional. Slow motion is intercut with normal speed with no regard for visual continuity. These aren't merely attention-grabbing tricks, either. It all serves to emphasize LaMotta's mental state.

In one moment, Vickie drives away with some mobsters. The scene suddenly drops into slow motion, music briefly rising to the top of the mix. In another, time crawls as she makes light conversation with these same men, Jake looking on from a distance. Sometimes sound slows down as the camera slows; sometimes it doesn't. Sometimes the two fall out of sync. The effect can be sinister, suggestive, ominous. In *Raging Bull*, slow motion (usually) doesn't punctuate violence or other such movie clichés. Here, it reeks of paranoia. Scorsese uses this technique again and again to place us inside Jake LaMotta's head, to make clear the depth of his focus and obsession. It's an obsession that will ruin him.

Things come to a head in one of the film's most memorable scenes. Jake and Joey are in Jake's home. Vickie arrives, says hello, and gives them each a kiss. Jake notes that she kissed his brother on the lips. He confronts Joey about it, first gently, but the conversation escalates until Jake flat-out asks Joey if he slept with Vickie. Joey thinks Jake has gone insane and tells him so in a monologue improvised by Pesci:

> I'm not gonna answer that. It's stupid. It's a sick question, and you're a sick fuck, and I'm not that sick that I'm gonna answer it. I'm leaving. If Nora calls, tell her I went home. I'm not staying in this nuthouse with you. You're a sick bastard. I feel sorry for you, I really do. You know what you should do? Try a little more fucking and a little less eating, so you won't have problems upstairs in the bedroom, and you pick on me and everybody else. You understand me, you fucking wacko? You're cracking up! Fucking screwball!

Joey leaves. Jake goes upstairs and confronts Vickie, smashing down the bathroom door and smacking her. She screams at him, telling him yes, she slept with Joey. She slept with *everyone*. He believes her. We have no idea if this is true. It's probably not. She's probably just winding him up. But maybe there's a kernel of truth in there somewhere; maybe she cheated, or maybe she merely *wanted* to cheat. Or maybe she's just trying to make clear to him that his accusations are outlandish. The truth of it doesn't matter. Jake storms out and heads to Joey's house, where he pummels his brother in front of his family and knocks Vickie out cold when she tries to intervene. It's perhaps Jake's darkest moment, the culmination of all the brooding and violence we've already seen.

We then see his final fight against Robinson, the one in which he's beaten to a swollen pulp, and that is the end for the youthful, dominating Jake LaMotta of *Raging Bull*. When next we see him, he's an embarrassment, slobbering over a politician's wife, kissing young girls, and entertaining fellow drunks with cheap party tricks, the scene made all the more sobering by De Niro's now-legendary decision to gain sixty pounds to play the older LaMotta. It's a commitment to acting Pesci said has been misinterpreted:

> Robert did it because he really wanted to feel what Jake LaMotta felt because Jake LaMotta had always had a hard time making the weight. That's all he talked about was the weight. Making the weight, making the weight. And he made such a big issue out of it talking to Robert all the time that Robert wanted to feel that sensation of blowing up like that. And he didn't do it to grandstand or to get an Oscar. I felt so bad for him because every asshole in the world, in Hollywood, says that kind of thing, and it's not true.[6]

De Niro's commitment to the role ensures that we feel the revulsion and pity we are intended to. The older LaMotta is a shell of his former self. He does a brief stint in prison for allowing underage girls in his club. He tries and fails to make amends with Joey. But if LaMotta was alone yet triumphant in the opening shot of the film, then here it's the opposite. He is alone, pathetic, and unaware that he was the architect of his own defeat:

> If his brother, and if Tommy Como, and if Salvie and if Vicky did everything he thought they did—he can do one of two things: kill them all or let it go. If you let it go, I mean, it's not the end of the world. But no, no, he's got to battle it out in the ring. He's got to battle it out at home. He's got to battle it everywhere until finally he's got to deal with that point where everyone else has disappeared from him and he's dealing with himself.[7]

His final monologue is the famous "I could have been a contender" speech from *On the Waterfront* (indirectly the second time De Niro played a character also portrayed by Marlon Brando). This decision is instructive. It tells us that, even now, Jake blames others for his own failings.

Jake LaMotta was a champion for a short period of time, a man of great skill whose downfall is his own doing. He is the definitive Scorsese protagonist in this respect, a deeply flawed person who becomes the engine of his own destruction. It's a theme we'll see many more times throughout the director's career but never so starkly as in *Raging Bull*.

CONCLUSION AND IMPACT

Upon release, *Raging Bull* barely crawled to profitability, garnering mixed reviews and a lukewarm box office. Despite this, the film earned eight Academy Award nominations, including Best Picture, Director, Actor, Supporting Actor, and Supporting Actress. It won two, one for Best Film Editing, thanks to Schoonmaker's invaluable contributions, and De Niro for Best Actor. Though met with only modest praise upon release, years later it would be hailed as the best film of the 1980s and is widely considered one of Martin Scorsese's masterworks.

Coming on the heels of the failure that was *New York, New York* and a tremendous personal health crisis—drug abuse and exhaustion had taken its toll on him—the director initially balked at making the picture. He couldn't wrap his head around it: "I resisted for a while—for a few years, actually—because I didn't understand boxing."[8] De Niro pushed and pushed some more. Scorsese still resisted. Then, one day the director collapsed in an exhausted stupor. He was rushed to the hospital, bleeding from multiple orifices. Future wife Isabella Rossellini believed he would die. There, in the hospital room, De Niro made yet another pitch. This time, Scorsese decided he needed to do the project in order to save his own life.[9] The director saw *Raging Bull* as a last gasp, as a chance to show the world he could still make great cinema. "I threw everything I knew into it, and if it meant the end of my career, then it would have to be the end of my career," he said.[10]

It's all but certain the film would not have been made were it not for De Niro. He had read LaMotta's memoir *Raging Bull: My Story* and was intrigued by it. "It's not so well written, but it's got heart to it. There's something interesting about the story," he said.[11] He brought the book to Scorsese, who read it in 1974 and later said he "never really understood sports." The director took considerable risks when making the film, casting the then-no-name actor Joe Pesci to act alongside De Niro, amateur actor Cathy Moriarty to play the female lead (for which she was nominated for Best Supporting Actress), and other amateurs like Frank Vincent, who would go on to have roles in *GoodFellas*, *Casino*, and *The Sopranos*, among others. He shot it in black-and-white. And he made no effort to make LaMotta a sympathetic character. It was a bold display at how bucking the norm could be made to work.

These days, many consider it the director's best work. It's a film that almost didn't get made but one that went on to launch what is arguably Scorsese's most adventurous decade of filmmaking, a decade that included populist fare; black comedies; meditations on religion; and, in the case of his next picture, strange forays into obsession.

8

THE KING OF COMEDY
(1982)

FILM DETAILS

RELEASE DATE: December 18, 1982
WRITTEN BY: Paul D. Zimmerman
STARRING: Robert De Niro, Jerry Lewis, Sandra Bernhard
RUNNING TIME: 109 minutes

ABOUT THE FILM

Martin Scorsese's creative career is many things, but predictable is not one of them. After a string of artistic successes marred only by the uneven *New York, New York*, all of them rooted in a tangible, uncompromising grittiness, the last thing one would expect is a black comedy costarring Jerry Lewis. Yet that's exactly what he delivered with *The King of Comedy*, a movie overlooked in its time but appreciated today as one of his great underappreciated works.

Though *Raging Bull* was a tremendous critical success, its lukewarm performance at the box office—it cost $18 million to make and earned $23 million, effectively a break-even movie—made Scorsese worry about his future.[1] Making films requires financing, and to secure financing, you have to demonstrate you can make money. It's a dilemma he'd grapple with throughout his career; despite being an acclaimed director, he's never been a guaranteed money maker.

The King of Comedy would offer him little help in that regard. Again praised by critics and ignored by audiences, the film bombed *big*, making under $3 million on a $19 million budget and for a time languishing in obscurity. *The King of Comedy*'s initial failure at the box office and later success as an underappreciated Scorsese gem is appropriate because this is a picture *about* failure, about not being appreciated, about being overlooked, and about the lengths someone will take to be seen.

De Niro had purchased the script from *Newsweek* writer Paul D. Zimmerman and repeatedly pushed Scorsese to direct, but the director kept declining. Then, one day, he didn't. Even then, he didn't initially find the personal connection he looks for in his pictures. "I didn't really understand where I stood in relationship to the film, the story, Rupert Pupkin, and Jerry Langford, too, until I was in the process of making the film," he said.[2] Then it clicked: the ideas of struggle, of rejection, of failure. He was exploring aspects of himself without realizing it. "The amount of rejection in this film is horrifying. There are scenes I almost can't look at," Scorsese said.[3]

Here we have Rupert Pupkin (Robert De Niro), a socially awkward loner on the fringes of society who dreams of becoming a big comedy star. He believes he can fulfill those dreams with the help of talk show host Jerry Langford (Jerry Lewis), but when Langford rebuffs Pupkin's aggressive salesmanship, Pupkin and his friend Masha (Sandra Bernhard) hatch a plan to launch Pupkin into stardom by force. The entire premise is just to the left of believable, but it's sold by a De Niro performance that is quietly among his most convincing and further cemented by an almost dreamlike approach by Scorsese, who would use a similar tone to even greater effect in his next film, *After Hours*. That dreamlike approach was appropriate, given that much of the film deals with being detached from reality.

ANALYSIS

Put a smile on Travis Bickle's face and give him a bad stand-up comedy routine, and there will still be something off-putting about him. That's essentially who Rupert Pupkin is: a man so isolated from society and detached from reality that his obsessions become dangerous.

The King of Comedy gives us a hazy form of reality that helps underscore just how disconnected from the world Pupkin is. In the opening scenes, we see a pushy, invasive Pupkin trying desperately to win an audience with his idol, talk show host Jerry Langford. He pretends to be part of Langford's security detail and helps push away a crowd of fans, then forces his way into a car with the host. Pupkin won't stop talking and won't stop insisting that he would make a great guest on the show. Langford agrees to talk with him again to discuss Pupkin's comedy act, but it's clear he's just brushing him off. We then cut to Pupkin having lunch with the host. Langford is asking him to take over the show for six weeks during Langford's absence. Then we're back to seeing Pupkin at home, practicing a conversation with Langford. There is no cue, visual or otherwise, that portions of this sequence are all in the character's head. This blending of reality and imagination is something the film often engages in. The result borders on the hallucinogenic.

Like a less-menacing Bickle, Pupkin cannot pick up on social cues. He doesn't understand when he is crossing lines or making others uncomfortable. He has little regard for or understanding of social norms. Also like Bickle, it appears that to some extent this has been worsened by isolation. Bickle's was a self-imposed isolation—his narrated correspondence with his parents indicates he once led a normal life but chose to flee it—whereas Pupkin's may not be. He still lives with his mother. She berates him from elsewhere in their home, screeching like Estelle Costanza (Estelle Harris), the perpetually complaining mother of George Costanza (Jason Alexander) from TV's *Seinfeld*. He sits alone in his room, recording demo tapes, practicing for a career he'll never have, and from the other room, she repeatedly tells him to quiet down. The only friend he appears to have is Masha, and she's just as screwed up as he is.

This idea of Pupkin's that he belongs onstage as an object of delight is echoed throughout the film via the movie's background characters, and it's disturbingly subtle. Typically, background actors are only meant to be set dressing. They exist to lend a scene life and believability. Here, they sometimes have a presence that looms large for the careful viewer and that can subconsciously get under the skin of casual viewers. In the most prominent example, Pupkin is out for dinner with Rita Keene (Diahnne Abbott), a bartender acquaintance, and attempts to impress her with his autograph book. Another patron quickly walks by and glances at their table. Pupkin looks over his shoulder, aware someone was there, but immediately goes back to what he was doing. For the rest of the scene, this patron is framed behind Pupkin's left shoulder, no focus on him, the same way any other restaurant scene would be shot. He's just another human-shaped blur in the background. Unlike your typical background actor, however, this one is *staring*. Though not in focus, his lack of movement and the fact that he's clearly looking at Pupkin's table gives him an odd presence in the scene. His stillness is off-putting. As Rupert tries to impress Rita by showing her his own autograph placed among autographs by legends like Marilyn Monroe, Ernie

Kovacs, and Woody Allen ("He's a personal friend of mine," Pupkin lies), the background actor begins mimicking Pupkin's gestures, just a few times, before walking off-screen. It's a fleeting moment, yet it's distracting because it's so far from the norm in movies. Later still, during an argument with Masha, the pair walk through the streets, bickering. Again, despite not being in focus, despite not being conspicuously framed, the background actors stare at Pupkin, watching him as if he is on a stage. (The restaurant scene also has a brief but telling insight into Pupkin's character. When he hands Rita his autograph and insists it will be worth a lot in a few weeks, she says, "Rupert, you have not changed," suggesting he's lived in this state of delusion for some time.)

If Pupkin is initially a less-threatening version of Travis Bickle, he doesn't remain benign. His persistence in trying to secure a meeting with Langford begins as overly forward, becomes annoying, but before long evolves into outright dangerous.

Pupkin deceives his way into Langford's home. The talk show host is understandably angry. He doesn't know yet to fear Pupkin because on the surface this stalker appears harmless. Obsessed, yes, but harmless. But Pupkin *is* a stalker, and stalkers are *not* harmless. Dr. Doris M. Hall, a criminology expert from California State University, said when dealing with stalkers, "Don't try to be nice; it

Overlooked in its day, *The King of Comedy*'s bleak look at celebrity obsession and the desire for public affirmation rings even more true in the social media age than it did in 1983. *Twentieth Century Fox Film Corporation/Photofest*

can only work against you."[4] That's the approach Langford takes after Pupkin deceives his way into the host's home. He tears into him, giving him a brutal dose of reality, telling Pupkin he suggested he follow up about his act only to get rid of him, saying he wants nothing to do with him, and demanding he leave.

If these tense scenes between De Niro and Lewis have a taste of realness to them, it's probably because they did. Lewis found De Niro's intense dedication to his roles off-putting, with De Niro going so far as to refuse dinner invitations from Lewis because the characters were rivals and he didn't want to befriend Lewis while making the movie. "De Niro has obviously never heard Noel Coward's advice to actors about remembering the lines and trying not to bump into the furniture," Lewis said. "He just could not forget this part at the end of the day's work."[5] Lewis had similar troubles with Bernhard, who was allowed to improvise most of her lines.

But the slap of reality by Langford doesn't bring Rupert Pupkin to his senses. Quite the opposite. It prompts him to dig in, double down, and become even more determined to get a guest shot on Langford's show—even if he has to break the law to do it.

Again harkening back to Bickle, Pupkin takes matters into his own hands. "That's the way they treated me," Pupkin says, "and now look where we are." He plans out a kidnapping in order to present himself as the comedy hero he longs to be. But where Bickle's approach is wild and unplanned, Pupkin's is fairly intricate and well-considered. Langford is kidnapped and held hostage. His safety is contingent upon Pupkin's demands to the studio being met. He doesn't wade in, guns blazing; he sets things up so that he'll end up on television, delivering the monologue he dreamed of delivering. That's it. That's his one goal: to tell his jokes on television. And he succeeds.

A common narrative in Scorsese films is the story of a man's rise and fall. We've already seen elements of it in *Who's That Knocking at My Door?* and *Mean Streets* and *New York, New York* and *Raging Bull*, and we'll see it again in *GoodFellas*, *Casino*, *The Aviator*, and others. *The King of Comedy* almost breaks that mold. Pupkin actually achieves his goal. He gets his moment of adoration, or perceived adoration. He's also jailed afterward. That's his fall. In his head, though, he won. He succeeded. He finished what he had started. If he suffers a collapse, then he does so with great satisfaction. He basks in the glow of that moment for the rest of his days, obsessing over it, turning it over in his head. Is it a victory for him despite having gone to prison? In some respects, it may be.

There is some debate among viewers as to whether *The King of Comedy*'s ending represents reality. Scorsese himself seems to suggest it is real, telling

Vanity Fair, "He becomes successful without being good."[6] Still, it's a curious way to perceive the sequence.

The picture ends with a montage showing Pupkin being released from prison and his autobiography going on sale; the montage continues with Pupkin calling Langford a friend and claiming he is entertaining numerous offers to perform his comedy. Finally, he takes the stage at the start of a TV special, and he is the star of the show. We experience a seemingly endless introduction, music that never stops, and an announcer introducing Pupkin over and over and over and over again. It's a sad and dark ending with almost sinister undertones. Though the film leaves it up to the viewer to decide whether what we see is reality, the presentation appears to answer the question for us. The obsessive repetition of his name, said like a mantra; the fixation on being in front of a crowd who goes wild at the mere mention of his name; and the almost hallucinogenic quality of the scene is a clear indication that we're inside Pupkin's head. We're experiencing what he experiences. We're in the same delusional state. It's presented like a dream sequence, unreal and beyond reality. Like Bickle glancing into his rearview mirror at the end of *Taxi Driver*, here we see that Pupkin is as deranged as he ever was.

CONCLUSION AND IMPACT

Pupkin had his success, but Scorsese did not. *The King of Comedy* was a box-office bomb. Critics loved it and still do, but audiences did not go see it. Perhaps the subject matter made them uncomfortable. After all, presenting a picture about the dark side of celebrity worship in a venue *designed* for celebrity worship (i.e., the movie theater) is a risky endeavor.

But time has been kind to *The King of Comedy*. Today, it enjoys a second life as an underappreciated and forward-looking Scorsese gem that is arguably more relevant today than ever. With its focus on media, celebrity obsession, and the protagonist's pathological need for attention, much of the picture rings with modern truth. Today, Rupert Pupkin would stalk a YouTube star or Instagram influencer rather than a talk show host, but the overall gist would remain unchanged. "We knew we were commenting on the culture of the time," Scorsese said much later, "but we were not thinking that it would blow up where it is now."[7] Significant elements were even borrowed from *The King of Comedy* for Warner Bros.' 2019 comic-book movie *Joker*, which features De Niro in a role suspiciously reminiscent of Jerry Langford. As of this writing, *Joker* is the highest-grossing R-rated movie of all time, and virtually every critical review notes the debt it owes to this and *Taxi Driver*.

That's today, however. At the time *Comedy* was released, it did little to boost Scorsese's career. The next several years would be a struggle for the director. He'd wanted to make an adaptation of Nikos Kazantzakis's 1955 novel *The Last Temptation of Christ*, but the road to making that picture was a rocky one. Dejected and needing to find his feel for filmmaking again, he ended up taking on a strange little picture set in an even stranger version of New York. It wouldn't lead to renewed box office success, either, but it *would* be delightfully weird.

9

AFTER HOURS
(1985)

FILM DETAILS

RELEASE DATE: September 13, 1985
WRITTEN BY: Joseph Minion
STARRING: Griffin Dunne, Rosanna Arquette, Thomas Chong, Linda
Fiorentino, Teri Garr, John Heard, Cheech Marin, Catherine O'Hara
RUNNING TIME: 97 minutes

ABOUT THE FILM

Predictability is not one of Martin Scorsese's strong suits. Though his touchstone works share common traits and themes that the public tends to associate with his name, he's long had a way of throwing curveballs at the audience. Following *Raging Bull* with something like *The King of Comedy* was an example of that, as was following *Casino* with the meditative *Kundun*. *After Hours* fits in the same category of movies that run against the prevailing perception of his work.

It was also a film made of necessity, in some ways, a stopgap picture the director gravitated toward when his plans for *The Last Temptation of Christ* (temporarily) fell apart, a pause for breath before launching into that difficult, controversial project. He was set to begin production on *Last Temptation* in Israel in 1983, but executives at Paramount got cold feet and canceled the picture

---

that December. That left Scorsese without an immediate project on the horizon. Without a big money maker on his resume since 1976's *Taxi Driver*, studios weren't exactly beating down his door to hand him bags of cash. "I went back to New York and really started to take stock of what my life was like and who I was and what movies I wanted to make," he said.[1]

Rather than pursue another sprawling, epic work, the director thought small, intimate, independent. A script by Joseph Minion caught the attention of actors and producers Griffin Dunne and Amy Robinson, who sent the screenplay to Scorsese. (Robinson previously had a small role in *Mean Streets* as Charlie's girlfriend, and Dunne read for the part of Tommy in *Alice Doesn't Live Here Anymore* but was too old for the role.) The script was a little strange—strange enough so that a young Tim Burton was almost tapped to direct—and a lot paranoid, and it featured a main character wracked with guilt for things he had never done. It was perfect for Scorsese and came at a pivotal moment in his career. "I really felt that if I don't pull this one off, it's completely over. I'll never make another film," Scorsese said.[2]

He pulled it off. *After Hours*, a paranoid black comedy littered with unusual characters and impossible coincidences, was a minor success at the box office, enough of a critical success to win him a Best Director award at Cannes, and an artistic success enough so that *After Hours* is now considered a cult classic and one of the great hidden gems of his career.

ANALYSIS

Martin Scorsese's best work is often deeply personal to him—and *After Hours* is probably more personal to him than viewers realize. Maybe even more than *Scorsese* realizes. The manic haze of the picture works in no small part because, as much as it seems like an outlier for the director—it's a wild, strange movie that feels more like a hallucination than something sliced from reality—it actually exists in a very familiar space.

After Hours continues Scorsese's love affair with the streets of New York City, once again exploring its seedy bars, dark alleyways, and unusual characters but this time doing it through a fever dream of a story. We'd previously seen a personal view of the city in *Mean Streets* and a view of the city through the eyes of an isolated loner in *Taxi Driver*, among other glimpses of life in the Big Apple. *After Hours* returns to the idea of the protagonist being an outsider but flips the notion on its head. *Taxi Driver*'s Travis Bickle was an outsider in the city around him, a man who was alone in a crowd, but the people around him were sane and stable. In *After Hours*, Paul Hackett (Griffin Dunne) is the opposite; he's the only seemingly normal person in a sea of misfits, kooks, and strange individuals. Here, the protagonist is sane and well-adjusted; everyone else is a Bickle cousin. The whole movie is a waking nightmare. "We just sweated blood over that thing," editor Thelma Schoonmaker said. "But he did want it to be a nightmare, because it was. Marty himself had even experienced that wild taxi ride, where the money flew out the window, you know? He had had that experience himself."[3]

That Hackett is going to have an unusual night is evident from the start. He meets a young woman in a diner, Marcy Franklin (Rosanna Arquette), who suggests he call her if he's interested in buying one of her roommate's sculptures of a bagel with cream cheese. Ignoring the weirdness, he takes that to be an invitation. He calls; she asks him to come by right away; and after an insane taxi ride through the streets of New York—perhaps the most realistic aspect of the film—he arrives at her apartment. Marcy's roommate, Kiki Bridges (Linda Fiorentino), hangs out the apartment window to toss him the keys. It's just a split second of rapid cuts, but it's the pivotal moment of the film and arguably the movie's best-known sequence. This fleeting image of the keys falling from above is the moment upon which the entire narrative hinges, the point in which Hackett leaps into a wormhole and jumps from our world to a much stranger place. Not literally, of course, but it certainly feels that way. As the keys fall, there is the faint sound of thunder. There is something sinister about them, like they are a harbinger of doom, so at the last moment, he steps aside and lets them fall to the ground rather than catch them.

But it's too late. By showing up at Marcy's door, he has already taken his first step into an alternate world. Marcy appears to be hiding some great secret. Kiki is hiding nothing. All '80s punk style and attitude, she creates papier-mâché sculptures, including one that reminds Paul of Edvard Munch's 1893 painting *The Scream*. We don't know it yet, but that sculpture is setting up several future plot points. In fact, virtually *everything* in this film quietly sets up future events because, as we come to discover, Paul's night will unfold in a series of horrible, awkward coincidences that plunge him deeper and deeper into circumstances that spiral well out of his control.

This early scene foreshadows what is to come in other ways, too, when Kiki makes a comment that ends up being a commentary on everyone else in the movie. As Paul massages her while waiting for Marcy to get home, he compliments her body. Kiki agrees with his positive assessment. "Not a lot of scars," she says. "Some women I know are covered with them head to toe. Not me." It's meant to be just one more item to add to the list of weirdness Paul has already experienced, yet it's more than that. All the people he encounters over the course of this long night *are* damaged in some way, some physically, most mentally, but every one of them is scarred in one way or another. The contrast here is noteworthy, too. On the surface, Kiki is the strange one, the one on the fringes of society, the one outside the mainstream. She chain-smokes and indulges in strange art and lounges around topless despite having just met Paul, and she's got that punk-infused style that is shorthand for "rebellious outsider." Despite this, Kiki is in many ways more grounded than anyone else but Paul. Most of the other people he encounters seem normal on the surface, but underneath they are *just* askew from the rest of us. They live with a hidden madness. Kiki, on the other hand, openly shows us exactly who she is. Kiki talks about literal damage, but most of the damage we see from *After Hours'* characters is internal, and much of this damage is revealed by the movie's most prominent device: improbable coincidence.

Paul tells Kiki a story about his childhood. As a child, he had to get his tonsils taken out. After the surgery, there was no room in the pediatric ward, so he was put in the burn ward with a blindfold on so he wouldn't see the people there. He was instructed not to remove it, or they'd have to operate again. That night he took off the blindfold anyway—and the story ends there. Kiki falls asleep. Marcy returns, and Paul goes with her to her room, where he spots medication for burns and later a book on reconstructive surgery for burn victims. He spots scars on her legs but doesn't mention them. "Tonight, I feel like I'm going to let loose or something. I feel like something is really going to happen here," she says, a tempting statement from an attractive woman, until she begins telling him about the time she was held at knifepoint in that very room and raped for six hours. Then she says it was her boyfriend who did it, and she slept through it all. What is truth here? Marcy's stories shift and change, always strange, always bleak. There is a sense that none of this is real, that the moment when the keys fell toward Paul was the flip of a switch that thrust him into a foggy dream world, and try as he might, he cannot escape it.

Paul deceives Marcy and leaves the apartment. He ends up in a small dive bar, where he meets a frustrated bartender, Tom (John Heard), and a weary waitress, Julie (Teri Garr). Paul doesn't have train fare to get home—it blew out of the cab he took to Marcy's—but he arranges to get the money from Tom. A series of improbable events leads him back to Marcy's apartment, where he finds her dead of an overdose. That's when he notices that Tom's keychain bears a skull identical to one of Marcy's tattoos.

More back-and-forths. He is in and out of Julie's apartment, where he sees that she is a sketch artist. She'll eventually sketch him for a wanted poster. Tom finds out his girlfriend killed herself, and of course, we find out his girlfriend was none other than Marcy. At Julie's apartment again, Paul sees that she has one of Kiki's bagel sculptures. Back and forth, back and forth. It's just one weird connection atop another, tying a knot so intricate it would take Alexander the Great to cut through it.

Paul thinks he finds some normality in another woman he meets, an ice cream truck driver, but this only digs him in deeper when she spots a wanted poster of him sketched by Julie. People in the neighborhood believe he not only killed Marcy but also that he is responsible for a series of break-ins plaguing the community. He has to run for his life.

Paul finally finds safety in the basement of a punk club, where he spends time with June (Verna Bloom), an older woman who is a blur of motherly caring and mature sexuality. He cuddles her, childlike, fearful of the mob chasing him, while she strokes his hair. Then they share a sensual dance to "Is That All There Is?" a 1960s hit sung by Peggy Lee. When the mob finally arrives, June hides Paul beneath layers of papier-mâché until he looks remarkably like Kiki's sculpture from earlier in the film. A pair of serial criminals played by comedians Cheech Marin and Tommy Chong steal him, thinking he is a statue they've been trying to get the whole movie. They drive away with him. He falls out of their truck right in front of his office, where the papier-mâché shatters. He cleans himself off, and he once again returns to the utterly mundane grind of office work.

There is something almost Hitchcockian in Paul's wrong-man-on-the-run flight from these people, except, unlike Hitchcock heroes who take flight in order to clear their names, Paul doesn't aim to clear his name. He has no hope to. He just wants to get back to his normal life. More Scorsesian is that Paul continually feels a sense of responsibility for things he is not responsible for. Overdoses, thefts, mistrust, betrayals: Everyone hangs their issues on him. This wasn't written as a film about Catholic guilt, but it's a minor thread the director was able to connect to.

After Hours may be a bizarre journey through the weirder side of an already weird city, but is it saying anything beyond that? When seen through the lens of Martin Scorsese's career, especially during a period when the project at the forefront of his mind was one concerning the life and times of Jesus Christ, it's certainly possible to see *After Hours* as a gentle probing of Catholic ideas. Paul's circular journey out of reality and ultimately back to it is a statement on our sense of place and belonging and on trusting what we know. The unknown can be alluring. Beautiful women can be seductive. But such temptations can lead to sin, and once wrapped in sin, it's difficult to unwrap one's self. Paul reached this place by following temptation, after all. He stuck around Marcy's apartment even after things got weird because he hoped for sexual gratification. Lust ruled him. Throughout his wild evening, he never truly turns his back on what initially brought him there, either; he simply tries to flee the situation. It's only after he encounters June, an attractive older woman in whom he instead seeks motherly comfort instead of sexual gratification, that he is finally offered a window out of the earthly hell he finds himself in.

That vague sense of guilt has been a hallmark of the director's work, though it's one usually treated with seriousness. Charlie's gloomy conscience in *Mean Streets*, for example, is a cloud that hangs over him and guides his (often poor) decision making. By contrast, here it's handled with humor. Paul is made to feel bad about things that aren't his fault or that he was no party to. His reactions, the things he does, the way he tries to retreat from the unforeseen consequences of his actions—this is an absurd but funny means of showing us how guilt can drive us to strange places.

In an early draft of the picture, Paul would not have escaped from his papier-mâché prison. Cheech and Chong were to have driven off with him, leaving his fate a mystery. This was deemed too dark by the studio. Another draft included a bizarre idea in which Paul effectively crawls inside June's womb and is birthed again on the West Side Highway, returning to the normal world that way.[4] Mercifully, both ideas were dropped. Paul's simple return to the working world provides needed contrast to his dreamlike experience of the night before. After all, one ceases to be able to recognize normalcy when one is always immersed in the abnormal.

The picture is also quite bleak. The absurdist humor of *After Hours* rings as strange and unsettling because it's not *treated* as comedy. The film doesn't offer you a wink and a nudge. When Marcy tells Paul how her estranged husband (if he even exists) has such on obsession with *The Wizard of Oz* that he screams, "Surrender, Dorothy," whenever he reaches orgasm, the oddness of the story is given no punchline or pause for laughter. It just hangs in the air, a story neither we nor Paul are equipped to process, before Paul is again launched into his next encounter with madness. It's perhaps the perfect kind of humor for a director known for his almost-manic tendencies.

In other hands, *After Hours* may have been a straight comedy, all playful misadventure and misunderstanding, but in Scorsese's hands, it becomes as much about people and their neurotic behavior as it does about the barrage of extraordinary connections Paul finds himself caught up in. The director is usually concerned about characters more than plot, about people more than narrative, so it's little surprise that in his hands this tightly plotted comedic thriller is as much a study of quirky city dwellers as it is a playful, Hitchcock-inspired suspense comedy. Paul Hackett's journey transforms him into an outsider in a neighborhood of outsiders, a place where seemingly normal people hide bizarre secrets. He's isolated, can't escape, and is repeatedly made to feel as if he's done something wrong despite doing his best to be a good person throughout.

"Marty really delighted in the awful things that happened to Paul Hackett," Dunne said.[5] The actor said at times he felt as if he was playing Scorsese himself at that point in his life. Scorsese was a man looking for purpose, looking for some way to continue making his art. Hackett's misadventures spoke to him in that regard. The character was "guilt ridden for nothing, which I adored," the director said, and the movie was made during a time when (in his mind, at least) his future as a director was in doubt, with a huge passion project having been swept out from under him after sets had already been built.[6] Indeed, Roger Ebert observed, "Each new person that Paul meets promises that they will take care of him, make him happy, lend him money, give him a place to stay, let him use the phone, trust him with their keys, drive him home—and every offer of mercy turns into an unanticipated danger. The film could be read as an emotional autobiography of that period in Scorsese's life."[7]

Movies like *Mean Streets*, *The Last Temptation of Christ*, and *Silence* are rightfully recognized as works that reflect important aspects of Martin Scorsese's inner self. Perhaps it's time that *After Hours* is added to the list.

CONCLUSION AND IMPACT

Today, *After Hours* enjoys a second life as an underappreciated Scorsese gem, a picture critics and fans alike cite as one worth revisiting. A lost masterpiece? That would be overstating the case. But it is an often-overlooked slice of bizarre brilliance from the most unpredictable director of the last fifty years.

More importantly, it lifted Scorsese during a period of self-doubt and temporarily got him away from the troubled *Last Temptation* project. He'd eventually get back to that project and the significant amount of controversy it stirred up, but first he'd take one other detour, and this detour would be to an even more unexpected place than *After Hours*: a follow-up to a twenty-five-year-old classic featuring one of the biggest movie stars in cinema history.

10

THE COLOR OF MONEY
(1986)

FILM DETAILS

RELEASE DATE: October 17, 1986
WRITTEN BY: Richard Price
STARRING: Paul Newman, Tom Cruise, Mary Elizabeth Mastrantonio
RUNNING TIME: 120 minutes

ABOUT THE FILM

By the mid-1980s, Martin Scorsese was on a four-picture streak of box-office failures. *After Hours* stumbled to profitability despite lukewarm audience reception, but *New York, New York*; *Raging Bull*; and *The King of Comedy* were all duds. No director, not even one as talented as Scorsese, can keep making movies when they consistently fail to turn a profit. With his passion project, *The Last Temptation of Christ*, seemingly dead in the water, his career was at a crossroads.

Salvation came from an unusual place: in a (sort of) sequel to a twenty-five-year-old movie about billiard players. Starring Paul Newman and Jackie Gleason, along with Piper Laurie and George C. Scott, 1961's *The Hustler* was widely considered a modern classic when Scorsese was tapped for a follow-up. The original had garnered nine Academy Award nominations, including Best Picture, Best Director, Best Actor, Best Supporting Actor, Best Actress, and

Best Writing—lofty shoes to fill by any measure. It told the story of "Fast" Eddie Felson (Newman), a pool hustler with his sights set on the best of the best, Minnesota Fats (Gleason), and helped cement Newman, who had previously been nominated for Best Actor for *Cat on a Hot Tin Roof*, into legend. And now, a quarter-century later, they were talking about revisiting Fast Eddie's life as an older man.

The thing is, Scorsese wasn't looking to make this picture. He didn't have a pool-hall flick in mind. He wasn't seeking an excuse to do one, either. He wanted to make *The Last Temptation of Christ*. *The Color of Money* hinged on the wishes of the aforementioned silver-screen legend: "Paul Newman liked *Raging Bull* and wrote me a letter. So it was basically worked around Newman, that's how we got it made."[1]

At this juncture in the director's career, it may have seemed like a no-brainer. Your recent movies have not done well, and you get a call from one of the most beloved actors of all time to do a sequel to one of his most beloved films? You jump at the chance.

It wasn't that simple for Scorsese, though. He wanted to ensure he could find something of himself in the movie. "If it's not personal, I can't be there in the morning," he said.[2] This was no small task, either, because the director had never worked with someone as big as Newman. Scorsese had worked closely with Robert De Niro, yes, but theirs was and remains a special kind of collaboration, a meeting of like minds that blossomed into artistic kinship and friendship. Scorsese was *used* to working with De Niro. They had worked closely together. They were collaborators. Their stars shined brighter together. And as acclaimed an actor as he already was, De Niro was not yet the enduring legend he is today.

Paul Newman was another matter altogether. He may not have won an Academy Award for Best Actor until *The Color of Money*, but it was his seventh nomination (out of nine overall), and the win was widely considered a nod to the previous six. He was also astonishingly popular. "How many teenage girls had that famous poster of Newman—his face in monochrome, his eyes a startling sky blue—tacked to their bedroom walls?" *Time* magazine wondered shortly after his death in 2008. "Then Newman did something really remarkable: he sustained that early promise for five decades."[3]

Scorsese had never worked with a star this big. But after a string of box-office failures, the director had to make a picture that could make money, especially with a star of this caliber in the lead: "Even when I try to make a Hollywood film, there's something in me that says, 'Go the other way.' With *The Color of Money*, working with two big stars, we tried to make a Hollywood movie. Or rather, I tried to make one of my pictures, but with a Hollywood star: Paul Newman. That was mainly making a film about an American icon. That's what I zeroed in on."[4]

The Color of Money tells the story of an older Fast Eddie who has turned from pool hustling to running liquor. After spotting a uniquely talented young player in a local pool hall, he decides to take the player, Vincent (Tom Cruise), under his wing. Vincent already has a manager-slash-girlfriend in Carmen (Mary Elizabeth Mastrantonio), but Eddie believes with the pair guiding him, the trio can make a lot of money. Vincent is too wild and intent on flashy wins instead of subtle scams, however, and after Eddie himself is roped in by a hustler, the two part ways. They meet again in a big tournament in Atlantic City, where Eddie defeats Vincent, only to learn that Vincent learned his lessons after all: He threw the game in order to make money betting on the match. Humiliated that Vincent let him win and determined to beat him for real, Eddie decides he's back in the billiards racket.

In many respects, the movie would live or die on Newman's stardom.

ANALYSIS

The Color of Money is about a talented man trying to reclaim a career that had slipped through his fingers. What better person to direct it than Martin Scorsese at this point in his life? Scorsese knew this was an opportunity to reinvigorate his status as a filmmaker, but he needed to do it right. In this case, "right" meant building the movie around Newman. "We shaped the story around him, to emphasize those qualities that he had in him, at that point in his life," Scorsese said. "He was a man who was getting older, he understood the nature of it. . . . But (Fast Eddie) had also to deal with his limitations as an older person. I wanted it to be a story of an older person who corrupts a young person, like a serpent in the garden of innocence."[5]

To say that the film was a love letter to Newman would be exaggerating, but it's hardly unfair to say that he gets a soft treatment throughout. At this point in his career, Scorsese's male protagonists were anything but sympathetic. Almost every single prior one is to some extent an unsympathetic person. Paul Hackett in *After Hours* is the sole exception. His protagonists tend to be selfish, self-centered, sometimes greedy, and always troubled. Fast Eddie is all of these things, too, but he's not only charismatic—with Paul Newman in the role, how could he be anything but?—but he also garners more audience sympathy than any other Scorsese lead until this point. Cruise's Vincent is brash and cocky to the point where it's sometimes vulgar, so we *want* Eddie to put him in his place. Dishonest hustler though he is, it's easy to root for Newman's character. One thing the film *wasn't* was a deeply personal work of self-expression for Martin Scorsese. He was a gun for hire, a movie mercenary. It's pure entertainment without a great deal of Scorsese in it, outside of some fabulously creative directing of pool matches that hearken back to his dynamic work on *Raging Bull*.

The Color of Money was a commercial film and was never going to be anything but, yet Scorsese only accepted the job after pushing for a rewrite of the script. He wanted at least *something* he could latch onto. That something ended up being Eddie's journey toward rediscovering his love for his art. The way Scorsese saw it, "He takes this young kid under his wing and corrupts him. And then somewhere along the road, in the education process, he reeducated himself and decides to play again. It's about a man who changes his mind at the age of fifty-two."[6] And there's his hook. There's what lets him bite in the story because there are elements in Eddie the director could see reflected in himself. After all, Scorsese had to again find not just his ability to make money with film but also his touch for winning over audiences. At a point in his career when he was considering other paths, it was either succeed or move on. The same choice was in front of Eddie. So though not personal, though not initially something that would express something inside himself, there is a little something here the director was able to work with.

And, of course, there is the delight the director took in choreographing the billiards matches. By his own admission, Scorsese is not much for sports competition. This did not prevent him from creating some of the most dynamic boxing scenes ever put to film. The same holds true here, though he did have a comfort level with the setting, given that he grew up around the kind of bars and pool halls where the action takes place. One of the most memorable scenes in *Mean Streets*, for example, is a fight that takes place in a dingy pool hall. So no, Scorsese is not a sports director. He doesn't gravitate to competitive events. But when it comes to focusing on the high-energy and adrenaline-rush moments of competition, few do it better. Much like *Raging Bull*'s carefully constructed fight sequences, each shot in Vincent's various matches were meticulously planned and staged for maximum effect. All were mapped out ahead of time, and Tom Cruise devoted himself to practicing under the tutelage of Michael Sigel, widely considered one of the best billiards players in history. (He won more than one hundred professional tournaments and at thirty-five became the youngest male player ever to be inducted into the Billiards Hall of Fame.) With one exception—a shot in which the cue ball leaps over two other balls—Cruise made all his own shots, and Scorsese captures them with dizzying camera work, shots from above, moving cameras, and deft editing, as always supported by editor Thelma Schoonmaker, his most important collaborator.

The story itself is fairly straightforward, though those elements that do fit in the Scorsese body of work are not explored with the depth of his previous films. Fast Eddie, twenty-five years wiser than the one we met in 1961's *The Hustler*, has been running whiskey, making money, and living comfortably doing it. He has cash. He flies under the radar. He spends time with beautiful women. But when he sees Vincent easily beat a local pool shark, Julian (John Turturro), with a touch that few players have, it sparks something in him. The allure of greatness calls to him once again but through someone else.

Eddie tries to teach Vincent the art of reading people, of the "human moves" that make hustling more than just winning pool games. Vincent doesn't understand, at least not at first. He's young and arrogant and addicted to the high of dominating other players. Eddie knows better. He knows scamming is a people game, not a pool game. With some basic social engineering, Eddie tricks Vincent at dinner, predicting he can pick up a woman Vincent doesn't realize Eddie already knows. It's the first of several lessons he'll learn.

The focus is on Eddie, on Newman, but the real character arc is with Vincent, who learns to hone his powers and use them to hustle. Eddie is a teacher. This is old hat to him. But he's also someone looking to recapture some of his former glory. Eddie wants to feel the rush of getting one over on people again, but this time he'll be doing it vicariously through Vincent. He never did stop hustling—as the film opens, he's selling bootleg whiskey—but pool hustling never left his blood, and there isn't anything quite like hustling someone face to face and them not even realizing you're doing it. "Money won is twice as sweet as money earned," he says, and for Fast Eddie, a big part of the fun is when you pull in someone who doesn't realize how badly they are about to get beat.

It's Vincent who fills him with that fire again. "I'm hungry again and you bled that back into me," he says. It's not that Vincent reminds him of his younger self. This isn't a father-son mentorship. It's that he sees Vincent as a tool, as something he can harness to continue hustling people without having to get his own hands dirty. First, however, he has to tame Vincent's youthful wildness. "You have to have two things to win," he tells the young player. "You got to have brains and you got to have balls. You've got too much of one and not enough of the other."

Eddie knows that the game isn't the game, it's all the stuff that happens *around* the game that matters. Vincent is too high on winning to see this. The trio set up a scam to lure in unsuspecting players, but when Eddie and Carmen act like a couple as part of the act, Vincent can't handle it. Carmen understands all short-term actions are in service to a long-term goal, but Vincent can't see beyond the shot in front of him. Eddie convinces them to go on a road trip so he can show them both the art of the scam. The end goal is Atlantic City for a big tournament, during which the best players in the country will be on hand. A lot of money could be made. In order to get there, however, they'll have to scam their way through town after town, learning how to take in unsuspecting rubes and pros alike.

It doesn't go well. Vincent is good, but he can't deal with losing, and losing on *purpose* is part of the scam. He shows off at one point, disgusting Eddie, who drives away in a fury. (Scorsese straps his camera to the side of Eddie's car in this shot, a dizzying way to get across his anger.) Vincent goes back into the parlor, easily beats anyone foolish enough to play him, and in his victory ruins any chance he had to hustle there ever again. "The town is dead to you," Eddie explains. You have to suck people in first. Only then can you exploit them.

Eddie tries to keep Vincent's ego in check, but his own pride is easily wounded, as well. Feeling a need to prove he can still hustle, he gets taken in by a pool shark, Amos (Forest Whitaker). He *knows* Amos is a hustler. He asks. Amos's evasive answers make clear what's happening here. But pride begins to drive him. Eddie goes back again and again, thinking he can win his money back but falling deeper into the hole each time. He gets taken. This destroys his ego. He bails out on guiding Vincent and Carmen, crushed with guilt and self-doubt, thinking himself unworthy.

When we finally get to Atlantic City for the tournament both Eddie and Vincent had been aiming for, the moment is initially treated almost with an air of reverence. The hall in which the tournament takes place is presented like a cathedral, the camera high above it all, drifting downward, the lighting soft, organ music introducing us to this place of wonder. Here, the tournament takes a predictable turn—Eddie faces off against Vincent, and the charming silver-screen icon wins, a story decision that borders on cliché—and subverts that predictable turn by revealing that Vincent threw the match. Eddie *didn't* win—not truly. It turns out that Vincent had learned his lessons well and by purposely losing had actually made himself a lot of money. When he gives Eddie his cut and reveals the truth, Eddie is deflated. This is a worse blow to his ego than losing to Amos. He forfeits the next match and gives the money back. This is not how he wanted to win.

The film flirts with the rise-and-fall theme that is so prevalent in Scorsese's work but doesn't see it through. What little fall Fast Eddie experiences here is short-lived. He briefly believes he failed to impart his hustler's wisdom to Vincent but realizes that Vincent actually had learned his lessons all too well.

Eddie's ego is crushed at his illegitimate win, but ultimately, it only serves to give him drive enough to prove himself. The pair arrange one last match: a private game, a legitimate competition.

The final shot of the picture is a freeze-frame of "Fast" Eddie Felson smiling right after a break, his final words: "Hey, I'm back." A fitting end to what might be the director's most populist, box-office-centric picture. This is a *hopeful* ending. An ending that suggests "Fast" Eddie still has some hustle left in him. It's not Henry Hill in a bathrobe in the 'burbs or Travis Bickle glaring into a rearview mirror or Jake LaMotta monologuing to himself. It's a man with a fresh start.

And so was Scorsese.

CONCLUSION AND IMPACT

In some ways the ending of *The Color of Money* was reflective of Scorsese himself, though he couldn't have known it when he was shooting the movie. Without a financial success since *Taxi Driver* a decade prior, there was the very real possibility that this could have been the director's last chance to make a major Hollywood picture. It would be stretching it to say that *The Color of Money* saved his career, but it certainly renewed confidence in his ability to deliver a profitable picture and corrected the downward financial (but not artistic) trajectory he was on. "*The Color of Money* was a good commercial exercise for me," he later said. "I learned a great deal about structure and style. Learned what may not have worked."[7]

The picture was a huge success, sitting at number 2 for five weeks straight—the popular comedy *Crocodile Dundee* prevented it from claiming the number 1 spot—and remaining in the top ten for nine straight weeks. It garnered strong critical reaction, too, with largely positive reviews and four Academy Award nominations, including another Best Actor nod for Newman, who this time won.

Much like Fast Eddie Felson, Martin Scorsese was back. So naturally, his next picture would be a hugely controversial reimagining of the life of Jesus Christ that many theaters refused to play.

11

THE LAST TEMPTATION OF CHRIST (1988)

FILM DETAILS

RELEASE DATE: August 12, 1988
WRITTEN BY: Paul Schrader
STARRING: Willem Dafoe, Harvey Keitel, Barbara Hershey, Harry Dean
Stanton, David Bowie
RUNNING TIME: 163 minutes

ABOUT THE FILM

In a career filled with controversial films, there is perhaps none made by
Martin Scorsese more controversial than *The Last Temptation of Christ*.
The same holds true for film as a personal statement. In a career in which his
best works are usually his most personal, few are more personal to him, arguably not even the semiautobiographical *Mean Streets*. But whether the film has
merits as a singular piece of work representative of a period in the director's
life will probably always be overshadowed by the hornet's nest of criticism
stirred up upon its release and the difficult gauntlet the director had to run
just to get it made.

The Last Temptation of Christ is based on the 1955 novel of the same name.
Written by nine-time Nobel Prize in Literature nominee Nikos Kazantzakis, the
Greek work was first translated into English in 1960, just one in an entire career

filled with works that grapple with spirituality, faith, and the juncture between man and myth and religion.

Both the book and the film take the same approach: They explore the ramifications behind the idea that Jesus Christ was simultaneously man and God, mortal and divine, a flawed human and the son of God. "I believe that Jesus is fully divine," Scorsese said, "but the teaching at Catholic schools placed such an emphasis on the divine side that if Jesus walked into a room, you'd know He was God because He glowed in the dark, instead of being just another person. But if He was like that, we always thought, then when the temptations came to Him, surely it was easy to resist them because He was God."[1]

Yet if Christ's sacrifice was *easy*, then would it have been a sacrifice at all? *Last Temptation* answers and says "no." For there to be meaning in the crucifixion, for Christ's death and resurrection to truly have significance, he must have struggled to rise above his earthly state and embrace his divine nature. This is the crux of the story and a central factor in why Scorsese had so much difficulty getting it made.

Growing up a devout Catholic, the idea of telling Jesus's life story had always intrigued the director, but it wasn't until 1972 when *Last Temptation* landed on his radar. While filming *Boxcar Bertha*, Barbara Hershey gave him a copy of the book. After reading it, Scorsese optioned the novel and enlisted Paul Schrader, who wrote *Taxi Driver*, to adapt it into a screenplay. He landed a deal with Paramount, and in 1983 filming was set to begin. He had a budget of $14 million, locations scouted in Israel, sets built, costumes in the works, casting completed (including musicians Sting and Ray Davies from the Police and the Kinks, respectively). But even before filming got under way, the budget was swelling, and protest letters were starting to come in from religious groups that didn't want the movie to get made. In December 1983, with production almost under way, Paramount decided to pull the plug.

Disheartened, the director went on to make *After Hours*, in part just to keep himself involved in film, then *The Color of Money* to show he could still sell tickets. He still didn't give up on the idea of making *Last Temptation*, however, and when Universal expressed interest, Scorsese said he could make the movie for just $7 million and complete filming in under two months. Universal agreed. The director and crew got to work, and an uproar resulted.

This was to be expected, especially in a 1980s United States that had taken a sharp turn toward the right. Censorship of supposedly morally questionable material was on the rise following a rather permissive 1970s. The Parents Music Resource Center (PMRC) formed in 1985 to push for warning labels on music with explicit content. Judith Krug, director of the American Library Association's Office of Intellectual Freedom in the 1980s, said incidents of libraries and schools banning books increased more than threefold starting around 1982.[2] Organizations like the American Family Association and Morality in Media became powerful lobbies that pushed the Federal Communications Commission to crack down on supposedly indecent television and radio broadcasts and more. This was the atmosphere in which Martin Scorsese released a film depicting Jesus Christ, doubting whether he was the Messiah or not.

The Last Temptation of Christ is clear about its origins and intentions. A title card at the start states, "This film is not based on the Gospels, but upon the fictional exploration of the eternal spiritual conflict." Unlike the biblical epics Scorsese grew up with and that audiences adored—*The Greatest Story Ever Told* (1965), *The Robe* (1960), *The Ten Commandments* (1956), and others—this picture is less a celebration of biblical stories and values as it is an exploration of what those stories actually *mean*, or at least from a certain point of view. That's in part what generated so much criticism.

ANALYSIS

"It is accomplished." Those three simple words mark the end of *The Last Temptation of Christ*'s potent and controversial exploration of what it means to be divine, though they apply as much to Scorsese's arduous journey in making this picture as they do to Christ's journey toward becoming the Messiah.

As the film opens, we see Jesus of Nazareth (Willem Dafoe) making crosses for the Romans. "I'm struggling," he tells Judas (Harvey Keitel), pain written on his face. From the first, this is a Jesus audiences were unfamiliar with: a Jesus who was just a man, as weak and vulnerable as any of us. This is a Jesus not yet convinced of his own divinity. Even in narration, he speaks of God as an entity separate from him, not recognizing the oneness of the two.

His very tangible humanity is emphasized again in his closeness to Mary Magdalene (Barbara Hershey). He sits in waiting as she services a line of men. He can see what is happening between the thin beaded curtains. Her sexuality is unhidden. Evening falls. The last of her clients leaves. Jesus approaches. He asks her for forgiveness, though for what we are not told. She tells him it's not that easy. "Just because you need forgiveness, don't ask me to do it," she says. This Jesus is emotionally fragile, vulnerable, *human*. "You're pitiful. I hate you. Here's my body. Save it," she says to him, pulling his hand to her belly. He pulls away. It is his first instance of resisting the most human aspects of himself while also emphasizing that he is, in fact, a mortal man. The director notes, "The point of that scene was to show the proximity of sexuality to Jesus, the occasion of sin. Jesus must have seen a naked woman—must have. So why couldn't we show that?"[3]

This scene and the doubt it conveys is echoed again and again in the film and always in small, human ways like this. There is little bombast in *Last Temptation* and certainly no scenes that could be described as epic. For the most part, *The Last Temptation of Christ* is shot with great simplicity. It's a sparse film, almost ugly in its barrenness. This was in part an aesthetic choice and in part a necessity forced upon the director by its relatively modest budget, just half of what he initially envisioned. But the grounded nature of the picture as far as themes and character are concerned was not a result of a tight budget. It was a creative decision meant to put the Jesus of the Gospels in a world the audience could understand and to differentiate this silver-screen version of Christ from other on-screen depictions. The Hollywood biblical epic was a proud American tradition, after all, especially during Scorsese's formative years in the 1950s and 1960s. As he tried to do with the musical genre in *New York, New York*, his goal was to strip away traditional Hollywood trappings in an effort to find truth.

"In those films, the characters were speaking with British accents. The dialogue was beautiful, in some cases, and the films look beautiful. They were

Willem Dafoe's depiction of a conflicted, very human Jesus Christ helped stir up one of the biggest controversies of Martin Scorsese's career. *Universal Pictures*

pageants. But they had nothing really to do with our lives," Scorsese said. "Jesus lived in the world. He wasn't in a temple. He wasn't in church. He was in the world. He was on the street. The picture I wanted to make was about Jesus on Eighth Avenue."[4] Which is not to say there aren't directorial flourishes of note. In one memorable shot, for instance, Jesus stands on a cliffside, talking with a follower. He says God wants to "push me over." As he utters the phrase, he gestures with his hand, and the camera moves as if flung away, twisting and tumbling over the edge of the cliff, a fleeting instant of dizziness. It's a visual way of telling us that Jesus does not feel in full control of himself; he cannot grasp who he is. He struggles with his own divinity. His disciples may be convinced of it, but he isn't. Not yet. The weight of his very real humanity is still heavy on his shoulders. He wonders, how can he also be God when he is so—ordinary?

"I don't steal, I don't fight, I don't kill, not because I don't want to, but because I'm afraid. I want to rebel against you, against everything, against *God*, but I'm afraid," Jesus says. "You want to know who my God is? Fear. You look inside me and that's all you'll find." A startling thing to think of these words coming from the Messiah, until you consider how relatable those words are. Who among us would not fear the idea that they are God in human form? Were the notion to come into your head that you were God manifested as a mortal man, would you not think yourself going mad? Would you not be concerned with your own mental health?

This struggle is the heart of the picture. For all its interpretations and reinterpretations of stories from the Bible—turning water to wine, the storming of the temple, meeting John the Baptist (Andre Gregory), raising Lazarus (Tomas Arana) from the dead, and of course the crucifixion—the narrative pulse is not in miracles and sermons; it's in Jesus coming to grips with his divine nature.

He intervenes when Mary is about to be stoned, asking the crowd who is without sin. This scene is especially potent because it lays bare Jesus as a man engaging in what must have been a terrifying and brave act. In a contemporary analysis of the film for *Crisis Magazine*, a Catholic publication, Richard Alleva observed, "To this mob, he's just a meddling fool who's asking for it." Depicting Jesus in this way, as vulnerable, as lacking superhuman powers but standing up for true righteousness anyway, means "we are allowed to eavesdrop on history and discover exactly what dangerous improvisation Jesus might have had to resort to in order to quell a mob."[5] Challenged to cast a stone only if without sin, an old man in the mob insists he has nothing to hide, but Jesus sees through him, says the man cheats his workers, says he knows about the time the old man spends with the widow, Judith. If the man casts a stone at Mary, Jesus asks, doesn't he fear God will wither his arm in payment for the deed?

Here, Jesus begins to realize his words have power. He is not yet convinced of his own divinity. He fears saying the wrong thing (and also the *right* thing), but he begins to understand the potency of his words. And so he begins to preach a gospel of love. Soon he has a flock following him. We even get an awkward 1980s minimontage, synth music and thundering drums by Peter Gabriel providing the score as Jesus walks toward the camera, the crowd growing behind him with each crossfade.

Sound is put to better use when he meets John the Baptist. When they first speak, the bustle of the crowd around them is suddenly muted, as if the two are alone despite being surrounded by scores of others. This isn't merely sound designed so the audience can better hear the conversation, either. It's meant to isolate them and emphasize the importance of their meeting. John the Baptist seems to recognize Jesus as the Messiah, yet they debate love versus anger. John argues that anger is God's way, citing the Bible. Jesus says anger is not the answer. So what *is* the answer, John asks? Jesus answers, "I don't know." The uncertainty is striking.

Until this point, the picture is fairly grounded in a reality viewers can understand. Jesus is a man. His followers are people inspired by his words. That there is a debate over his divinity, even in his own mind, is understandable. His disciples debate whether he is the Messiah, too. Then he experiences strange visions in the desert: a snake with a woman's voice, a lion with the voice of Judas, he bites from an apple that is filled with blood. And then when he hears his followers wondering aloud if he truly is divine, if he is God made flesh, he reaches inside his own chest and tears out his heart—literally. This truly is a miracle.

Initially, Scorsese resisted such overt displays of the supernatural, but eventually he relented, leaving the truth of some of the miracles a question for the audience to ponder. "Paul (Schrader) wrote the first version of the script coming out of the psychological trauma of his mother's death, and it was a very heartfelt piece of work. He felt that the supernatural should exist alongside the natural, so he added Jesus taking His heart out, as well as a literal version of the Last Supper in terms of swallowing the flesh and blood of Jesus," Scorsese said. The duo ended up paring down some of those elements, but many remain in the finished work. "This approach still applies to the way the miracles are done in the film. It's as if to say: What was hypnosis, what was a real miracle and what was a kind of curing?"[6] (By "curing," Scorsese is referring to actual remedies practiced during the day, such as using saliva and herbs to treat ailments.)

It would be easy to mistake *The Last Temptation of Christ* as a film about faith, but in truth it's a film about doubt—and though the two seem a pair, there is a distinction. Faith is about finding your path toward something you cannot see but believing it is there all the same, about thinking, *knowing*, there is salvation at the end of an arduous road. Doubt is having such truths presented to you and turning away from them all the same, about being on a path and never being certain that it's the correct one. This is a Jesus who questions his role almost to the last.

It is only when upon the cross, beaten and bloodied and tempted by Satan in the guise of an angel, that he realizes what he truly is. Satan comes as a little girl, sweet, pure. "Your father is the god of mercy, not punishment," she tells him. Here, the most controversial sequence of the film begins, a lengthy vision of what Christ's life could be if he lived out his life as an ordinary man rather than be crucified. Is it a dream? A vision? A longing fantasy? The latter is how it was spun in much of the contemporary criticism of the picture. A report in the *Los Angeles Times* noted, "Evangelical Protestant protests, starting last month and recently joined by Southern Baptist and Eastern Orthodox condemnations, have particularly focused on a scene showing Jesus making love to Mary Magdalene in a dream episode."[7]

But it's not a dream sequence. This is Satan making one last-ditch effort to tempt Jesus. In the vision, he sees the girl taking him away from the cross. She tells him he is not the Messiah, and he feels a sense of relief that this terrible burden has been lifted from him. He sees himself as married. He makes love. His wife is pregnant with his child. He has a family. It is a pure life, a good life, the life men are meant to live under God. For the director, there is no shame or blame in this. "You know, the one sexual thing the priest told Catholic boys they could not be held responsible for was nocturnal emission. It was like an involuntary fantasy. And with Jesus, it's the same thing. How can you hold him responsible for this fantasy?"[8]

The vision continues. Jesus sees a preacher speaking of the life of Jesus and his accomplishments and crucifixion. It is the apostle Paul. Jesus tells him these stories are lies; he was not crucified; God saved him, and he was allowed to live out a normal life. Jesus threatens to tell people the truth, but Paul says none will listen. People need God; they need faith in Jesus Christ, the Messiah, their salvation. The idea, Paul tells Jesus, is more powerful than the reality.

And for the first time in the film, Jesus of Nazareth fully embraces his Godhood. He begs God to take him back. "I want to bring salvation!" He *wants* to be crucified. "I want to be the Messiah," he says. And with that he is on the cross again, the vision ended. He's dying. Through his pain, he smiles. "It is accomplished!" he declares. "It is accomplished."

And then shrieking voices and colors like overexposed film flapping on the reel. Jesus Christ cast aside temptation, overcame his humanity, and gave himself for mankind. Surely a potent, moving sacrifice? Much of the religious community did not see it that way. But for Scorsese, at least, he had fulfilled his mission.

CONCLUSION AND IMPACT

Rather than being welcome as a heartfelt examination of faith, *The Last Temptation of Christ* was met with scathing criticism by religious groups across the country, threats of boycotts, and a general atmosphere of outrage. It was called "sacrilegious," a "deliberate act of blasphemy," "morally offensive," and "exploitation . . . for greed."[9] Organization after organization called for boycotts of the film despite never having seen it.

Scorsese knew the picture would stir up some controversy, but not only was that not his intent, but he also believed any controversy would lead to productive conversation. "I thought there would be some people who would be set against it completely. But I also thought it would open up a healthy discussion," the director said. "I expected some controversy. But I expected it to be intelligent. I expected discussion and dialogue."[10]

That is not what he got. A group of southern California Protestant ministers called it a movie about a "mentally deranged and lust-driven man who convinces Judas Iscariot to betray Him."[11] Mother Angelica of the Eternal Word Television Network declared, "Every Christian ought to be incensed about this blasphemous film."[12] And on and on.

It's true that, for much of the picture's run time, we have a flawed Messiah. He is a man, and he is *also* God. That seeming contradiction, the miracle of both being true, *that* is the area Scorsese explores (through ideas initially written by Kazantzakis, it's important to note). The director wanted "to make him more like a person who would be in this room, someone you could talk to."[13]

In many respects, this picture was the director's attempt to get to know Jesus better, to meet him and "talk" with him through the medium he knew best. Roger Ebert observed that Keitel had previously played two autobiographical characters for Scorsese, J. R. and Charlie, from *Who's That Knocking at My Door?* and *Mean Streets*, respectively, and here he plays Judas. "Perhaps Judas is Scorsese's autobiographical character in *The Last Temptation of Christ*. Certainly not the Messiah, but the mortal man walking beside him, worrying about him, lecturing him, wanting him to be better, threatening him, confiding in him, prepared to betray him if he must. Christ is the film, Judas is the director."[14] And indeed, in this version of the Messiah story, it is Jesus who essentially convinces Judas to betray him. Judas must commit a terrible deed in order for Jesus Christ to fulfill his destiny.

To what extent *The Last Temptation of Christ* succeeds as a film, both as art and as entertainment, is debatable. It lacks much of the dynamism one associates with Scorsese's work. It's visually barren, and its nearly three-hour run time is perhaps longer than it needs to be. But as an exploratory piece, as a thought experiment, it is a potent piece of work.

Potent, but another failure as far as breaking through to a wider audience was concerned. Scorsese would take a quick detour to Soho for a short piece as part of an anthology with Francis Ford Coppola and Woody Allen, but the next major movie percolating in his head would bring him back to familiar territory: criminals, the city streets, and a hazy view of morality. It would become his signature picture.

12

NEW YORK STORIES: LIFE LESSONS (1989)

FILM DETAILS

RELEASE DATE: March 10, 1989
WRITTEN BY: Richard Price
STARRING: Nick Nolte, Rosanna Arquette, Steve Buscemi
RUNNING TIME: 124 minutes (full film), 40 minutes (Scorsese's contribution)
NOTES: This is an anthology film, with two other segments, *Life without Zoë* and *Oedipus Wrecks*, directed by Francis Ford Coppola and Woody Allen, respectively.

ABOUT THE FILM

Following *The Last Temptation of Christ*, Martin Scorsese began working with author Nicholas Pileggi to adapt his bestselling book *Wiseguy* into a film. Before launching into that project, however, he got pulled into a collaborative project with two other directors who also rose to prominence in the 1970s, Francis Ford Coppola and Woody Allen. Together, the trio would create an anthology film called *New York Stories*, each of the three pieces related to the city in some way.

Scorsese used the opportunity to take another crack at exploring the themes in Fyodor Dostoevsky's *The Gambler*. Starring Nick Nolte and Rosanna Arquette, *Life Lessons* explores the psyche of a man who subconsciously sabotages his own relationships in order to fuel inspiration for his art. Often overlooked when discussing Scorsese's body of work, the short film proves to be one of the director's most personally revealing pictures.

ANALYSIS

Life Lessons is a story about obsession: about obsession so crippling it paralyzes a man but also sets him free. And it's about manipulation: about a man who manipulates young women like he manipulates paint, casting it here and there in a frenzy, searching for something he can't grasp or identify but that he knows he'll find if he just keeps probing. Emotional wrecks are left in his wake. He was divorced at least four times, he says. Each woman is a canvas. Blank when he first meets them, a whiter shade of pale, a series of parts and images to capture and control, and then he's done.

Nolte plays Lionel Dobie, a Soho painter with a dark style and an avid following. As the piece opens, Lionel is freaking out prior to an upcoming show, unable to paint, unable to express himself. He needs his muse. She arrives in the form of Paulette (Arquette), his live-in assistant who is more than an assistant. An aspiring artist herself, she sleeps with Lionel in exchange for a place to stay and mentorship on her art (which he never provides). The arrangement isn't merely one of convenience and sexual gratification, though. We see this when she is introduced. He's at the airport, waiting for her. Shown from his subjective point of view, most of the frame is blacked out, as if he has tunnel vision. He can't see the world until she appears. Only then does the lens open up. It's an effect the director uses repeatedly over the course of this short, an expression of Lionel's single-minded focus.

We see it again as she unpacks, this highly subjective camera work. Lionel's eyes linger on her panties. They focus on her foot, a delicate chain of gold on her ankle. Always on tiny details. He's apparently promised Paulette he won't ask to sleep with her anymore, but once the promise is made, she is all he can think about. When she expresses interest in other men, he interferes. When she expresses interest in other artists, he interferes. When she does nothing more than lay in bed, talking on the phone, he hovers over her like an expectant dog, at once needful and dangerous, as capable of attacking as he is of smothering her in unwanted love.

Lionel does offer Paulette a thought on art that resonates, but it's difficult to credit him with doing so out of any sense of benevolence or desire to share wisdom. When asking for feedback on her work, he tells Paulette, "What the hell difference does it matter what I think? It's yours. You make art because you have to. 'Cause you got no choice. It's not about talent. It's about no choice but to do it." This is perhaps the most honest thing he says. His cries of "I love you" are selfish and needy; his warnings about other men, defensive and jealous. But this? This is a slice of truth. Art isn't merely a vocation or pastime. For many, it's a *need*. It's an outlet. It's their only real means of expression. Certainly, this is the case for Scorsese, who from an early age found that expressing himself visually wasn't just a natural talent; it was the only real way he had to pour out what was boiling inside him.

Lionel, however, doesn't merely express his inner self through art. His muse, his trigger, his *fuel* is emotional abuse. He needs it. What ends up on the canvas stems from it. Late in the picture, after Paulette has left him and he's displaying a fabulous new body of work, a fan approaches Lionel during an exhibition and gives him a strange yet telling compliment: "I look at your stuff, and I just want to divorce my wife." Appropriate, given the extent to which Lionel's art is propelled by toxic relationships.

In this respect, Lionel has a lot more in common with the standard Scorsese protagonist than he appears to on his artsy Soho surface. Most are streetwise and grounded in some way. The Howard Hugheses of his filmography are rare. More common are the Henry Hills and Rupert Pupkins, men who are not lofty and thoughtful and expressive but who walk in the same muck as the rest of us. But look closer, and you see a trait that surfaces in Hill and Pupkin and Travis Bickle and Jake LaMotta and so many others, including in the otherwise aloof Lionel: a propensity for self-destruction, a subconscious need to sabotage his own life, a self-destructive streak he doesn't even know is there. In this case, it *drives* him.

But where Lionel differs from so many other Scorsese protagonists is that he has all the rise and none of the fall. Put another way, his knack for self-sabotage actually *works* for him. Controlling women to the point where their entire relationship is a cesspool provides grist for his artistic mill, and his career as an artist thrives as a result. No tragic collapses. No falls from grace. Just artistic success and a string of emotionally scarred women left in his wake.

How much of this is Martin Scorsese himself reimagined as a painter? It's no secret that his work is often deeply personal and that he often seeks out characters that reflect some aspect of his own inner workings. When making *Life Lessons*, Scorsese was on his fourth marriage, and it was falling apart. Though married to producer Barbara De Fina, who worked on *GoodFellas*, *The Color of Money*, *The Last Temptation of Christ*, *Kundun*, and *Casino*, he was dating actress Illeana Douglas, who had small roles in *Last Temptation*,

GoodFellas, *Cape Fear*, and this short film. And previous relationships had been turbulent, especially his second marriage, to writer Julia Cameron. Certainly, he was no stranger to the cycle of collapse and rebuilding that relationships can go through.

And in *Life Lessons*, it is indeed a cycle. The piece ends when Lionel, at another showing of his paintings, encounters a beautiful, young, aspiring artist fascinated with his work. The camera again moves to a subjective point of view, leaping from close-up to close-up of various parts of her body, his obsessive eye kicking in once again. He offers her a job as a live-in "assistant." The cycle begins anew.

CONCLUSION AND IMPACT

New York Stories was a modest success, with Scorsese's and Allen's segments winning praise, but it would quickly be overshadowed by the director's next project, a crime film that is his definitive work.

13

GOODFELLAS (1990)

FILM DETAILS

RELEASE DATE: September 9, 1990
WRITTEN BY: Nicholas Pileggi, Martin Scorsese
STARRING: Ray Liotta, Lorraine Bracco, Robert De Niro, Joe Pesci, Paul Sorvino
RUNNING TIME: 145 minutes

ABOUT THE FILM

" As far back as I can remember, I always wanted to be a gangster." With those simple words, the third of Martin Scorsese's three greatest masterpieces begins. And they're magic words. Alluring and aggressive. Tempting. Off-putting. Unsympathetic. Enticing. Martini-sipping cool. A simple line that sets the stage for a narrative that pushes and pulls the viewer over the course of two hours and twenty minutes.

Based on the book *Wiseguy* by Nicholas Pileggi, *GoodFellas* is less a story and more an experience, a series of vignettes following the rise and fall of midlevel mobster Henry Hill (Ray Liotta) and his two closest friends, Jimmy Conway (Robert De Niro) and Tommy DeVito (Joe Pesci). Henry gets involved with low-level mobsters as a teen; by his early twenties is flush with ill-gotten cash; meets and marries his wife, Karen (Lorraine Bracco); starts slinging drugs during a brief prison stint; continues to sell after he is released; gets busted; rats out his friends; and enters the witness protection program with more frustration than remorse. That's the whole story.

Free of the constraints of telling a tight, focused story and instead intent on immersing us in the criminal underworld in a way that had never been seen before, *GoodFellas* is a picture that ignores Hollywood's unwritten rules and forges new ground, not just for the director, but also for every edgy, too-cool-for-school director to follow.

The book upon which the movie was based was a best-seller, a book in which real-life criminal Henry Hill "prefers to describe the details and recall the prevailing mood rather than convince the reader of his own stand-up behavior."[1] Scorsese encountered Pileggi's work while making *The Color of Money* and was immediately intrigued by the honesty of it. The pair collaborated on the screenplay, going through draft after draft, with Scorsese taking a rapid-fire, music-video-like approach to the narrative. The director described his vision as being like a two-hour trailer, something to capture the breathless energy and constant tension of being a career criminal. The results changed modern cinema.

ANALYSIS

GoodFellas is *the* Martin Scorsese picture. Throughout this book, I repeatedly emphasize the eclectic nature of the director's filmography, one that is among the most varied and unpredictable of any auteur of the last fifty or sixty years. While a number of common themes tie his work together, that Scorsese has been pigeonholed by casual audiences as someone who only does gangster movies has long been unfair, given the variety of tone, genre, and approach in his work.

Despite all that, *GoodFellas* is *the* Martin Scorsese picture of all Martin Scorsese pictures. Not the best, which is far too subjective a judgment, nor the most important but rather the one that best defines him as a filmmaker because it best represents his disregard for the "right" way to make a movie. Though *The Color of Money* proved he could appeal to a mainstream audience, it did not reestablish him as an artist of note to a general public that had forgotten how good he could be. *GoodFellas* was in many ways a total reinvention, an example of an artist taking everything he had learned and applying it to something new. This movie *feels* like Scorsese, yet he had done nothing like it before. Embryonic elements showed up in works like *Mean Streets*, *Raging Bull*, and even the unusual *After Hours*, but this picture was a new invention and one that would set the tone for the rest of his career.

What makes *GoodFellas* work is its total disregard for the unwritten rules of Hollywood productions. Element after element should not work, yet it does. Wall-to-wall narration. A *second* narrator appearing out of nowhere. Copious freeze-frames. A sudden fourth-wall break two hours into the movie. Or even the fact that *GoodFellas* doesn't really have a *plot*. It's a series of vignettes, with few movie-length narrative threads tying all the vignettes together aside from the characters themselves. It's entirely possible to watch a random twenty-minute chunk of the movie and have a satisfying, nearly complete experience. What narrative arc there is follows the Scorsese template—like so many others, it's a rise-and-fall story, with the protagonist responsible for his own downfall—but it's not a standard story by any means. There is no goal, no real obstacle to overcome. For Henry Hill, no central character conflict aside from the basic desire to make money and stay alive. He has ups and downs with his wife, but they are not the story. The story is just a series of glimpses into the crazy lifestyle he leads.

In a sense, the film opens at what turns out to be the beginning of the end for Henry, Tommy, and Jimmy, with made man Billy Batts (Frank Vincent) in the trunk of a car, beaten and bloodied. It's the incident where everything went wrong for the trio, though they didn't know it at the time. It's an immediate dose of savage violence, all thrusting knives and sickening sound effects, a shock to the system that tells viewers right from the start that these are not good people and this won't be a romanticized or "classy" mob story. That makes the contrast of the sudden cut to soaring swing music all the more potent. It's glamour set next to gore.

It's easy to walk away with the impression that *GoodFellas* glorifies the criminal lifestyle, at least at first. "As far back as I can remember, I always wanted to be a gangster," Liotta intones in his first bit of narration, and from there we launch into song, the first lyrics we hear saying, "I know I go from rags to riches." Our first shot of young Henry Hill (Christopher Serrone) is a deep close-up, the glow of Tuddy's (Frank DiLeo) cab stand reflected in his eyes. It's a classic image of youth, as if he's gazing out at a carnival or amusement park, but it's tainted by what lies behind those glowing lights. In that way, that first shot of Henry's eyes is a reflection of the film as a whole: rich promise followed by harsh reality. For now, jumping into gangster life almost seems kind of *fun* and appealing. There are some ugly moments in his early life—a freeze-frame of his father beating him shows us how his entry into the lifestyle alienates him from the normal life the rest of us live, for example—but there is a vicarious delight in seeing his mailman almost thrown headfirst into a pizza oven. Anyone who had difficulties with authority in their youth will smile inwardly. There is something attractive here, something alluring. We almost root for Henry to get one over on authority figures. There are brief moments when the shine is not so strong, such as Henry being scolded for helping out a guy who had just been shot, but the overall image is an appealing one. Scorsese is going to smother that shine later in the film, but in the early going, it's a wild ride.

The director's work is never as immersive as it is here. He puts you in the world with these criminals and lowlifes, deep enough into it so that you almost feel sympathy for them, as if they are part of your extended family. A dysfunctional family, to be sure, but family all the same. This kind of immersion comes not through a trick or two but through a full-frontal assault on your senses: voice-over narration presented as if Henry is telling his story directly to you, startling use of period music throughout, bold cuts from scene to scene that play more like flashes of memory than scenes from a movie, and of course Scorsese's brilliantly considered camerawork. The Copacabana entrance is perhaps the picture's most heralded scene, but two others make this point just as well.

The first is early on, shortly after we're introduced to the adult Henry Hill. We enter a smoky bar filled with mobsters, seeing it through Henry's eyes. One by one we're introduced to a series of crooks with colorful-sounding nicknames, quick introductions that don't really *matter* as far as story is concerned but that are essential in establishing the environment and atmosphere he exists in. It's

Martin Scorsese and Robert De Niro's career-spanning artistic collaboration is arguably matched only by the work Akira Kurosawa and Toshiro Mifune did together. *Warner Bros./Photofest*

one long shot, everyone greeting the camera directly, tossing off small hellos or referencing events we never see and never hear about again. The camera continues around some tables, through the back of the bar; then we follow a rack of fur coats into a back hallway, where we see Henry doing some business; then the camera follows the coats into the kitchen. It's a shot that doesn't get the same accolades as the Copacabana sequence but that is just as daring, immersive, instructive, and effective.

The other is a different type of scene entirely, one shot in a far more traditional manner. This is perhaps the most famous scene of the movie, though it's famous for being so quotable, not for its directorial bravado. Yet consider the choices Scorsese made here, and it becomes apparent that every choice was weighed and considered with careful thought. We're talking about the "funny" dialogue between Henry and Tommy. Tommy's tirade here and the growing tension it displays is potent because of its *lack* of directorial bravado. The sequence is carefully staged with nothing more than two simple medium shots, Tommy in one flanked by onlookers, Henry in the other with more of the same—pure simplicity.

It's that simplicity that brings us into the scene in such a powerful way. The strength of the "funny" scene isn't in Pesci's performance or the dialogue; it's in the scene's honesty. By now the story has become a minor part of Hollywood legend: An incident similar to this actually happened to Pesci; he suggested playing with the idea to Scorsese; it was worked out in rehearsals through improvisation; and once they had it, they rolled cameras. One of the most memorable scenes in movies was born. It works because it doesn't feel like clever dialogue. It doesn't sound like something a screenwriter would come up with. It rings with authenticity because it *is* a true story, and anyone who has been around someone like Tommy—a firecracker looking for an excuse to explode, someone who baits others and wields social power like a gunslinger—knows how situations like this can appear unexpectedly and fly out of control before you've even had time to process them. Scorsese's choice to stage the whole scene in static medium shots underlines this because it keeps the people surrounding Henry and Tommy in the shot at all times. We can see their slow realization that things may take a dark turn at any moment. Scorsese and editor Thelma Schoonmaker hold the moment just long enough so that tension fills the room. If Henry makes a misstep, he'll either have a violent confrontation with a hyperviolent man or back down in front of everyone and look spineless. In either case, he loses a significant amount of credibility with this crowd, so Henry does the best he can do and takes a risk: He calls Tommy's bluff. Laughter. A violent incident with the owner of the establishment. More laughter. And the moment has passed.

Scorsese's willingness to allow his actors to improvise and contribute their own ideas resulted in one of *GoodFellas'* most iconic scenes, during which Henry Hill must answer a simple question: "How am I funny?" *Warner Bros. Pictures/Photofest*

And we were *in* the moment because we knew that, in the midst of a film with a restless camera, bringing the camera to a stop during that confrontation was the best possible choice. It's these seemingly small moments that sink you into the world and allow you to live vicariously through the characters, feeling the highs and the frightening lows of mobster life. No other gangster movie had ever done it this effectively. (The "funny" scene is also an effective bit of character work, setting up the monster lurking inside Tommy and providing valuable context for his sudden murders of both Spider and Billy Batts.)

A major factor in allowing us to live in this world is the fact that Henry grabs us by the hand and takes us there with him. We are Karen being led by Henry through the bowels of the Copacabana to the best seats in the house. This is accomplished through a device generally frowned upon in filmmaking: voice-over narration.

Voice-over narration is often cited as a weakness in film, used primarily to fill in aspects of the plot or characterization that for one reason or another could not be presented on-screen, as a means of dumping exposition onto the audience, or a lazy way to fix script problems. To be clear, I do not endorse that view, but it's a widely held one, or at least it was before Scorsese proved (repeatedly) that voice-over can be a strength. "Show, don't tell" is perhaps the most oft-repeated rule of writing, after all. *GoodFellas*' narration isn't about correcting flaws in the script or dumping exposition onto the audience, however. It's a character unto itself. In fact, it's *the* character of the movie. It's Henry Hill himself, looking back on his life and telling you stories about how he used to live, in the same way mobsters spin stories for one another. They're brags. They're tall tales. It's entertainment built on half-truths. The entire flavor of the picture changes without that narration. The narration is what puts us inside Henry's head. It justifies the highly subjective camerawork Scorsese employs throughout, the dizzying Steadicam shots, the freeze-frames, and so on. The allure of *GoodFellas* isn't in its plot. It doesn't draw you in with intrigue or surprises. The interest is in Henry's state of mind as he recalls the crazy life he used to lead. These aren't "real" events, after all; they're Henry's memories of them. The narration lends connective tissue to the vignettes that come together to make the film. The narration is the tie that binds.

It also enhances the feeling of collapse one gets from Henry's rise and fall—and that collapse is the heart of the movie. The early portions of the picture, during Henry's golden age of sorts, look remarkably appealing. Henry has everything he could want: money, booze, women, access to the hottest spots in town, free rein at fancy restaurants, people bending over backward to please him. The life looks alluring. You can hear the excitement in his voice.

It doesn't take long for this to be turned on its head, however. The pivotal moment is the killing of Billy Batts, though signals that the mob life isn't as glamorous as Henry believes dot the picture well before this scene. Karen at a gathering of worn-down, unhappy housewives. Henry insists to Karen that "Nobody goes to jail unless they want to, unless they make themselves get caught," which is transparent nonsense. Karen's mother is upset that Henry is out all night. The young assistant Spider (Michael Imperioli) is shot and killed by Tommy. Henry does a stint in prison. Time and again, the attractive parts of the lifestyle are contrasted with things that would make a normal person say, "This is not for me."

Contrast is a major part of the picture's power, and this is often seen in the sharp, frantic editing. Witness the cut after Henry brutally beats Karen's neighbor for sexually assaulting her (itself a fantastic single-shot take that follows him across the street, to the beating, and back). Henry, sweaty and bristling with anger, hands her a bloodied handgun. Slight slow motion as it dawns on her that Henry is a dangerous man. Cut to their wedding, a joyous affair. The contrast between brutality and joy makes the viewer feel as overwhelmed as Karen is. And then that bright day filled with smiles and love cuts directly to Karen's mother (Suzanne Shepard), furious that Henry has been out all night, happiness contrasted with turmoil and domestic tension.

Scorsese often does the same with music. Scenes of horrific violence are often contrasted with beautiful or uplifting music ("Atlantis" by Donovan during the beating of Billy Batts, the outro of "Layla" when all the victims of Jimmy's hits are being discovered). The result is that we feel continually off-balance. The contradictions, the conflict between the high of owning the town and the low of what that really means, the stark reality of how quickly things can end in this world makes *GoodFellas* fantastic voyeurism but terrible wish fulfillment. We might daydream about what we'd do in Michael Corleone's shoes, but *GoodFellas* does not provide the same sort of operatic thrill as *The Godfather*. Once we get a real taste of Henry's life, we want no part of it.

The killing of Spider, for example: Spider is a young man, just like Henry was at the start of the film, hanging around, helping out, but not yet a criminal. He's just slinging drinks at private card games. He could have been another Henry, or he could have straightened out and lived a normal life. We never find out because, in a fit of bruised ego, Tommy kills him for talking back—this shortly after having shot him in the foot while making him dance at gunpoint. That's how fast it can end when you're around these people.

As if to signal that life is falling apart for Henry, the movie cuts right from Spider's death to Karen mashing the buttons at an apartment building, shouting for Henry's mistress (or *goomah*). So while Henry's friends slaughter young men with little provocation, his marriage begins to disintegrate. Scorsese called the picture a "nostalgia of a world of gods," but really, it's about the *collapse* of the gods.[2] It is their twilight years, the end of the ill-gotten heaven they created, shattered when the mob got involved in dealing drugs.

The "pure" pre-drug-running days of the mafia are something of a myth, of course, injected into pop culture by Vito Corleone's opposition to drug dealing in *The Godfather*. The truth is that any illicit trade that could bring in money was open game, though some mob bosses forbid it within their ranks: "FBI documents do indicate that bosses such as Paul Castellano and Vincent 'the Chin' Gigante in New York and Angelo Bruno in Philadelphia banned members of their organizations from getting involved in narcotics."[3] Much like *GoodFellas*' Paulie Cicero (Paul Sorvino), however, this wasn't a moral objection on their part; it was a pragmatic decision based on the realization that running drugs exposed them to greater legal risk, especially as the so-called war on drugs began in the 1970s. Things did change during that era, though. There was just too much money to be made for these mobsters to ignore it; "The 'Pizza Connection,' for instance, was a Sicilian Mafia heroin ring that dominated the trade in New York and other East Coast cities between 1975 and 1984, bringing an estimated $1.6 billion worth of heroin into the United States."[4] The drug trade is what Henry got roped into, and it's what ended up bringing down Paulie and his underlings. It was the end of an era, the decay and death of the old image of what gangsters were—well-dressed gentlemen running the neighborhood through the veiled threat of violence—and replacing that image with coked-up, frantic criminals.

And frantic is what Henry Hill was on May 11, 1980, the day during which the movie's most dizzying, dynamic sequence takes place. This is when Henry gets busted for running drugs, the bust that ultimately brings *everyone* down, and it's a whirlwind of editing that is disorienting and exhausting and a fitting end to Henry's climb through the criminal world: cocaine, fast cuts, rambling narration, blaring music, no focus on any one thing as the most important object of Henry's attentions. As a helicopter appears to follow him around as he sets up deals and preps to run drugs, we're not sure if he's just being paranoid or if he's really being tailed, but we're pretty sure it's the latter. Meanwhile, he's obsessing about his pasta sauce and bickering with his babysitter over her lucky hat, even though he *knows* he's probably being watched. His head just isn't screwed on right. Through maddening editing and Liotta's breathless narration, the viewer's head feels out of sorts, too.

Henry Hill gets busted. Once out on bail, he reaches out to Paulie for help. He gets a small wad of cash, and that's it. "Now I gotta turn my back on you," Paulie tells him. "Thirty-two hundred bucks," Henry says in the narration. "That's what he gave me. Thirty-two hundred bucks for a lifetime. It wasn't even enough to pay for the coffin."

Nearly two hours prior, after we saw Henry get pinched for the first time, Jimmy congratulated him on handling it well. "You learned the two greatest things in life: Never rat on your friends, and always keep your mouth shut." But this time, in an effort to save his family, Henry rats everyone out: Jimmy, Paulie, *everyone*. He goes into witness protection. Everyone else goes to jail.

Henry's turn at the end does not fill him with remorse for his past deeds, however. Though *GoodFellas* represents Scorsese at the height of his filmmaking prowess and showcases many of the hallmarks of his best work, it does lack one of his most prominent themes: guilt. Guilt runs through his entire filmography, informing the narratives of many of his pictures and serving as an integral part of his most personal characters. It's an inescapable aspect of his work and an essential part of understanding what makes his art so singular. Yet guilt is nowhere to be found here. Henry Hill gets caught in the end and rats out his friends, and the only real concern he has is that he can't get a good dish of pasta anymore. He's just another working schmuck like the rest of us. There are no lessons learned, no moral transformations, no remorse whatsoever. Hill is frustrated with where his life ends up but only because it inconveniences him. "It'll be phony if he felt badly about what he did. The irony of it at the end I kind of think is very funny," Scorsese said. "I think the audience should get angry with him. I would hope they would be. And maybe angry with the system that allows it."[5]

The first thirty minutes of *GoodFellas* seems to glorify mob life, and Henry's utter lack of remorse seems to solidify the idea, but in the end we see that the life wasn't so magnificent after all. That didn't stop people from being outraged at the picture. "People got so angry that they stormed out of the theater. They thought it was an outrage that I had made these people so attractive," Scorsese said. But he "liked the everyday banality of it," the idea that these gangsters, privileged in so many ways, also argued about sauce, had problems with relationships, and were generally *human* rather than caricatures.[6] Henry tells us that, when it comes to the sauce a fellow inmate made while in prison, "I felt he used too many onions, but it was still a very good sauce." It's a seemingly unimportant detail, but these small, mundane details are the flavor of the movie, just as the pork is the flavor of the sauce Vinnie makes. The entire prison sequence is a good example of this because it has little to do with looking at actual life in prison. It could even be excised from the film, except that it reinforces the idea that these men live in a kind of privilege most of us could never understand. Being in prison doesn't *matter* to them. They chat, they cook, they scam, they make money. It's just another place for them to be. From a narrative standpoint, one might ask why it's necessary to include the prison sequence at all, but again, *GoodFellas* isn't a film about narrative. It's a series of glimpses into a lifestyle that fascinated Scorsese. No, *GoodFellas* is not a condemnation of the lifestyle. It makes no efforts to rebuke it, but it doesn't celebrate it, either. It simply puts us in that world, and it's a world in which everything appealing is matched by something horrible. Henry's friends end up dead or in jail. Violence touches everything they do. Just getting into Jimmy Conway's orbit results in countless dead bodies. Karen can't even accept a gift of clothes from him without wondering if she is going to be killed. (It was a brilliant decision to leave it unclear whether her fear is justified. We never find out if she really is going to be whacked in that scene.)

Even the final music sends mixed messages. It's a snarling, nasty version of "My Way," best known for Frank Sinatra's rendition but here performed by Sid Vicious, bassist for the punk band the Sex Pistols. On the surface it seems a middle finger to the world, a loud announcement saying, "Screw the plebes.

Screw you if you don't like it. I lived my life my way, and I don't regret it." And it does say that, to an extent, yet there's more beneath the surface.

On February 1, 1979, just released on bail after having been arrested for assault, Sid Vicious died of a heroin overdose on his first night of freedom. His reputation was so bad, his survivors couldn't even find a funeral home willing to hold a service for him.[7] Fitting, then, that it should be his version of "My Way" that closes the door on Henry Hill's on-screen life. It's a snarling bit of rebellion spit out by someone who self-destructed, not unlike Henry Hill himself. The music also serves as a commentary on the end of an era. The picture opens in the midst of the heyday of swing, a time when Frank Sinatra and Dean Martin ruled the stage, but ends with a sneering Brit spitting out one of Sinatra's best-known works, a perfect musical summation of the close of the supposed golden age of Italian mobsters.

Through music, through fast cuts and long takes, through copious use of the word *fuck* and shockingly real violence, Martin Scorsese painted a picture of gangster life unlike any we had ever seen before, then pulled the rug out from under it, with Henry Hill ending up just an anonymous homeowner in an anonymous suburb, scooping the paper up from his front porch. It was the end of the glory days of the mob, but the start of a new era for Martin Scorsese himself.

CONCLUSION AND IMPACT

GoodFellas' legacy looms large. It's widely considered both a classic of the genre as well as one of the great films in cinema history. Few crime movies that came after could help but owe it some debt. Quentin Tarantino cribbed much of his style from *GoodFellas* (along with a generous helping of spaghetti westerns and kung fu movies, of course). HBO's game-changing television show *The Sopranos* changed the medium forever and ushered in a golden age of quality dramatic TV, and that show wouldn't exist were it not for *GoodFellas*—and not just because six regular cast members on *The Sopranos* and twenty-seven of its actors previously appeared in *GoodFellas*.[8] The dynamics and energy in many modern crime and antihero movies can be traced directly back to *GoodFellas*. Pictures like 2013's *American Hustle* by David O. Russell, which garnered ten Academy Award nominations; Paul Thomas Anderson's *Boogie Nights* (1997); and Ted Demme's 2001 movie *Blow* are just a few that clearly took inspiration from Scorsese's work, borrowing much of the tone, style, and approach. The picture did what few pictures do: It changed cinema; "Throughout the 1990s, the sense of cinematic liberation engendered by Scorsese's masterpiece would yield experiments of a type unthinkable in a pre-*Goodfellas* Hollywood—Molotov cocktails like Oliver Stone's *Natural Born Killers* and David Fincher's *Fight Club*, and the Hughes Brothers' heavily Scorsese-influenced *Dead Presidents*."[9]

The picture would change Scorsese as a filmmaker, too. Works like *Casino* and *The Wolf of Wall Street* are so thoroughly built on the foundation he created here. *GoodFellas* is now widely seen as Scorsese's primary style by mainstream audiences. It's not an entirely fair assessment of his work—the variety of tone and style in his career is laudable—but it's not entirely *unfair*, either, seeing as *GoodFellas* is arguably the definitive Scorsese picture. Even works that on the surface have little resemblance to *GoodFellas*, such as his druggy Nicolas Cage vehicle *Bringing Out the Dead*, are extensions of the style he pioneered here.

To some extent, the picture has become an anchor on the director, with audiences expecting another rehash and disappointed when they don't get one. Pictures like *Kundun* and *The Age of Innocence* and *Silence* and *Hugo* are seen as departures rather than as a reflection of the director's wide range of interests and talents. When the director returned to mob movies in 2019 with *The Irishman*, Schoonmaker was quick to temper expectations, knowing people would expect a movie similar to this one. "It is not *Goodfellas*," she said. "It's completely different. It's wonderful. They're going to love it. But please don't think it's gonna be *Goodfellas*, because it isn't."[10] Even I am guilty of perpetuating the idea, above framing this as *the* Martin Scorsese picture.

Yet when a picture leaves such an indelible mark on the face of popular cinema, it's easy to understand why. Even Martin Scorsese himself understood that, revisiting remarkably similar material just five years later with *Casino*. But in the interim, he'd show us the stuffy world of 1870s upper-crust New York City, and with his next picture, let us observe a family being torn apart from within. That picture would be *Cape Fear*, and it would end up being one of his biggest box-office successes.

14

CAPE FEAR
(1991)

FILM DETAILS

RELEASE DATE: November 13, 1991
WRITTEN BY: Wesley Strick
STARRING: Robert De Niro, Nick Nolte, Jessica Lange, Juliette Lewis
RUNNING TIME: 128 minutes

ABOUT THE FILM

One thing Martin Scorsese has never been is a populist film director. He's had his popular successes, to be sure, but much of his catalog is made up of work that only just made back its money (if at all); personal, often-experimental films that tend to be at odds with Hollywood trends. For every *The Wolf of Wall Street*, which made $392 million worldwide on a $100 million budget, there is a *Bringing Out the Dead*, which couldn't even earn $17 million to match its $55 million budget. The struggle to secure funding for his pictures and the precarious balance between commerce and art—*art* with a lowercase *A*, as Mr. Scorsese is averse to labeling his work as "Art"—has been a hallmark of his career.

That makes *Cape Fear* something of an anomaly, though an intentional one. Much like *The Color of Money*, this was an attempt by the director to show that he could make pictures that could also succeed at the box office. Originally attached to Steven Spielberg, *the* populist director of the era, as well as partially produced by him (albeit without credit), *Cape Fear* is a mainstream thriller and a remake of the 1962 film of the same name.[1] Scorsese's version leans heavily on talent—Nick Nolte during one of the most fruitful periods of his career, Jessica Lange coming off her fifth Academy Award nomination, and Robert De Niro in his third Oscar-nominated role for Scorsese, not to mention Juliette Lewis with a remarkable, career-making performance—and also aims to infuse the thriller genre with the topic Scorsese knows best: human turmoil.

In *Cape Fear*, Max Cady (De Niro) is released from prison after serving fourteen years for raping a sixteen-year-old girl. His fixation through all those long years has been his defense attorney, Sam Bowden (Nolte), who, horrified at his client's crime, buried evidence that may have lightened Cady's sentence. Once released, Cady begins a campaign of harassment against Bowden; his wife, Leigh (Lange); and his daughter, Danielle (Lewis), and it's a clever one that makes Sam look like the bad guy. "The law considers me more of a loose cannon than Max Cady," he complains. As things escalate, Cady begins to manipulate Danielle and drive wedges between her and her parents. After he kills two people in their home, the Bowdens flee to a beloved vacation spot, Cape Fear. Cady follows, and they barely escape a final confrontation with him with their lives. Standard thriller stuff, at least on the surface.

The original script was far more traditional than it became. It was written with Spielberg's Amblin Entertainment in mind, after all, ending up with Scorsese only after Spielberg decided it wasn't right for him. The pair traded film rights, *Schindler's List* for *Cape Fear*, and Scorsese got the picture. (The idea of what a Scorsese-directed *Schindler's List* would have looked like is tantalizing, though Spielberg was clearly the right man for the job.)

But screenwriter Wesley Strick said the director was quick to take a figurative knife to the screenplay's most conventional traits. "Marty had quite a radar for every bit of slickness and hyperbole," Strick said. "Anything that smacked of television, all the dialogue he perceived as being 'clever,' everything that was too well-reasoned, too neat, too clean, with ideas that were somewhat predigested—he wanted it gone."[2] This wasn't going to be a standard thriller. It was going to be a Martin Scorsese picture.

ANALYSIS

Cape Fear is a film about the erosion of family, disguised as a traditional thriller. On the surface, the central conflict appears to be the Bowden family versus Cady, a fairly straightforward tale of people being tormented by a madman.

Beneath the surface, however, the film is more concerned with turmoil within the family and the unseen wounds that threaten to tear it apart from the inside. "I had read *Cape Fear* three times. And three times I hated it," Scorsese said. "I thought the family was too clichéd, too happy. . . . They were like Martians to me. I was rooting for Cady to get them."[3] Once injected with marital turmoil, professional malfeasance, and an uneasy exploration of a teen's awakening sexuality, however, the picture becomes much more than a conventional thriller.

Opening with Danielle and bookending the film with close-ups on her face suggests that, though most of the focus is on Sam Bowden and Max Cady, the real journey here is hers. It is she who is transformed. The key murder of this thriller is not of a person; it's of her innocence. In the opening narration, she reminisces about family times at the coastal region of North Carolina called Cape Fear, "when the only thing to fear on those enchanting summer nights was that the magic would end and real life would come crashing in." And in fact, that is what happens. Real life destroys that special place, her father's past sins made flesh in the form of a tattooed, sexually charged madman.

The next cut is to Cady's jail cell, the walls covered in dictators and comic-book characters. He is the real life she fears—real life twisted into a horrid form but real life all the same. His body is covered in tattoos: Bible quotes and slogans about justice, about righteousness, about vengeance smiting the false. A storm boils in the sky behind him as he struts away from prison, now released to the world. He is a horror.

Back at the Bowdens', Leigh Bowden is designing a logo for a client when we first see her. She explains what she is looking to get across: "Stability. A company you can trust." An appropriate theme, given the lack of stability in her own family. It appears normal and stable at first, but Cady will exploit the cracks in that stability and upend their trust in one another. It's a brilliant, subtle bit of foreshadowing. This is what Scorsese is most concerned with. De Niro's Max Cady is a suitably frightening monster, and his escalating war with Sam is tightly plotted and gripping throughout, but it's the drama of flawed people making a mess of their own lives that makes this a Scorsese picture.

In this case, the protagonist is at least *trying* not to screw up his own life. Sam is far from perfect—no Scorsese protagonist is—but he appears to be trying to move on from his past transgressions. He had a past of infidelity, and that infidelity remains a bruise on his marriage. It almost broke Leigh's spirit. They picked up the pieces and moved on, but the hurt and mistrust lingers. Sam plays racquetball with a clerk at his law office, Lori Davis (Illeana Douglas), and though they're both attractive and seem to enjoy one another's company, he gently turns aside her suggestion that there is something between them. Still, he

Robert De Niro's transformation for *Cape Fear*, a mainstream thriller by the mainstream-averse Scorsese, earned him an Academy Award nomination for Best Actor. *Universal Pictures/Photofest*

doesn't even tell his wife that Lori exists. Lori is surprised by this. Sam explains that he's married and that's why he can't tell his wife, but this is no answer. "Is marriage synonymous with deception?" she asks, and though she intends the question to be a light one, just a joke, it rings deeper for Sam. He's been down this road before. He has cheated before. He's trying to avoid temptation, trying to stay faithful, but Lori's question digs at a more difficult truth for him because it's his own deception that is going to put his family in danger: not the deception of having an affair—there is no suggestion that he plans to pursue Lori (though he is quick to invite her to play another game)—but deceptions from years prior. This idea of past sins returning, of past misdeeds lying in wait before their consequences finally arrive is a central one to the picture, and it's one Cady exploits.

It's fitting that Cady is covered in biblical passages. The ideas of sin and redemption and guilt and holy justice are familiar in the director's work, and it's a prevalent theme here, too. Cady is anything but a good man, yet Sam Bowden's actions fourteen years prior are also questionable. He was tasked by law to defend his client to the best of his ability, but he knowingly suppressed information that could have aided him. Whether he was justified in that gets into murky moral territory. The truth is, it's likely that Bowden's deception saved any number of young women from torment at Cady's hands. At the same time, Bowden is neither judge nor jury. In a world governed by laws, it was not his place to decide Cady's fate. Just as Bowden must atone for his past marital sins, he must atone for his professional sins, as well. The difference is that there is no clear path to redemption for him. How could he possibly redeem himself? And more difficult still, does he truly need to?

In Max Cady's eyes, he does. Cady seeks to corrupt the family, to immerse them in the same sin he himself was immersed in. He does this by baiting Sam into acting against his own interests, but far more insidious is the way in which he twists the family from within. He does not succeed in killing the family (though he does kill two other victims). He does not rape members of the family, as he plans (though Lori is brutally raped and disfigured at his hands). He doesn't even seriously injure any of the Bowdens (though he does kill their dog). But what he does succeed in doing to the family is to twist the Bowdens' daughter away from them and perhaps turn her onto a darker path. He does so by exploiting her newly blossoming sexuality, and in *Cape Fear*, sexuality is the opposite of purity and goodness. There is no healthy sexuality here, no true intimacy. Sex is infidelity; it's the loss of innocence; it's violent rape. There is an echo all the way back to *Who's That Knocking at My Door?* here, a film in which the lead (J. R.) was put off by the discovery that his girlfriend had been raped—not because she had been violated in such an intimate way but because it meant she wasn't a virgin. Here the director's Catholicism finds its way into the work, subtly suggesting that sex is sin and corruption. "Punishment for everything you ever felt sexually," he said. "It is the basic moral battleground of Christian ethics."[4]

We see early on that Danielle is ripe for this sort of corruption, too. After Cady starts stalking the family, Leigh tells Danielle to watch out for him; he might be a stalker or flasher. (She does not yet know the depths of his crimes when she says this.) "You think I've never been flashed before?" Danielle asks. It's evident she hasn't. She's sexually naïve, saying this simply to wind her mother up, but she's curious. This curiosity is what Cady will exploit. Later, when attempting to emotionally manipulate Leigh at the end of the Bowden driveway, Cady spots Danielle in the yard. At the sight of her, he races away, as if understanding that he couldn't be in her presence, not yet. There is too much temptation there for him. But it shows him the way he can cause the family the deepest possible hurt.

Cady tricks Danielle into meeting him in her school theater. The result is the film's most memorable scene and the performance that won Lewis an Oscar nomination. It's a difficult scene to watch. De Niro was around forty-seven when it was filmed, Lewis was seventeen, and this chasm-wide age gap is only a small part of what makes it so disturbing. Danielle's girlish awkwardness veers back and forth between naïve innocence and adolescent curiosity. Max Cady, on the other hand, is all greasy sexuality and exploitative manipulation. He knows how to push her buttons. She's a teenager in a tension-filled home, rebelling against her parents and desperate to feel like a grown woman. He exploits that. "Your parents don't want you to achieve adulthood. That's natural. They know the pitfalls of adulthood, all that freedom. They know it only too well," he tells her. They discuss *Tropic of Cancer*, the sexually explicit book by Henry Miller that was once banned in the United States. It's a provocative work, made all the more provocative by being something she's "not supposed" to be reading.

If the scene were merely this weathered-looking, obsessive older man pushing a young girl to discuss her sexuality with him, it would be disturbing enough, but then he caresses her face and inserts his thumb in her mouth. She sucks the thumb, an off-putting blend of childlike innocence and burgeoning sexual discovery, highly suggestive, and then he kisses her, long and deeply. When he walks off, she's overcome with a swirl of conflicting emotions, expressed without words: fear, confusion, arousal. There is a sense of danger and a sense of discovery here that both delights and frightens her. She runs from the theater in tears, unable to fully grasp what she is feeling.

This scene is especially remarkable because it was partially improvised by De Niro and the much-younger Lewis. The director set up two cameras so the pair could just work out the scene, and he rolled. They did just three takes. The first take is what you see on-screen. When De Niro puts his thumb in Lewis's mouth, she did not know it was coming. She stayed in character, reacting as she thought Danielle would. The mix of emotions Danielle feels, the desire to please coupled with the feeling of having been violated, is a complex cocktail. And despite her questioning eyes looking up at Cady as if seeking approval, it was indeed a violation. "He put his thumb in my mouth all the way, and then he pulled it all the way out," Lewis recalled. "I'll tell you exactly what it felt like, emotionally—like someone walked up, penetrated you and then walked away."[5]

Cady's advances may have terrified most young women, but he chose his target well in Danielle. Her tumultuous home life leaves her vulnerable. Later, at home, Sam tries to impress upon her the danger Cady poses to the family. While doing so, he scolds her: "Put some clothes on. You're not a little kid anymore." Again, sexuality as sin. Urging her away from Cady does not have the intended result. You tell a rebellious young adult what they can't do, and it only strengthens their resolve to do it. She grows defensive. "He didn't force himself on me. I know you think that he did, but I think he was just trying to make a connection with me," she tells her father.

Sam asks if Cady touched her. She smiles but doesn't answer. He asks again. No answer. Sam grows angry, grabs her face, fiercely scolds her. His fatherly concern is understandable—Cady went to prison for raping a girl Danielle's age—but his reaction hurts far more than it helps, exacerbated by the wedge Cady had already driven between them. There is already poison in the well. All of this makes Danielle's sexuality the real battleground, the arena in which Cady knows he can hurt Sam the most. Sex is sin, and by awakening Danielle's latent curiosity, he's led her down the path.

Her parents fight over Sam's sexual transgressions, too. When Leigh overhears him on the phone with Lori, she believes he's cheating again. Leigh calls them "stupid, sophomoric infidelities." Danielle hears the fighting and calls a friend to escape. "I'm just losing my mind here," she says. As the couple argues, each dredges up the past and uses it as a weapon against the other. They bludgeon one another with it. Past pains, past hurts, the past pulled back into the here and now in order to hurt again. It's what drives Cady. The past he believes he lost drives him, and so the idea of past hurts is something he weaponizes and injects into the Bowden marriage.

When the family finally retreats from Cady's escalating war with them, they retreat to the past, too, to Cape Fear, where they vacationed in better times.

It's here, in a geographical embodiment of years gone by, where the situation finally reaches a head. Scorsese is known for his dynamic, visceral approach to violence, but violence is not the same as action, and to this point he hadn't done much that looked like mainstream action. The action of *Raging Bull* was poetry; of *Taxi Driver*, dark fantasy; of *GoodFellas*, street-corner storytelling. But here in *Cape Fear*, it's a straightforward thriller ending. We have a raging river, a family trapped in a small place, and a madman after them. Cady continues to push Danielle's buttons, but in the end, she chooses family over temptation. Cady is killed. The end.

But the last shot of Danielle is an unspoken message to the audience. Cady awakened something in her, shook her from her childish daydreams, broke her away from her family. In the end, Max Cady won.

CONCLUSION AND IMPACT

Cape Fear was a huge box-office hit, among the most successful of the director's career, raking in $182 million worldwide on a $35 million budget. It was also a success with critics, earning two Academy Award nominations (for De Niro and Lewis) and positive acclaim among reviewers.

The movie was quite a different beast from the Hitchcockian original, which stars Robert Mitchum and Gregory Peck, both of whom have small roles in the remake, though it does pay homage to the original by using a version of the original score by Bernard Hermann, reworked here by Elmer Bernstein. In the 1962 version, Max holds a grudge against Sam because Sam testified against him, and his confrontation with the Bowden daughter is a fairly standard suspense-and-chase sequence, among other more subtle alterations in tone and approach. The changes made this *Cape Fear* less traditional and more modern, lending it an intellectual and emotional depth not present in the original. Perhaps more importantly, it made the movie far more *Scorsese* than would be expected of a mainstream thriller.

But Martin Scorsese's career is filled with the unexpected. His next picture, for instance: a lush, colorful, talk-heavy, costume drama about unrequited love set in 1870s New York City.

15

THE AGE OF INNOCENCE (1993)

FILM DETAILS

RELEASE DATE: September 17, 1993
WRITTEN BY: Jay Cocks, Martin Scorsese
STARRING: Daniel Day-Lewis, Michelle Pfeiffer, Winona Ryder
RUNNING TIME: 139 minutes

ABOUT THE FILM

A costume drama is perhaps the last thing you'd expect from Martin Scorsese, a man who made his reputation on profanity-soaked meditations on greed, guilt, and violence, yet in many ways Scorsese's secret weapon as a filmmaker is the kind of unpredictability that allows him to make movies like this. Pictures like this may not resemble the work people best know him for, but they allow him to indulge in ideas and techniques he can then use to great effect in his more Scorsesian works.

The Age of Innocence is a lush adaptation of Edith Wharton's Pulitzer Prize–winning 1920 novel of the same name, a story about New York's so-called gilded age of the 1870s. On the surface, it is an anomaly in the director's career, a quiet, deeply literary look at unrequited love. Yet elaborate costumes and social rituals or not, this is another exploration of New York by the most New York director there ever was. The period is changed from his norm. So is the strata of society he explores. But the heart and soul of it remains. It's Scorsese picking at the fabric of the locale he knows best, the city that made him who he is. Rage is traded for repression, guns for gossip, and crime for superficial cordiality, but the hallmarks of the director's love for the darker side of human drama are etched all over this living painting.

The Age of Innocence follows Newland Archer (Daniel Day-Lewis) and his passion for Countess Ellen Olenska (Michelle Pfeiffer), a woman he cannot be with due to his pending nuptials to Ellen's cousin, May Welland (Winona Ryder). The pair's longing for one another sets off whispers in the upper-crust society that already sees Ellen as an outsider, compounded by May's subtle machinations to keep them apart. Despite some false starts, Newland never gets to be with the woman he truly loves, instead living out his life as a loyal but quietly unfulfilled husband.

Following the frenetic energy of *GoodFellas* and the brooding tension of *Cape Fear* with a visually lush formal drama is the kind of left turn that makes a study of the director's career both surprising and challenging. This is a picture that has more in common with Stanley Kubrick's 1975 visual masterpiece *Barry Lyndon* than it does with anything in Scorsese's own catalog, yet dig under the surface, and the heartbeat is still Scorsese's.

ANALYSIS

Martin Scorsese did not grow up in a life of wealth and privilege, but the social sparring he witnessed on Little Italy's street corners was not all that far removed from the wordless wars of New York's Victorian-era elite. Less bloodshed, perhaps, but an equal amount of posturing and positioning.

The picture opens in a theater, New York's wealthiest closely observing one another as much as they are observing the show onstage. This opening scene does double duty, providing some simple exposition to give us a sense of the key relationships—Newland is engaged to May, but it has not yet been announced, and Countess Ellen has returned to New York after living in Europe for some years with her husband—but it serves a more important purpose in quickly and efficiently showing viewers that appearance, image, and the power of gossip are major forces in this corner of society. "This was a world balanced so precariously that its harmony could be shattered by a whisper," the unnamed narrator tells us. The next scene is an aloof, playfully pretentious variation on the introduction sequence in *GoodFellas*, in which the camera winds its way through an array of colorful mobsters as Henry Hill tells us who each are. Here, the mobsters are replaced with stuffy, overdressed New York elite, but the effect is the same. It's our introduction to a world that will seem alien to most viewers, one in which words uttered with a smile are as deadly as daggers.

The Age of Innocence is a *quiet* film, one that seems all the quieter when set next to Scorsese's other work. The rigid formality, that every dramatic turn is prompted by words rather than actions, that the literary pomp is cloaked in manufactured smiles and cordiality—it all seems quite out of place in his work, but it's not. Though this is a world that seems a stark contrast to the one depicted in, say, *Raging Bull*, for the director they were merely different sides of the same coin. "The gracefulness of the prose has a kind of scathing, ironic violence to it," Scorsese observed.[1]

Both Newland and Ellen are prisoners of a society with a strict set of unspoken rules. Just as the gangsters Scorsese often depicts have a code regarding what can and can't be said, so do these people. That's a great frustration to the pair, especially to Ellen, who, having lived in Europe for a number of years, feels out of place with the delicate walk one must walk to remain relevant in Gotham high society. Here, image is everything: putting on the perfect face, putting on the perfect air, putting on the perfect performance. All see through one another, but none acknowledge it. It's a ceaseless chess game. People enjoy talking, she

The lush costumes and restrained formality of *The Age of Innocence* do not seem to fit with Martin Scorsese's other work, but the director saw familiar cruelty in the novel's social interactions. *Columbia Pictures/Photofest*

says, "as long as they don't hear anything unpleasant. Does no one here want to hear the truth, Mr. Archer?"

Newland's own truth is his love for Ellen, one he at first tries not to acknowledge, just as New York society has trained him, but one that slowly grows in his heart. Though the countess is beautiful—this was when Michelle Pfeiffer was one of the era's most prominent silver-screen icons—it's not her beauty that draws Newland to her. Rather, it's her attitudes about the New York culture he has such difficulty navigating. She is honest, whereas high society is not. She embraces her emotions, whereas others suppress them. She believes in breaking norms, whereas others see them as sacrosanct. "It seems stupid to discover America only to make it a copy of another country," she says, mocking the way in which the city's upper crust tries to model itself after the elite of London and Paris. When Newland notes that something is not fashionable, she asks, "Fashionable? Is fashion such a serious consideration?" He replies, "Among people who have nothing more serious to consider."

She even has the cheek to be late to her own gathering, one to which she invited all the city's social elite. It's all a bit much for most—one man even comments later in the film, albeit indirectly, "Society has a history of tolerating vulgar women"—but Newland sees a kindred spirit in her.

Through this struggle against societal constraints, *The Age of Innocence* explores sexual repression, social pressures, temptation, desire, and the way in which social circles control our lives. Tear away the audacious costumes and extravagant meals and ostentatious displays of wealth, and these people are little different than those huddled around Henry Hill and Tommy DeVito, looking on as the pair navigate the verbal minefield Tommy threw them into when he asked Henry what made him so funny. The minefields Newland and Ellen must navigate may not be matters of life and death, but when the result of a misstep could be ostracism from their professional and social circles, it may as well be. Alienation is its own kind of death in a world such as this.

Throughout all this verbal fencing, Scorsese delights in painting this world with meticulous attention to detail and startling creative flourishes. On several occasions, the screen fades to vivid washes of color, each shimmering yellow and fiery red chosen for what it says about the scene. Characters sometimes turn to the camera and address the viewer directly, as if telling us a story. Meals are sumptuous visual feasts of foods few viewers will ever be served, plated on dinnerware few could afford. A shot of dozens of men in near-identical garb, all holding their formal hats atop their heads in the face of a windstorm, speaks to the anonymity of city life and the conformity to which all eventually succumb. Sometimes the camera peers and probes like a voyeur peering into the window at an unreachable strata of society. Other times it is still, the image like a painting come to life, calling to mind Kubrick's similar approach on the equally lush *Barry Lyndon*. Scorsese knew the rapid-fire, high-energy approach he so excels at would not work for this time and place, instead taking a directorial approach that is as literary as the narration that spans the film, as elegant and understated as it is formal and extravagant. Far from being mere window dressing or indulgence, all these directorial flourishes and splendid visual designs are an essential part of helping us understand the rarified air Newland, Ellen, and May breathe, and the precarious position Newland's longing puts them all in.

But the lure of the relationship is too strong for him. He makes excuses to see Ellen. They largely remain chaste, the extent of their physical intimacy limited to a pair of kisses, but their passion is palpable. This is most evident in a carriage ride they take late in the film. It is the most erotic sequence Scorsese ever shot, and there is nary a bit of sex in it, a bared wrist the only skin we see. Newland slips off Ellen's glove, the removal of each clasp filled with aching. Slipping the glove off becomes a deeply sensual moment when seen in the context of the repressed emotion at the heart of the film. Kissing her wrist is like kissing her most intimate parts. They do not consummate their love. Newland's infidelity is (almost) purely one of the heart. Regardless, it's as passionate a scene as the director has ever filmed, burning with longing and terribly erotic, yet also laced with sadness because the pair know they can never be together.

The scene may be dressed in the elaborate garb of the Victorian-era New York elite, but it represents a kind of sexual repression Scorsese knows all too well, one seen in J. R.'s unwillingness to sleep with the Girl in *Who's That Knocking at My Door?* and Jake LaMotta's awkward intimacy in *Raging Bull* or even in the way in which sexual liberation is tied to unhappiness and punishment in *Cape Fear*. Newland is not experiencing the kind of Catholic sexual repression Scorsese is familiar with, but the effect is much the same. Neither Newland nor Ellen can fully embrace their feelings for one another, not merely because both are married—either could seek a divorce, but both dismiss the idea as infeasible—but because they live in a society that frowns upon overt expression of one's genuine feelings. Appearances are more important than truth, and most are all too eager to pointedly look away from truth, provided the object of their observations is willing to play the game, too.

What Newland and Ellen don't initially realize is that, despite her seeming wide-eyed innocence, May sees what is going on and takes subtle but precise measures to undermine it at every turn. Newland believes he is being discreet about his desire for Ellen, but May is more insightful than he realizes, her ability to suss out truth from fiction hidden behind a seemingly innocent veneer. When he returns from his ride with Ellen, May says to him, "You haven't kissed me today." They hug, and over his shoulder we can see uncertainty in her eyes. She knows something is amiss. And she has far more guile than we are initially led to believe. That evening, she wears her bridal gown to an opera. In this corner of society, women often wore their bridal gowns out during their first two years of marriage, but this is the first time she's done it. That evening at home, May reveals to Newland that Ellen wrote a note saying she is returning to Europe. The news crushes him, but he must suppress it in front of his wife. What is left unspoken is that May helped manipulate Ellen's decision. When May thought she was pregnant, the first person she told was Ellen—secretly, knowing full well the effect it would have on her. It worked, too. The countess leaves New York shortly thereafter. Two weeks later, when May finally tells her husband, only then does he realize that May had perceived his true feelings all along.

This is a devastating blow on multiple levels. Newland cannot pursue Ellen, not without losing everything. Yet, as the nameless narrator points out, he is now trapped in a world in which he holds no sway and has none of the skill of manipulation his wife possesses. "The separation between himself and the partner of his guilt had been achieved," the narrator says, "and he knew that now the whole tribe had rallied around his wife. He was a prisoner in the center of an armed camp." As we hear this, we see Newland at an elegant dinner with friends and family, people chatting around a table laid with finery, he and his wife at the heads of the table, Ellen next to him but a thousand miles away. Newland is left alone in a crowd, ostracized and scrutinized. There is a ritual to their social interactions, one May has mastered and he has not. Everyone pretends things are perfect; everyone knows they are not. People believe Newland and Ellen truly had a consummated affair, but none will say it. May believes the same, but she won't say it, either. It's all false faces and perfect words, a dance of sorts, pointed and cutting without being direct.

Most of this is masked in the first two-thirds of the picture. It is only in the end that we realize just how cunning May had been all along and how effective yet subtle her machinations had been. Look all the way back to the yellow roses Newland buys Ellen, flowers that become a symbol of their desire for one another. When Newland sends them, May expresses her approval, then casually mentions all the flowers the countess receives from others, too. Her observation appears innocent; her seeming obliviousness, naïve. In truth, she is making Newland believe his gesture is nothing special. Even when she later asks if Newland's request to move the date of their wedding means he believes he's marrying the wrong woman, his assurances seem to placate her. Yet May is perceptive and adroit at nudging situations to her favor. She *does* move the date of their wedding forward, just as Newland is beginning to build courage enough to pursue Ellen. And, as already noted, when Ellen returns after another long absence, once again stirring Newland's longing, May frightens Ellen into returning to Europe by telling her she and Newland are having a child, two weeks before she even tells her husband. It's only once she has driven the countess away that May tells Newland the news. It's terrifically manipulative, played with quiet confidence by Ryder.

Finally, seeing the writing on the wall, Newland abandons the idea of ever being with Ellen and falls into domestic life with May. This is depicted in one of Scorsese's most clever sequences, a passing-of-the-years montage that isn't a montage at all. May reveals to Newland that she is pregnant. The narrator begins to tell us about all the important milestones Newland would experience in that same room (the christening of his child, etc.), the camera slowly panning around, around, and around, the years falling away behind us, until we land on Newland again, still in the same room, visibly older and on the phone talking with his adult son.

The narrative ends here, but there remains an epilogue of sorts. At the age of fifty-seven, Newland has three grown children. May has passed, a victim of pneumonia. His grief at her passing was genuine. He takes a trip to France with his son, Ted (Robert Sean Leonard), and Ted arranges a meeting with Ellen. Newland has not seen her for twenty-five years. Ted confesses to his father that, just before she passed, May shared a family secret: that Newland, Ted's father, was once in love with the Countess Ellen Olenska. She did not worry, however, because "once when she asked you to," Ted says, "you gave up the thing you wanted most." But that is not how Newland remembers it. "She never asked," he says, pained. "She never asked me."

Outside the building where Ellen lives, Newland declines to go see her. The sun glares off a window swung closed by a servant. The sun calls back a memory of seeing her standing by the sea, a sailboat passing before a lighthouse. At the time, he told himself he would go to her if she turned before the boat reached the lighthouse. She never turned. But now, in his vision, he sees her turning, the sun bright as if called down from heaven, and she is radiant. His vision ends. He stands, and Newland Archer walks away.

Throughout his life, Newland Archer faced neither bullets nor knives nor criminal madmen. He merely faced words and glances. But words and glances were all it took to deny him everything he ever wanted.

CONCLUSION AND IMPACT

The Age of Innocence did not light the box office on fire, but it was a critical darling, garnering five Academy Award nominations (winning for Costume Design) and winning praise by most contemporary critics. It largely remains an anomaly in the director's body of work, matched perhaps only by *Kundun* and *Silence* in its quiet, meditative nature.

Fans wanting more of the crime-and-music whirlwind Scorsese is known for would not have to wait long, however, as his next picture would take everything that made *GoodFellas* great and drop it into an appropriate place for vice and indulgence: the city of sin, Las Vegas.

16

CASINO
(1995)

FILM DETAILS

RELEASE DATE: November 22, 1995
WRITTEN BY: Nicholas Pileggi, Martin Scorsese
STARRING: Robert De Niro, Sharon Stone, Joe Pesci
RUNNING TIME: 178 minutes

ABOUT THE FILM

It would be inaccurate to call *Casino* a clone of *GoodFellas*, yet the description wouldn't be entirely without basis, either. Presented with a similar tone and approach and dealing with similar subject matter, the picture is a spiritual successor to *GoodFellas*, a continuation and expansion of the aesthetic developed there and proof that the artistic success of that movie was no anomaly.

It all began with an article in the *Las Vegas Sun*. Nicholas Pileggi, Scorsese's writing collaborator on *GoodFellas*, read a piece about Frank "Lefty" Rosenthal having a dispute with his wife, Vegas showgirl and socialite Geri McGee. Intrigued, Pileggi began further research. Before long, he fell down a rabbit hole investigating organized crime in Las Vegas. It looked to be a story worth telling. His initial aim was to write another book similar to *Wiseguy*, the book upon which *GoodFellas* was based, then pursue a film adaptation with Scorsese, but the director persuaded him to instead begin working on a script right away.

The pair again collaborated on the screenplay, piecing together a narrative from the growing pile of unfinished notes Pileggi was accumulating. Names and details were changed, but the essential truths remained in place: In the 1960s and '70s, the mob was making big money in the growing city out in the desert: "The skim at the Stardust was $7 million per year; at the Flamingo, it was $36 million from 1960 to 1967; at the Tropicana it was $150,000 per month."[1] Here, a trio of characters would find themselves walking a dangerous tightrope between interpersonal conflict and keeping this massive criminal operation running, to inevitably deadly results. It's pure Scorsese: a rise to wealth followed by a greed-driven fall from grace. "Gaining Paradise and losing it, through pride and through greed—it's the old-fashioned Old Testament story," Scorsese said. "Ace is given Paradise on Earth. In fact, he's there to keep everybody happy and keep everything in order, and to make as much money as possible so they can take more on the skim. But the problem is he has to give way at times to certain people and certain pressures, which he won't do because of who he is."[2]

In *Casino*, sports-betting savant Sam "Ace" Rothstein (Robert De Niro) is tasked with running the Tangiers casino by his mafia bosses so their skimming operation can proceed uninterrupted. He runs the casino as a legitimate operation, though he does so without a gaming license by taking advantage of loopholes in gaming laws. His old friend Nicky Santoro (Joe Pesci) flies out to Vegas to join him. Nicky is an erratic, brutal mob enforcer who is there to milk the town of every dollar he can, no matter the attention it draws. When Sam sees socialite grifter Ginger McKenna (Sharon Stone), he's immediately smitten. He asks her to marry him. She reluctantly agrees, drawn by promises of wealth despite carrying a torch for her con man pimp, Lester Diamond (James Woods). Things begin to disintegrate after Sam fires the brother-in-law of a local county commissioner, which leads to him having his gaming license application rejected. At the same time, Ginger spirals into drug and alcohol addiction, while Nicky's crime rampages become an increasing problem for their distant mob bosses. Sam's marriage falls apart, Ginger steals a load of money from him, and the FBI descends on the casinos. Nicky ends up being whacked in the desert for the problems he caused, Sam survives an assassination attempt, and the old status quo of the Vegas casino collapses, ending the golden age of mob rule over Sin City. There's a lot packed into these three hours.

ANALYSIS

With all its elaborate costumes—the picture allegedly had a $1 million budget for costumes alone—flashing lights, and clattering jewelry, it's easy to say *Casino* is about greed and the things we bring upon ourselves in the pursuit of money.[3] After all, it's set in the greed capital of the world and basks in audacious displays of wealth. Yet look closer, and you see that much of the struggle is not between greed and selflessness; it's between legitimacy and crime, between playing by the rules (but toeing the line) and making your own rules, between doing things the old mob way and doing things in a way suited for the money mecca that is Vegas. And most of all, it's about trust.

Sam Rothstein's two foils are the two people he is closest to, Nicky and Ginger. Both relationships contain elements of the previously mentioned conflicts. Ginger can't break herself away from her attachment to her con man flame and fully embrace the life of a married woman; she's still stuck in the world of pimps and petty scamming, even as she lives an increasingly opulent lifestyle with Sam. It's Sam's relationship with Nicky, however, where these themes truly come to the fore. The pair are constantly at odds over the reason they are in Vegas in the first place. Nicky believes they are there to rob the place blind, to rake in the bucks while the city is flush with cash, and then move on to greener pastures. Sam recognizes that the goal is to operate a successful, legitimate business in such a way that profits can be illegally skimmed without anyone noticing. If done right, it's an operation that could last in perpetuity.

But Nicky is a short-term, impulsive thinker, effectively a less-boisterous Tommy DeVito. (A scene early in the picture in which he repeatedly stabs someone in the neck with a pen for insulting Sam makes clear this character is dangerously close to being a retread of Pesci's character in *GoodFellas*. He's distinguished from Tommy largely by Pesci's acting talents rather than through the writing.) This divide between Nicky and Sam is one of two major fulcrums upon which the picture pivots, the other being Sam's relationship with Ginger and the inordinate amount of trust he places in her. These two things are the backbone of the film. All its themes spring from them.

Beyond those very human-focused themes, the picture broadly ends up being about the rise and fall of mob rule in Las Vegas, the city's supposed transformation from playground of the mafia to legitimate greed-centric capital of the world. "Supposed," of course, because when it comes to whether the mafia still has a hand in Vegas operations, the "answer depends on who you ask. A couple of businesses are reportedly mobbed up. But the jury is still out."[4] For the purposes of *Casino*, however, that era has come to a close.

This idea of exploring the heyday of a group of criminals and their eventual downfall, fueled in no small part by the inevitable internal strife that arises when a lot of illegal money is at play, is one of many commonalities that make *Casino* a spiritual sequel to *GoodFellas*. The picture even starts with the same technique, opening up with a pivotal later scene, then jumping back in time and working back toward that scene. Here, we see Sam (dressed in an audacious peach-and-white outfit) get into his car, turn the key, and trigger a car bomb, presumably killing him. (It doesn't.) We then jump back in time to see the events that led up to this moment.

The structure is familiar, and so are the varied, often-daring techniques Scorsese employs to immerse us in this world. Narration guides us through the entire three hours, led by De Niro and Pesci. Music is central. Fast cuts, swirling camerawork, scenes abbreviated to their barest essentials, breaking the fourth wall, shocking violence and copious use of profanity—it's all here.

Though *Casino* reuses a slew of tricks from *GoodFellas*, it also employs enough new and fresh tricks to distinguish itself from its older cousin. Characters talking in code to one another are supplemented by subtitles that say what they *really* mean. Title cards indicating time and place are sometimes playfully vague and mirror the narration ("Back Home" or "Back Home Years Ago"). Frank Vincent suddenly provides some narration two hours and fifteen minutes into the film. And in one fourth-wall-breaking example, Pesci's narration is interrupted when, in the scene he's narrating, his character is hit with a shovel, causing both the on-screen character and the narrator to cry out in pain. This in particular casts the narration in a whole new light. In *GoodFellas*, we were being told a story by Henry Hill (and, to a lesser extent, Karen). Here, we can't be told a story by Nicky because Nicky is dead. Not only is he dead, but also we heard Nicky the narrator get slammed in the head *in the narration itself*. It makes little sense, and it doesn't need to. The effect is more important than adherence to realism.

Even the tricks *Casino* does reuse are used in a different way. This is most prominent in the picture's use of music. Here, music doesn't just punctuate key scenes. It permeates *everything* from the first frame to the end. There are only a few moments that don't have a soundtrack playing, and those brief instances of silence are meant to emphasize something important, such as the first moment Sam sees Ginger. Otherwise, the music never stops. This isn't merely Scorsese at his most self-indulgent in terms of using popular songs in his movies. The relentless assault of sound is not unlike the sensory battering you'll get in any casino, where the lights and sound never cease. There is an almost-claustrophobic effect to it, a way in which it skews your sense of the passage of time because there is never a pause for breath. Your senses are overwhelmed. Casinos use this to great effect to keep people at the tables and spending money.

The music often comments on the movie, too, a subtle touch that rewards close viewings. For example, when Sam first walks Ginger into their new home

Every aspect of *Casino*'s audacious displays of wealth was as tightly controlled by Scorsese as the Tangiers was by Sam "Ace" Rothstein, portrayed by Robert De Niro. It would be De Niro's last role for Scorsese for twenty-four years, until 2019's *The Irishman*. *Universal*

following their marriage, the first lyric we hear is, "What a difference a day makes," from the song of the same name by Dinah Washington. In another shot of Sam casting his steely gaze over the betting floor, watching for cheats, we hear Muddy Waters croon, "Everybody knows I'm here." It's not just background music; it's a carefully chosen symphony of music and message and audience manipulation.

As was the case for every Scorsese film from *Raging Bull* forward, three-time Academy Award–winning editor Thelma Schoonmaker worked with the director to piece together a whirlwind picture that feels half the length of its three-hour run time. It's a tour de force of editorial talent, with noteworthy choices and techniques coming so quickly it can be dizzying trying to keep up with them all. The needle-drop music cues that gave *GoodFellas* so much life are in place, but they are only the beginning. Witness the first moment Nicky meets Ginger in Sam's apartment. There is a rapid-fire triple-fade cut when she walks into the room that borders on the unnecessary, yet it effectively gets across the idea that Nicky is stunned to see her there and momentarily has his breath taken away. Or the quick cuts from person to person as we take a tour of the casino floor. Or the documentary-like approach to much of the first hour, when we take a deep dive into how Vegas and crime intertwine to form a massive money-making machine. And many more.

If there is a Copacabana shot in *Casino*, it's our introduction to the money-counting room, the heart of every casino and the room where the mob's most important work takes place. In this shot we follow someone through the floor of the casino, past the gaming tables, and into the room where millions of dollars are counted daily. The camera probes the room, still in one continuous shot, showing how the counting is done and, more importantly, how cash is skimmed. From there the shot continues, following a courier holding a huge bag of cash out of the count room, onto the casino floor, out the front door, and into a taxi. It's a dynamic sequence that is more than just showing off. That count room is the most integral part of the mob's operations in Vegas, the place from which all their cash comes, and entering it in this way provides a more vivid picture of how there is a hidden world behind the lights and sounds and chips and characters that populate an active casino.

If the approach rings familiar, it's meant to. Both these cinematic cousins are concerned with introducing us to a world and lifestyle most will never come in contact with, much less be intimately familiar with. Even setting aside new directorial indulgences, however, *Casino* distinguishes itself in ways better suited to its sleazy-glitz setting. This is clear by the picture's look alone. Smoke-filled clubs and dingy backrooms are traded for brightly lit casino floors and lavish homes and apartments. Timeless men's suits are replaced with ostentatiously loud sports jackets and jewel-studded sequin dresses. A tremendous amount of money was poured into the wardrobe in order to capture the look and feel of a Las Vegas busting at the seams with cash, and that wardrobe was essential to telling us who these people are. "Pay attention to the characters," said Rita Ryack, lead costume designer for the film. "Look at their clothes—every little detail means something, even on the extras. Sharon (Stone) looks one way when she was a girl in that flappy mod sequin dress throwing chips in the air. When she's a junky at the end, she's lost all of that weight, and she dies in her pajamas—you follow her rise in that gold sequin dress, and then you witness her decline."[5]

The way *Casino* most effectively distinguishes itself is not merely through being glitzier and more creative, however. It does so through the characters, Sam in particular. He's a corrupt man who believes he runs a legitimate business. He's also a man who can spot any attempt to rip off his casino but who also marries an untrustworthy con artist still pining for her pimp. Early in the film, Sam narrates, "That's the truth about Las Vegas. We're the only winners. The players don't stand a chance," yet his inner life is at odds with the image of power and command he displays. Sam's attention to detail is extraordinary, as it must be in his line of work, though sometimes he misses the forest for the trees. When he complains that the blueberries in the casino's blueberry muffins are not evenly distributed, he says he's trying to ensure the casino functions well. Yet his attention to this kind of unimportant detail is in stark contrast to the lack of attention he gives to Ginger, or rather to Ginger's true nature. He's seen her operate. He knows what she is all about or thinks he does. Yet he thinks he can rein her in in the same way he reins in thousands of gamblers and millions of dollars. He sees her but doesn't *see* her. From the moment he agrees to give her access to his safety deposit box, we know she will eventually rip him off. It's inevitable. Sam sees so much yet cannot see this. Perhaps this man, so used to always getting what he wants, simply saw her as another trophy rather than a fully realized human being with the same complicated nature as anyone else.

He does question her when she asks for large sums of money without explanation, so it's not as if he's *completely* blind. He appears to have at least some understanding of the position he's put himself in. He's not Jake LaMotta, though; he seeks to control Ginger's behavior only when it appears he's being taken advantage of. He confronts her and Lester at a diner when he realizes she's shoveling money Lester's way, arranging to have him beaten as a lesson. But he continues the relationship (and maintains Ginger's access to his emergency money) anyway. Ginger turns to alcohol to wash away her misery, and he watches her spiral downward until finally filing for divorce. Here, too, he does not cut off her access to his emergency stash. She remains a blind spot for him even as he directly confronts signal after signal that his relationship is a ticking time bomb. It's only after she flees the state with their daughter and Lester that he finally pulls the plug and cuts off her access to the money, which unleashes a series of events that tears apart not only their marriage but also Sam's already rocky relationship with Nicky. Like so many Scorsese protagonists, Sam Rothstein is the architect of his own downfall. Driven in part by hubris, by a feeling of being untouchable, by a feeling that he can control Ginger and Nicky—two people *no one* can control—he puts himself in a position to collapse.

Though Sam was taken by Ginger, she's not a purely malicious scam artist. This is a woman stuck in a cycle of abuse. The film doesn't fully explore her background, but there are enough hints to piece it together. Lester took her under his wing when she was still in school. He strung her along from an early age, pimping her out and using her to scam money from others. Whatever successes she has, whatever status she enjoys, she always ends up running back to him. Even on her wedding day, she calls him and cries, wondering if she did the right thing. Lester, meanwhile, is at home snorting cocaine with some other woman, urging Ginger to stick with the marriage. He uses her to get access to Sam's wealth, but he says the right thing, playing to her insecurities and acting as if he is the only stability in her life.

None of the characters can avoid their status quo being shaken, though. Ginger cannot exist both as Sam's wife and Lester's plaything. The two are incompatible, and in the end both must fall apart. Nicky cannot continue to run amok without fear of reprisal, either. There is too much money at stake. He ends up in a ditch as payback for the trouble he causes. And Sam cannot keep one foot in the world of crime and one (very public) foot in legitimate business. In the end, this arrangement must collapse, too. "Ultimately, it's a tragedy," the director said. "It's the frailty of being human. I want to push audiences' emotional empathy with certain types of characters who are normally considered villains."[6]

The FBI sweeps in and busts the mob bosses who pulled strings from afar. Ginger dies of a drug overdose, and Sam returns to being a sports handicapper for organized crime. The picture ends with images of real-life casinos being demolished, fleeting, temporary landmarks of vice torn down to pave the way for newer, larger, more extravagant landmarks of vice. So *Casino* does not depict the rise of today's Las Vegas. It depicts the end of yesterday's. And more importantly, it depicts the end of a triangle of relationships, people torn apart by drugs, violence, and of course greed. And it's that human toll that hits hardest.

CONCLUSION AND IMPACT

Today, Sin City doesn't just embrace its historic ties to mafia rule; it also proudly profits from its questionable past with shows, museums, and dinner events that center around the mob theme: "Las Vegas is exploiting the public's love for goodfellas as a curious hyper-local form of cultural tourism, like the Mission architecture of California or a Civil War battlefield in Virginia. Since its 2012 opening, Mob Museum has ranked in the top 20 of national museums."[7] As with so much else the city is built on, it's a crass, tacky bastardization of something real, turned into money-making artifice for millions of tourists each year.

As for the film, it was fairly well received but criticized for being a retread of *GoodFellas*, which was released just five years prior, and did only modestly at the box office ($42 million in the United States, $116 million worldwide). It's only in retrospect that some critics have reassessed the picture and declared it the more mature, refined work. "*Casino* is a more substantial, artful, and engrossing movie than *GoodFellas*," *GQ* argued. "It's partly because Ace Rothstein, *Casino*'s main character, is a far more fascinating creature than Henry

Hill. It's also because *Casino* is a dazzling period piece, a penetrating historical work that captures Las Vegas better than any other movie that has come before or after it."[8]

It's not accurate to say that, with *Casino*, Scorsese said his final piece about organized crime. He'd take a look at it again from different angles with *Gangs of New York*, *The Departed*, and *The Irishman*. It also wouldn't be accurate to say he had his fill of the style he pioneered with *GoodFellas*. He'd revisit it again with *The Wolf of Wall Street* and even to some extent with *Bringing Out the Dead*. But, for the moment at least, he'd take a rest from such rapid-fire, music-infused violence and with his next film would instead turn toward the polar opposite of worldly indulgences, casual criminality, and deeply unsympathetic characters: He'd turn his gaze toward Tibet and the rise of the fourteenth Dalai Lama.

KUNDUN (1997)

FILM DETAILS

RELEASE DATE: December 25, 1997
WRITTEN BY: Melissa Mathison
STARRING: Tenzin Thuthob Tsarong, Gyurme Tethong, Tulku Jamyang
Kunga Tenzin, Tenzin Yeshi Paichang
RUNNING TIME: 134 minutes

ABOUT THE FILM

What would a man sacrifice in order to bring salvation to others? At what cost does it come? And can one overcome violence through peace?

There are no easy answers to these questions. The fourteenth Dalai Lama, spiritual leader of the Tibetan people and the foremost figure in Tibetan Buddhism, is one of the few who could. Fleeing Tibet at the age of twenty-four in the wake of the 1959 Tibet uprising, the Dalai Lama has lived his life in exile, awaiting a day when he can return to a free Tibet. He is eighty-three years old as of this writing. It's unlikely he will see his dream fulfilled in this lifetime, though for the Dalai Lama at least, there is always next lifetime.

Kundun explores the early life of Tenzin Gyatso, the fourteenth Dalai Lama, from shortly after his birth in 1935 to ascending as the leader of Tibetan Buddhism in 1940 and finally his flight from Tibet during the 1959 Tibetan uprising, with a focus on his spiritual growth as a young man and how his compassionate brand of spirituality ran headlong into the behemoth that was (and remains) communist China, at the time led by Chairman Mao.

ANALYSIS

Prior to *The Age of Innocence*, few would have looked to Martin Scorsese for a meditative art film focused on an Eastern culture little seen in the West at the time and a culture best known for its embrace of nonviolence. Screenwriter Melissa Mathison (*E.T.: The Extra-Terrestrial*) thought otherwise, suggesting Scorsese be brought on as director. And indeed, the director found himself intrigued with the material: "I'm fascinated by one person in the world who is full of compassion and full of love, the idea of this enlightened being who has unconditional love for all sentient beings. Is this possible? I don't know if the film answers that; perhaps all it can do is give an impression of what Tibetan culture was like."[1]

There is an understated beauty to *Kundun* that is apparent from the title cards, with striking Eastern-tinged music by Philip Glass guiding us over vivid depictions of sand art. It's an immediate signal that we'll be in a different time and place than seen in other Scorsese pictures. So, too, is the tone dramatically different from what we've seen before—though perhaps the first surprise is that much of the picture features child actors, a rarity in his filmography. It wouldn't be for another fourteen years, with *Hugo*, that the director would again make young actors this prominent a part of a movie.

Here, the very young Dalai Lama (Tenzin Yeshi Paichang), prior to his discovery by spiritual leaders, is a precocious, demanding child of two who appears to have an inflated sense of his own place in the world. At dinner, he insists his father move so he can sit at the head of the table. He demands that others tell the story of the night he was born. He shows fierceness unlike other children his age. Later, when a lama shows up during their search for the next Dalai Lama (in the Gelug school of Tibetan Buddhism, the Dalai Lama is reborn after death, necessitating a search for the new Dalai Lama in order to maintain succession), the boy points to the lama's beaded necklace. "This is mine," he declares. In another child this might seem forward and unwanted. Here, it's a sign.

The boy's true inner nature is depicted in a scene in which he sees two beetles in conflict. He separates the two, placing them at a distance from one another as if to say, "You can coexist." A naïve belief, perhaps, given the experience he will later have with China's Chairman Mao (Robert Lin) but also a *beautiful* belief. Violence rules the world, it seems to say, but there can be another way.

These signs of potential divinity are prominent throughout the early discovery sequences. Scorsese takes the reality of resurrection, of death and rebirth, and of the Dalai Lama's divine nature as a matter of course. *Kundun* does not question his divinity, nor does it question the idea that this long cycle of resurrection is reality. Faith and belief are paramount. We are never shown anything that could be described as supernatural. No hearts pulled from chests or water turned to wine, as in *The Last Temptation of Christ*. Most of what we see could be explained in real-world terms though sometimes involving extraordinary coincidence, such as the boy correctly choosing items that belonged to former Dalai Lamas. The one moment that leaps past this and ventures into the realm of the near unbelievable is when the child says his teeth are being kept in a cupboard. Unprompted, he opens a cabinet, goes through some items that have obviously been there a long time, and opens a package that contains the jawbone of a former Dalai Lama. This borders on the supernatural, yet Scorsese treats it straight, with unquestioning belief.

Certainly, the lamas who find, educate, and serve the young Dalai Lama believe. Their hands shake when they recognize him for who he is. When he is told of his true nature, we see through his eyes in a wonderful shot through another lama's robes, the boy not yet part of this strange new way of living but also shielded within it as if in a womb. He is the Buddha returned again but will have to grow into the role with the help of these men, just as Scorsese's version of Jesus of Nazareth needed his disciples to fully embrace who and what he was. For the moment, he is still very much a child. When the boy is finally named the fourteenth Dalai Lama, his family bows before him, his older brother giving him a puzzled and annoyed look as Kundun (one of the names given to him in Tibetan Buddhism) smiles back with delight. It's a charming moment that speaks to the human side of this divine person.

And he is indeed human. There is no healing lepers or resurrecting the dead. This is a boy (and then a young man and then a man) who is rebellious and willful and intent on enjoying his life. He takes a car and crashes it. He looks on as a rat drinks from a cup, the others around him deep in meditation, a combination of joy and mischief and compassion and wonder etched on his face. At one point, he asks one of his friends and advisors if the lamas found the wrong child. Could it be that he isn't the Dalai Lama after all? No, his friend replies with utter certainty. But like the Jesus of *Last Temptation*, the Dalai Lama is not always certain. The things he is forced to confront in *Kundun* are not obstacles to be overcome with divine power; they are obstacles to be overcome with will and focus and devotion to nonviolence. In the midst of a director's career typified by how we engage in and react to violence, here is a film about *avoiding* it. The Dalai Lama succeeds in that task, at great cost to himself and his people, but fails in his greater task of keeping Tibet free.

His father passes away. As practiced by Vajrayana Buddhists in areas of Tibet, Sichuan, and portions of Mongolia, his body is subjected to sky burial, a practice in which a corpse is placed on a mountaintop to decompose naturally or, more often, to be eaten by vultures. The idea is that the body is but a shell, an empty vessel once the spirit has departed, so the body is given back to nature as intended, thus preserving the circle of life. Here, the Dalai Lama witnesses his father's sky burial—in this case, the body is cut into pieces—just as he hears the news that Tibet has been ordered to become part of China and succumb to Chinese rule. The layers here are fitting, the loss of his father set alongside the potential loss of his land and people, a pair of endings, each emotionally complicated in their own way.

Tibet finds itself "crashing into the Twentieth Century, they find themselves face-to-face with a society that is one of the most anti-spiritual ever formed, the Marxist government of the Chinese communists," Scorsese said. "What interests me is how a man of non-violence deals with these people."[2]

Soon, speakers are blaring Chinese pride music outside. "They have taken away our silence," the Dalai Lama laments. Things are about to change. Again, echoes of previous Scorsese movies in a seemingly unlikely place. *Casino* depicts the end of the era of mafia rule in Las Vegas; *GoodFellas*, the end of the golden age of the classic Italian mobster; *The Last Temptation of Christ*, the end of the old laws and the beginning of the new; and even *Alice Doesn't Live Here Anymore*, the end of one life and the birth of a new. So, too, is that theme present in *Kundun*. The Dalai Lama travels to China to meet Chairman Mao in the hopes of preserving both peace and Tibet itself. But it's not to be. Mao tells him, "Religion is poison. . . . Tibet has been poisoned by religion." Though said with feigned concern and a smile, this is, spiritually at least, a declaration of war. "That's exactly what the Dalai Lama told us he said," Scorsese remembered, "and how Mao moved closer to him on the couch. And that the Dalai Lama couldn't look at him anymore, he just looked at Mao's shiny shoes, and knew that that man is just going to wipe everything away."[3]

It does not take long for Mao's veiled threats to become reality. The Dalai Lama meets with him several times, always in good faith, initially believing he can be reasoned with, but there is no reason here. Mao believes Tibet is his, that it is China's. And the Tibetan people are in no position to stop him.

When the Dalai Lama was a child, his parents would often tell the story of the night of his birth. The great point of the anecdote was that he did not cry when he was born, a trait that set him apart. But he weeps when he learns of the atrocities the Chinese army perpetrates upon his people, massacres and butchery, rapes, people being forced to fornicate in the streets, children being made to shoot their own parents. Kundun envisions himself in a sea of bodies, bloodied lamas by the hundreds, stretching as far as he can see, like blood-red flowers in a field, an image of horror and beauty.

He realizes he must sacrifice his ancestral home so that he may continue on as a spiritual leader for his people. He must leave Tibet. He vows, "I will liberate those not liberated. I will release those not released. I will relieve those unrelieved," and with that, he begins his difficult flight from the lands in which he had been born, died, and reborn again and again. Glass's music surges as the beautiful sand art first seen in the title cards is swept away. Each advance of the Chinese, each violent act, each person who dies in rebellion—all of them are symbolized in this destruction of beauty. Tibetan sand mandalas, as this art is called, are lush, beautiful "paintings" of sand, painstakingly created by a team of monks and depicting deities and other imagery. They are then ritually destroyed as a representation of the transient nature of life. Once destroyed, the sand is returned to a body of moving water and returned to nature. All things must pass. All things are cyclical in nature. Just as the sand mandala is destroyed, so, too, is the Tibet the Dalai Lama knew. For different reasons, of course, but a new mandala will one day arise again from the same sands, and (or so goes the hope) a free Tibet will arise again, too. That is the fourteenth Dalai Lama's lifelong mission, even today.

In the final sequences of the film, he flees Tibet, always just one step ahead of the Chinese who wish to take him into custody. Glass's music never ceases for the final ten minutes, building and building until it becomes both tense and hypnotic. The Dalai Lama and his guides reach the border of India. They bow to him. As he looks back, he sees a vision of them dead on their horses, killed, presumably by those who hunt them. He does not speak of it. Instead he nods a thanks to them, seeing that they are still among the living, and he crosses the border. There, one of the border guards asks him, "Are you the Lord Buddha?"

"I think I am a reflection," he says, "like the moon on water. When you see me, and I try to be a good man, see yourself." Bereft of his spiritual home, exiled from the place from which he belongs, all the fourteenth Dalai Lama can do is serve as an example of how to live, how to be, how to *exist*. When faced by violence, to exist in peace. When faced by turmoil, to exist in calm. When faced by oppression, to exist in the perpetual hope of freedom springing anew.

Like so many Scorsese films, *Kundun* ends with collapse and loss, the protagonist left without something they cherish or desire or hold dear: admiration and the thrill of victory for Jake LaMotta; access to an easy life for Henry Hill; a successful music career for *New York, New York*'s Jimmy Doyle; passion for Newland Archer; family stability for Sam Bowden; and many more. But unlike so many Scorsese films, *Kundun*, through the spirit of the Dalai Lama, ends with something often scarce in his filmography: hope.

CONCLUSION AND IMPACT

Today, the fourteenth Dalai Lama is still in exile. He lives in India and travels the world speaking on the plight of the Tibetan people, who still live under the yoke of Chinese rule. He still preaches the gospel of nonviolence.

Whether there will be a fifteenth Dalai Lama remains an open question. The Chinese government will not recognize one chosen on the basis of reincarnation. If Tibet remains under Chinese control, the Dalai Lama says he will not reincarnate within Tibet. The Chinese government insists otherwise. In 2014, a Chinese Foreign Ministry spokeswoman said, "The title of Dalai Lama is conferred by the central government, which has hundreds of years of history. The (present) 14th Dalai Lama has ulterior motives, and is seeking to distort and negate history, which is damaging to the normal order of Tibetan Buddhism."[4] Yet in 1994, when the Dalai Lama named a Tibetan boy the reincarnation of the Panchen Lama, the second-highest figure in Tibetan Buddhism, the Chinese government captured the boy and put another in his place, seeming to confirm the Dalai Lama's observation that "there is an obvious risk of vested political interests misusing the reincarnation system to fulfill their own political agenda."[5] So the struggle continues up until today.

Unsurprisingly, *Kundun* stirred up political controversy in China. For a time, Scorsese was even banned from the country. He couldn't get his films distributed there, either, until *Hugo* received a small release in 2012. And it didn't just cause problems for the director: "The picture seriously damaged business relationships between China and The Walt Disney Co., which had produced and distributed the film over Beijing's objections. Relations weren't normalized until the studio apologized, as part of the negotiation process leading up to the creation of Shanghai Disneyland."[6]

The picture was another box-office failure, receiving a highly limited release and only bringing in $6 million, but it was generally praised by critics for its visual beauty and garnered four Academy Award nominations (Art Direction,

Costume Design, Cinematography, and Score). Michael Wilmington of the *Chicago Tribune* said of the picture, "In the post-1980s movie era of blood-drenched demolition derbies and explosive high-tech extravaganzas, it may be the kind of artistic feat that gets insufficiently appreciated."[7]

But by this point smaller, more personal films that fail at the box office had become standard for Martin Scorsese, a director often at odds with the financial realities of Hollywood productions. Yet that wouldn't stop him for making his next picture, a bizarre, druggy look at an insomniac ambulance driver obsessed with a dead homeless girl, a concept that was about as appealing to mainstream audiences as it sounds.

18

BRINGING OUT THE DEAD (1999)

FILM DETAILS

RELEASE DATE: October 22, 1999
WRITTEN BY: Paul Schrader
STARRING: Nicolas Cage, Patricia Arquette, John Goodman, Ving Rhames,
 Tom Sizemore
RUNNING TIME: 121 minutes

ABOUT THE FILM

Death is an ever-present entity in Martin Scorsese films, but it wouldn't be accurate to say that the director is preoccupied with the subject. Rather, death is a mere fact of life, something unavoidable, something many of his characters take as a matter of course. *Bringing Out the Dead* takes the theme of death and brings it to the fore, blending it with more prominent Scorsesian themes like redemption and guilt—lots and lots of guilt. It's also a meditation on how being in close proximity to death on a regular basis drives a person to a mental place just askew from reality. Though saving lives, the paramedics and ER nurses of the film are as twisted, callous, and antisocial as any of the gangsters in the director's crime films, in no small part because their daily exposure to the worst humanity has to offer has made them numb to the idea of compassion.

The film is based on the bestselling book of the same name by Joe Connelly, who described it as semiautobiographical. The movie focuses on Frank Pierce (Nicolas Cage), a paramedic working a bad Manhattan neighborhood in the early 1990s, a period when violent crime in New York City had spiked past its 1970s highs. He and Larry (John Goodman) respond to an elderly man in cardiac distress, assuring the man's daughter, Mary (Patricia Arquette), that they can revive him. They do, but the man remains in a coma. Frank and other partners respond to a series of calls, largely to drug dealers and users, drunks, and other less-than-savory characters. Frank grows increasingly disoriented as the picture wears on. Unable to sleep and seeing visions of a homeless girl, Rose (Cynthia Roman), he had earlier failed to save, he rescues a drug pusher from a fatal fall, protects a disturbed drug user from a beating, then realizes what he has to do in order to free himself from visions of Rose. Frank goes to the hospital where the man he saved at the start of the picture is being kept on life support, unplugs him, then goes to Mary to tell her that her father has passed. Only then does Frank appear to have found peace.

ANALYSIS

Death is everywhere. It surrounds Frank Pierce. It hangs over his shoulder as he works, often with a kiss of religious and spiritual imagery. He talks of "spirits leaving the body and not wanting to be put back, spirits angry at the awkward places death had left them," and in the neighborhood he works, awkward places abound. The people he treats are addicts, drug dealers, prostitutes, the mentally disturbed, homeless who have lost touch with wider society, drug users deep in the throes of their addictions, street criminals, *victims* of street criminals, the sick, the mad, the deranged. His city is filled with miserable people leading miserable lives. This is Travis Bickle's world but seen through the eyes of someone who wants to save it rather than purge it in bloodshed.

The apartment where we first see Frank work is a picture of normality by comparison. There, he must revive an older man (Cullen O. Johnson) who has gone into cardiac arrest. A cross hangs on the wall over the bed. (How many times have we seen this in a Scorsese movie?) He asks the family to play the old man's favorite music, Frank Sinatra, and the victim's pulse returns. He provides aid and saves the man's life.

What Frank doesn't know is that this is someone who did not want to be saved, someone who was ready to depart this life. It's one of a pair of guilts that torment him throughout the picture, each in contrast to the other. The old man was ready to pass, but ER doctors keep reviving him, more than a dozen times bringing him back from the brink. Keeping him alive only prolongs his suffering, and as the movie progresses, Frank begins imagining the old man is talking to him from his coma, asking to be allowed to die. Seeing him cling on against his wishes is an anchor on Frank's psyche.

The other guilt that plagues him is a larger anchor, however: Rose. Rose was an eighteen-year-old homeless girl whom Frank could not save. As his insomnia increases and his shifts become more chaotic, he sees her face more and more. It's painted on everyone he sees. She is beneath every hoodie, around every corner, etched on every pedestrian. These phantom versions of her ask why he didn't save her. He has no answer. This pair are his spiritual burdens. They are the emotional trauma he must work through even as he helps others through their physical trauma. The elderly man wanted to die. The young woman wanted to live. Frank feels as if he's failed both of them.

This sets Frank apart from many other Scorsese protagonists. His is a different sort of guilt than the usual Scorsese guilt. In earlier pictures, the nature of a character's guilt was often vague or unspecified (*Who's That Knocking at My Door?* and *Mean Streets*) or stemmed from things they couldn't fully confront or acknowledge (*Raging Bull* and *Cape Fear*), usually their own behavior. Here, Frank's guilt takes a specific form and specific substance. It is guilt for failure on his part, failure to save the lives he is tasked with saving, as represented by Rose. It's not about the individual. Rose is a stand-in for all of them. In his narration, Frank says, "After a while I grew to understand that my role was less about saving than about bearing witness. I was a grief mop. It was enough that I simply showed up." He is, in some sense, a temporary Messiah for the people he serves, there to absolve them of sin as much as he is to lift them from pain. Those brief moments of being cared for, of being attended to, of being treated like a *human* are powerful to people who have largely been ignored by wider society. "He knows he's not God," Scorsese said, "but there's a pride because he has the power to bring someone back to life. He thinks he is divine to a certain extent, and it's very moving when it strikes him that he may not be."[1]

That's the role Frank is fulfilling, and it's why his failure to save Rose looms so large for him. Unlike such squadmates as Tom Wolls (Tom Sizemore) or ER workers like Nurse Constance (Mary Beth Hurt), Frank doesn't want to forget that those he serves are *people*. The people he and his colleagues serve can make that difficult, however. Like several other pictures by the director, *Bringing Out the Dead* doesn't have much in the way of plot. Instead, it's a series of interconnected vignettes depicting Frank's life as a tired, tormented paramedic. Each of these vignettes gives us a glimpse of people torn down by poverty or addiction and a city that considers them second-class citizens. He's accompanied by one of three different partners throughout: the pragmatic Larry, who represents what Frank could be if still of sound mind; the religiously hopeful Marcus (Ving Rhames), who represents the kind of hubris that can come of taking your role as a life-saver too close to heart; and the violently psychopathic Tom, who represents someone who has lost sight of what they are and why they do what they do.

When riding with Marcus, Frank is told that he has to accept that death is just a part of the job. You don't think about it; otherwise it will consume you. Seeing Rose's face everywhere makes Frank want to quit. In fact, a running gag in the film is that he wants to be fired, but his boss refuses to do so, always making excuses to put off his firing for a few more days. But Marcus knows quitting won't work, anyway: "You think just 'cause you quit, them ghosts is gonna quit you? It don't work that way, Frank."

Bringing Out the Dead's often-hallucinogenic approach to exploring character can be disorienting. Frank discovers himself not through direct experiences but through visions, dreams, and hazy images of the world. This isn't merely a stylistic choice by Scorsese. Rather, it ties into the spiritual journey Frank is on and the disconnect between our bodies and our souls. Mary's father lives on in a shell and wishes to depart the world. Rose has already passed, but her spirit lives on in Frank and in his memories. He keeps her here, tied to the world through his regret and guilt. We see the streets of New York as strange, twisted visions, the people and their *essence* seeming to be two different things. We get fleeting impressions of them rather than an actual view of their humanity. It's that latter view that Frank must recapture if he is to cast guilt off his shoulders and find the redemption he so desperately needs.

When Frank returns to a drug den where he had earlier found Mary (and where he experienced a horrifying hallucination of Rose's death), he finds Cy (Cliff Curtis), the guy who runs the place, speared on a wrought-iron balcony fence and teetering precariously over the side of the fourteenth floor. Emergency workers have to blowtorch the fencing to remove him, sparks flying into the night air, their beautiful lights turning into fireworks. It's strangely beautiful. When Frank was here last, he sought escape in drugs and rest but could not find it. He sought peace and instead found haunted memories. But his return is different. Though tainted with death and injury, it's an awakening. The sparks and fireworks are a celebration, or the gates of his mind being opened, the moment when the purpose of his work comes back into focus. He's not there to judge or condemn people. When they're vulnerable and on the brink, people are just people. His role is to save them, even drug dealers.

This is further solidified in his final encounter with Noel (Marc Anthony), a disturbed drug user who has been losing his grip on reality. Throughout the picture, Frank encounters Noel—on the streets, in the ER, and even with Mary, with whom Noel once stayed. Each time, Noel grows increasingly erratic and detached from the real world. Frank and Tom chase after him, but then things get dark. Tom is a psychopath, a violent man who looks down on the people he serves. They're not human to him. A part of him seems to enjoy their suffering. It's almost a game to Tom, but this time, it's a violent game that snaps Frank out of his mental fog. The New York here is plucked from *Taxi Driver*, all wet streets and decaying people and hopelessness. The presentation and approach are similar to what Scorsese developed in *GoodFellas*, with a needle-drop pop music soundtrack, narration, and aggressive scene shifts. But the *heart* of it is quite different from either. Though it touches on common Scorsese themes, guilt being the most prominent, *Bringing Out the Dead* resolves itself with an air of distant, dreamlike hope that is rarely present in his work. It manifests itself in this alleyway with Frank, Tom, and Noel.

After Tom beats Noel with a bat, Frank chases off Tom and performs mouth-to-mouth on the beaten addict. In any other film depicting the lives of paramedics, this procedure would appear normal. In *Bringing Out the Dead*, it's a noteworthy decision on Frank's part because, for most of the picture, the paramedics have talked about how they avoid doing it. Most only did it once. They had a bad experience, or more commonly, they just didn't want to perform such an intimate procedure with the kind of people they serve. There is a habit of dehumanizing the people in the neighborhood, seeing them as something filthy and *other*, which infects the entire crew. So when Frank performs mouth-to-mouth, it's a big moment. It's a *redemptive* moment. This is Frank's sacrifice. His giving of himself to save another. It's not as potent as volunteering to be nailed to a cross, but the spirit of the act is the same. In saving Noel, in a way Frank finally saves Rose, too. He sets her spirit free and gives her peace.

This selfless act—he's no longer just going through the motions—awakens something in him, a memory of why he does the job in the first place, perhaps, or an acknowledgment that the people he serves are indeed *people*, something many of his colleagues seem to have forgotten. He travels to Mary's father's hospital room, hooks himself up to the equipment monitoring his vital signs to throw off the readings, and then allows the old man to die. He *becomes* the old man, in a sense, temporarily serving as a stand-in for him so he can finally pass in peace. This is a case where saving a life means allowing someone to die rather than suffer. Death is natural. You can't always stop it. Sometimes, you *shouldn't* stop it. By freeing the old man from his torment, Frank frees himself of his final burden.

With this weight off him, he goes to see Mary. He tells her that her father has passed. In response, she tells him something he said to her at the start of the film: "You have to keep the body going until the brain and heart recover enough to go on their own." As she says this, she wears Rose's face. The picture ends with Frank and Mary sitting in quiet contemplation, the morning sun streaming in through the apartment window, bathing them in light. Through death, they've each rediscovered life.

Death has been a presence in almost all Scorsese films to this point, but he never dwelled on it the way he dwells on it here. In his crime pictures especially, death is a matter of course. It's just part of the fringe world these people exist in. Here, however, death is something different. It's a fact of life, yes, but it's an aspect of life deeply connected to people and the lives they lead. It's a movie about forgotten deaths, about the daily tragedies we either don't see or pointedly look away from. It's also about embracing a life well led and the peace that comes at the end. Frank's redemption isn't about saving Rose or allowing Mary's father to die; it's that he came to recognize these people *as* people. He came to understand the role he plays in their lives and accept the sacrifice he is tasked with making. *Bringing Out the Dead* has more in common with *The Last Temptation of Christ* in that regard than any other Scorsese picture. Frank Pierce is no Messiah, but he does give a part of himself so that others can live.

CONCLUSION AND IMPACT

Bringing Out the Dead failed at the box office despite garnering positive reviews, but the picture's success is secondary to what it accomplished: It proved that the aesthetic and style and formula of *GoodFellas* could be used for something other than a gangster picture and still result in an artistic success. The rapid-fire pace, MTV-infused soundtrack, high energy, narration, and creative camera choices were all worked out there (and further refined in *Casino*), then were cast in a completely different context here while still working to great effect. That makes it interesting, then, that his next picture would be a return to crime yet would be markedly different than any crime picture he had ever done before.

19

GANGS OF NEW YORK (2002)

FILM DETAILS

RELEASE DATE: December 20, 2002
WRITTEN BY: Jay Cocks, Steven Zaillian, Kenneth Lonergan
STARRING: Leonardo DiCaprio, Daniel Day-Lewis, Cameron Diaz
RUNNING TIME: 168 minutes

ABOUT THE FILM

Somewhere in an alternate universe, there is a Martin Scorsese who crafted a five-season, fifty-hour dramatic television series on the history of New York City, of which *Gangs of New York* is but a part. Even in *this* universe, *Gangs of New York* fits into a tapestry of Scorsese pictures that, when taken as a whole, sketches out a broad history of life in New York, usually (but not always) focused on life in the streets.

Gangs is an ambitious picture, as far as scale is concerned, arguably the most technically ambitious of his career, aside perhaps from *The Irishman*'s CGI wizardry. It's one that had been in his mind for many years—literally decades—and one that even after being made fell short of what he hoped to accomplish with it.

It's little surprise he was drawn to the material. In some respects, it's *Mean Streets* set in the 1860s, albeit with a plot driven more by standard tropes than personal experience. The setting is pure Scorsese, though, exploring the deeper past of the neighborhood that made him who he is. "I grew up in that area. And when I became aware of St. Patrick's Old Cathedral and the graveyard around it, with the names on the tombstones, I realized the Irish were there before the Italians," he told Richard Schickel.[1]

He first encountered the book by Herbert Asbury from which the movie is drawn in 1970. He started working with Jay Cocks (who wrote *The Age of Innocence* and *Silence* screenplays) to carve stories from the book and craft them into a screenplay. By the late 1970s, he had a "beautiful" script, but being neck deep in *New York, New York* and in the midst of one of the most volatile and draining parts of his career, Scorsese decided he couldn't pursue the project. By 1990, they had revisited the project again, reshaping the story around Bill the Butcher and a boy named Amsterdam seeking to avenge his father. But he still needed a studio willing to fund such an ambitious picture. It would be yet another decade until it was made. And it turned out ambitious, indeed—so ambitious that it swelled way over budget, causing Scorsese to invest millions of his own money into the production and prompting sharp clashes between the director and now-disgraced producer Harvey Weinstein.[2]

Daniel Day-Lewis returns to Scorsese's work as Bill the Butcher, playing a character of roughly the same time and place as he does in *The Age of Innocence* (a touch earlier, actually) but at the polar-opposite end of society. Every bit as composed, genteel, and refined as Newland Archer is, Bill is the opposite, a brutal, ostentatious man who chews the scenery to pieces and murders without qualm. A number of notable actors have small roles throughout—Cameron Diaz, John C. Reilly, Liam Neeson, and others—but the most important addition to the Scorsese roster is Leonardo DiCaprio as Amsterdam Vallon. This would be the first of five films and counting for the pair, effectively dividing the director's career up into the De Niro era and the DiCaprio era. The tale here is a simple one: Bill killed Amsterdam's father. Once old enough, Amsterdam infiltrates Bill's gang, earns his trust, and attempts to kill him. He fails, but in the midst of Civil War–era riots, the pair clash one last time, and Amsterdam is able to get his revenge.

ANALYSIS

Scorsese films are most often preoccupied with exploring the human condition in some way, with setting and genre merely an excuse to explore similar themes from different angles. *The Age of Innocence* looks and feels much different than, say, *Mean Streets*, but at their heart they're both about the complexities of human needs and interactions. *Raging Bull* isn't about boxing; it's a movie about the human condition that happens to feature boxing. *Casino* isn't about how organized crime in Las Vegas works; it's about the conflict that comes when incompatible wants are pitted against one another. And so on.

Gangs of New York largely lacks this element of the director's work. This isn't to say the key characters don't have inner lives and understandable motivations. Amsterdam is clearly driven with a specific purpose, and though the script doesn't appear to give Bill much in the way of inner complexity, he's given so much depth by Daniel Day-Lewis that it's easy to read far more into the character than what you find in the screenplay (surely a factor in his casting in the first place, given that Lewis delivered the same kind of depth in *The Age of Innocence*).

Yet what does the picture *say*, exactly? Fitting for its ambitious scale, there is little in the way of exploration of the individual. Instead, Scorsese explores a slice of New York society in the 1860s. We don't learn about what makes Amsterdam tick; we learn about what makes this part of *America* tick. Our complex historical relationship with immigration, our long history of racial segregation, political corruption, the way in which demagogues can whip people into such a fearful frenzy that they will act against their own best interests—this is a film that peels back the layers of society rather than of individuals.

This makes *Gangs* more relevant today than it was upon release. Bill is a principled man, but his principles are twisted and driven by fear of the other. He controls his neighborhood through fear and not merely by fear of the violence he will inflict on people who cross him. It's fear of the other, fear of foreign invaders to American soil, fear of being supplanted by people who aren't "real" Americans. Bill puts himself between the supposed "natives" who were born in America and the immigrants coming to her shores. He positions himself as serving the interests of the people of his neighborhood, as being willing to speak aloud about the fears they secretly have, yet he *sows* that fear. He waters it and nourishes it. And he makes every effort to dehumanize the Irish he so clearly despises. They're not real Americans, he says. They're not legitimate. They don't respect our ways. The message rings familiar. Not much has changed in the United States, save perhaps the targets of the Butcher's xenophobic ire.

The opening fight sequence provides some backstory for a variety of characters and motivation for Amsterdam, but the more important role it plays is introducing the world of Five Points in Manhattan, a place the *New York Times* said was once the "world's most notorious slum." "The newspapers dwelt interminably upon its alleged violence and depravity. Readers were thrilled and repulsed by tales of murder, mayhem and sexual license. By the late 1830s the

Five Points was already infamous enough that tourists from around the world made regular 'slumming' trips," the *Times* reported, while also noting that most of the claims of rampant violence appear to have been greatly exaggerated. "The overwhelming reality of the Five Points, and the one thing that all observers seem to have gotten right, was the misery. The endless drudgery and the low pay. The appalling sanitation and the firetrap tenements. The plagues of cholera, measles, diphtheria and typhus that struck hardest at children and infants."[3]

The picture opens in torch-lit caves filled with grimy-looking people wielding archaic weapons. If this is to be an urban drama, there is no sign of it here. It's not until the doors are kicked open and the streets of Five Points are revealed that we realize we're in the middle of the city. That contrast between the primitive and contemporary is symbolic of the savagery within a supposedly civilized place we'll see throughout the movie. Consider the terms we often use to discuss organized crime: *underground* and *underbelly* and the like, always suggesting something hidden from view beneath an otherwise normal exterior. Here, that idea is literalized.

It's only the Irish immigrants who are truly underground in *Gangs*, though. Bill the Butcher operates openly and apparently with the blessing of his neighborhood (though some of that support is driven by terror at his violence). The fight for the neighborhood is between those "born right wise in this fine land, or the foreign hordes defiling it," according to Bill, pitting his gangs against an array of Irish immigrant gangs, led by "Priest" Vallon (Neeson). When Priest is killed, he instructs his son just before he dies, "Don't ever look away." It's important that he knows the sacrifice people like his father made to live free.

Sixteen years later, Amsterdam is released from the orphanage where he had lived. As he departs for his old neighborhood, he tosses away his pocket Bible. It sinks into the waters surrounding New York. Faith is fine, but it won't protect him on these violent streets. Amsterdam finds his freedom and returns home just as slavery is abolished in the southern states. This synchronicity doesn't just foreshadow the draft riots that will explode in the final act of the film; it sets the stage for the moral conflict that is central to the narrative. Amsterdam versus Bill isn't merely a story about avenging a boy's father; it's a story about fighting for the heart of the American ideal. That slavery was abolished is in theory a transformative moment in US history, but the truth is that such racial and ethnic hatreds could not be abolished with a pen. They still linger today, and modern-day Bill the Butchers still stir up mistrust of foreign "invaders."

Early on, Amsterdam takes us on a tour of the neighborhood, introducing us to each of the five avenues of Five Points through narration and an instructive overhead shot, with further narration outlining the political climate of the

The sprawling sets of *Gangs of New York* served as the backdrop for what would be the start of the director's second great collaboration, this time with Leonardo Di-Caprio. *Miramax/Photofest*

neighborhood, the various gangs who call it home, and more. It's an info dump of exposition, the sort of thing most directors seek to avoid, but by this point in his career, Scorsese had turned it into something of an art form, using it in *Casino*, *GoodFellas*, and others. Again, this doesn't merely provide the setting within which Amsterdam's pursuit of vengeance takes place; it provides the context for the broader themes of xenophobia, fear of outsiders, and what it means to be a "real" citizen of a place.

The vengeance narrative that provides us a reason to explore this world is fairly straightforward. Bill killed Amsterdam's father. Amsterdam wants revenge. Bill has no idea Amsterdam is Priest's son and allows him to get close. Amsterdam bides his time, has some conflicted feelings, and Bill discovers who he is before he can act. Amsterdam is beaten nearly to death, branded, and let loose, after which he gathers a gang of sympathetic Irish and then confronts and kills Bill. It would be gripping if it wasn't so predictable, though Scorsese makes each step along this otherwise clichéd path work on multiple levels, in no small part thanks to the work of Day-Lewis.

When Amsterdam tells Johnny (Henry Thomas, "Elliott" of *E. T.* fame) he won't kill Bill the Butcher at his first opportunity because "you kill a king; you don't stab him in the dark; you kill him where the whole court can watch him die," we know Amsterdam is making excuses because he finds Bill's power and lifestyle uncomfortably alluring, but it also sends a second message: Unless exposed to the light of day, corruption and evil perpetuates itself. When Amsterdam thinks of a way to skirt the law and keep their illegal boxing matches going, Amsterdam getting pulled into Bill's orbit is secondary to the idea that, in this slice of the United States, the *image* of abiding by the law is more important than the law itself. Legendary New York political figure William "Boss" Tweed (Jim Broadbent) even says, "The appearance of the law must be upheld, especially while it's being broken."

The very presence of Tweed as a character enhances the secondary concerns of the picture. He's not just a figure from old political cartoons; he's a *person*, and what he represents is the system's willingness to look away from wrongdoing provided that willful ignorance lines one's pockets. These are truths still inherent in today's American politics. Time and again, we see Tweed and Bill flex on one another, each attempting to hold their power over the other—one power "legitimate," the other not, but both all too real in this environment—and as a result, neither paying much attention to the people they supposedly represent. When Amsterdam suggests moving the unsanctioned fights just outside the Manhattan boundaries onto floating barges, it's not merely an illustration of Amsterdam ingratiating himself to Bill; it's also a nod at how easily the spirit of the law is subverted with the help of politicians willing to look the other way. Tweed allows it to happen in exchange for Bill delivering immigrant votes to him (a proposal Bill refuses because he hates immigrants). As a further example, when the brawling former mercenary Walter "Monk" McGinn (Brendan Gleeson) is elected sheriff, he's almost immediately murdered by Bill. It happens in broad daylight, in front of witnesses. Tweed again looks the other way.

Similarly, the Union's supposed defense of slaves and potential slaves is, as we see later, not necessarily representative of the people *in* the Union. Many still want to see black citizens as lesser or not as citizens at all. The government is signing up immigrants right off the boat to go die for a cause and for their new country, but there are few signals that the cause is genuine. It's just politics.

This isn't to say Tweed (movie Tweed or otherwise) was on par with Confederate leaders. Rather, it's to suggest that Tweed's presence is a commentary on how *buyable* morals are in politics. One understands that, while Tweed knew he had to take a pro-Union view, there was still a portion of the populace who supported slavery. His concern is not with taking a clear moral position; it's with playing both sides to garner votes.

The murky morality of 1860s United States is perhaps best depicted in a single tracking shot showing immigrants right off the boat being made into citizens, being signed up to go to war, then marching onto a second boat to go fight for the Union. As the camera follows the boarding new soldiers, a coffin swings into view, and the camera switches course to follow it as it's hoisted onto the dock with dozens of other coffins. In setting the reality next to the promise, new citizens going to fight for their new country set next to the bodies of those who came before, it's a stark reminder of the human toll of war and the way in which the victims of war tend to be the poor and desperate.

The vengeance narrative comes to a head at the same time the political narrative comes to a head. New York City explodes with violence during the draft riots of 1863. This true historical event lasted four days and consumed most of Lower Manhattan and remains today one of the largest civil insurrections in US history. Working-class Irish rioted, attacked African Americans, and destroyed property. President Abraham Lincoln was forced to dispatch militia regiments to regain control. The riots were sparked by the drawing of draft numbers pulling working-class young men into the war effort—you could buy your way out of the draft for three hundred dollars, effectively inoculating the rich—though the tinder had already been in place well before the draft, as white laborers worried that the Emancipation Proclamation would flood the city with black workers and provide competition for work. (Again, echoes of this mentality still reverberate in today's political climate, with Hispanic and Latino immigrants the new targets.) Herbert Asbury, the author of the book upon which the movie is based, estimated the death toll of the riots to be nearly two thousand, though that number is widely disputed. Leslie M. Harris puts the number closer to 120.[4]

In the film, this explosive violence takes place just as Amsterdam and Bill have their final confrontation, staged similarly to the first, the cycle of violence and vengeance coming full circle. But this time, it's Bill who is bested. Amsterdam gets his revenge.

The final shots are of a cemetery, the Manhattan skyline dominating the horizon across the river. The years fade by, the city changes, until finally we're looking at a contemporary New York City (though even that skyline now appears archaic, shown in its pre-9/11 form). The years have moved on. The city has become something new, but the seeds of what made it remain. Just as individuals are molded and shaped by their past, so, too, is a society. *Gangs of New York* is not merely a period piece and a revenge tale. It's a fable about the soul of America.

CONCLUSION AND IMPACT

With a huge $100 million budget—large even today, and this was a 2002 picture—a nearly three-hour running time, and a sprawling recreation of Five Points that involved the construction of dozens of buildings, *Gangs of New York* was by far Martin Scorsese's most ambitious production to date. He eschewed the digital effects that were starting to become commonplace in the industry, instead taking an old-Hollywood approach to recreating the time and place of the story on a grand scale. Though it was nominated for ten Academy Awards, including Best Picture, Best Director, and Best Actor for Daniel Day-Lewis, it did not take home a single statue. It also faltered at the box office. Prerelease expectations suggested the picture would be Martin Scorsese's magnum opus, decades in the making. Instead, it turned out to be an entertaining period piece that doesn't fully explore the many themes it introduces.

One can't fault the director's vision. *Gangs of New York* is in some ways a big-picture culmination of Scorsese's exploration of New York City, a way for him to say, "I've explored the city's underworld from every angle, now let's see how we got here in the first place." But Scorsese works best when his focus is on *individuals*, which is why, despite the subject matter seeming to be unusual for him—a wealthy mogul and aviation genius who succumbs to mental illness—his next picture would be far closer to his sensibilities as a storyteller.

20

THE AVIATOR
(2004)

FILM DETAILS

RELEASE DATE: December 14, 2004
WRITTEN BY: John Logan
STARRING: Leonardo DiCaprio, Cate Blanchett, Kate Beckinsale, John C.
   Reilly, Alec Baldwin, Alan Alda
RUNNING TIME: 170 minutes

ABOUT THE FILM

Even when one accomplishes great things, things so great they seemed lifted out of myth and legend, there remains a human being behind those accomplishments, one as flawed and troubled as the rest of us. Sometimes even more so. Such is the subject of Scorsese's 2004 biopic on Howard Hughes, an exploration of genius and madness that at times also doubles as a love letter to the cinema of Hughes's era.

The screenplay by John Logan had been kicking around Hollywood for a few years already, with Leonardo DiCaprio attached almost from the start. After nearly ending up in the hands of director Michael Mann (*Heat*, *Collateral*), New Line Cinema hired Scorsese. The move helped solidify the director's fertile new working partnership with DiCaprio, which has resulted in five films as of this writing (with a sixth in preproduction, *Killers of the Flower Moon*), and again proved that anyone pigeonholing Scorsese as a crime director has an unfairly narrow view of his vision.

The Aviator focuses on Hughes's life from the late 1920s to the late 1940s. Obsessed with completing his epic air-combat movie *Hell's Angels* (1930), Hughes (DiCaprio) hires Noah Dietrich (John C. Reilly) to run the day-to-day operations of his businesses. His film debuts, he becomes romantically entwined with legendary actress Katharine Hepburn (Cate Blanchett), and then becomes obsessed with setting a world speed record in his H-1 Racer airplane. He smashes the record and, high on his triumph, purchases Transcontinental and Western Air (TWA), with his sights set on offering not just nonstop coast-to-coast flights in the United States—a first at the time—but also international flights from New York to Paris. Unfortunately for Hughes, Pan Am owner Juan Trippe (Alec Baldwin) and his bought-and-paid-for US senator Owen Brewster (Alan Alda) plan to block Hughes's move through legislation. Hepburn leaves Hughes, and the aviator's obsessive-compulsive disorder (OCD) symptoms worsen as he pursues two major government projects, a spy plane and a huge air-transport vehicle dubbed the Hercules (and disparagingly called the "Spruce Goose" by critics). Falsely accused of war profiteering by Brewster, Hughes has a major mental break and locks himself inside a room for months, stuck in a fit of repeated phrases and behavioral obsessions. He snaps out of it just in time to successfully defend himself in front of the US Senate and show the world that the "Spruce Goose" can actually fly—but his madness never truly goes away, and the picture ends with Hughes teetering on the verge of another major mental break.

ANALYSIS

Genius and madness often go hand in hand. Decorated professor Dean Keith Simonton, PhD, once noted that, according to peer-reviewed research, "on average, the more eminent the creator, the higher is the expected rate and intensity of the psychopathological symptoms."[1] Few in the twentieth century have been as eminent as Howard Hughes, and few men of prominence have been madder. For Scorsese, the trick of *The Aviator* was in how to depict both in a way that is simultaneously honest and entertaining without being exploitative.

The director had been down this road before. Nick Nolte's character in *New York Stories* is a creative genius who has to put himself (and his partner) through emotional torture in order to wring out his art. The Jesus of Nazareth depicted in *The Last Temptation of Christ* seems to waver back and forth between vivid insights into the human condition and bouts of mania. And in the tail end of *Goodfellas*, Henry Hill's incessant drug use leads to a manic day of paranoia.

We also have examples of Scorsese depicting characters who are disconnected from reality. In *Raging Bull*, for example, when Jake LaMotta's obsessive observations have him fixated on Vickie, we see it in a subjective viewpoint that lets the viewer understand the deep paranoia in LaMotta's mind, even if we don't relate to it. We can feel Frank Pierce's growing detachment from reality as *Bringing Out the Dead* progresses. And even in *Mean Streets*, a scene of a drunken Charlie stumbling through a bar is potently immersive, letting the viewer feel the fog he is in.

But the director had never so directly confronted the subject matter as he does with *The Aviator*, a picture that pulls few punches in showing how both genius and madness consumed Howard Hughes. Hughes was a titan. After initially making his splash as a movie producer with films like *Hell's Angels* and *Scarface* (1932), which in 1983 was remade by Brian De Palma, Hughes went on to become a dominant force in the aviation industry, breaking flight records, helping conceive of innovative new aircraft, and making absurd amounts of money. Yet Hughes also suffered from OCD, an affliction that would grow to debilitating levels over the course of his life, until he eventually became more famous for being a recluse than for being an innovator.

DiCaprio brings Hughes to life in one of the actor's great performances, bouncing effortlessly between egomaniacal heights of achievement and humiliating lows stemming from his condition. Though DiCaprio first worked for Scorsese in *Gangs of New York*, this is where their partnership truly blossomed. It's a mirror of Scorsese's relationship with Robert De Niro in that regard, with De Niro debuting in a crime picture (*Mean Streets*) and their creative partnership truly flowering with a picture about a man disconnected from society (*Taxi Driver*). Further pictures featuring the actors would explore delusional obsessions (*The King of Comedy*; *Shutter Island*); audacious levels of greed (*Casino*; *The Wolf of Wall Street*); and, of course, trust and betrayal in the world of crime (*GoodFellas*; *The Departed*). (Interestingly, given the fact that he effectively replaced De Niro as the director's go-to actor, DiCaprio was initially recommended to Scorsese *by* De Niro.[2])

Hughes struggles through each triumph and accomplishment, a successful genius on the outside but filled with torment on the inside. One wonders to what extent Scorsese saw himself in the maverick, pushing himself through masterpieces like *Raging Bull* even while struggling to maintain his grip on his health, career, and even his own sanity. Certainly, the director had some tough periods when his health and difficulties with drug abuse made it harder to tap into his creative genius, times when his personal torment could only be exorcised through cinematic expression. Still, even with such struggles, the director never had the kind of near-mythical mental breaks Howard Hughes had. "In my mind, his obsessive-compulsive disorder is like the labyrinth that he gets stuck in," Scorsese said, "sort of like the Minotaur. He's got wings, like the ones Daedalus makes for his son, Icarus, the wings to get out of that labyrinth, but he flies too close to the sun and the wings melt, and he comes down. There's a Hughes metaphor there. His pride and his ego destroyed him, too."[3]

Saying his pride and ego destroyed him, too, is unfair, though. Scorsese pictures are often about endings, about collapse, about the end of an era or golden age of a person's life. There is a seed of that here. The picture ends with a triumphant Hughes having proven his impossible beast of an aircraft can fly but with Hughes also on the verge of another serious mental break. Collapse is coming. Just as often, Scorsese protagonists bring their downfall on themselves. Loss permeates his work. There is a degree to which the Travis Bickles, Jake LaMottas, and Henry Hills of his world are responsible for their own troubles. They are culpable in their own collapses. But that cannot be said about Howard Hughes. He was proud, yes. Arrogant to the point of being reckless, sure. Brimming with ego, albeit well-deserved ego, no doubt. But his mental illness was not his fault. He did not choose his affliction, and there is little in the film to suggest he acted in a way to exacerbate his problems. His condition was beyond his control. At best, he could have withdrawn from his pursuits as a business magnate, aviator, and filmmaker and focused entirely on seeking help, yet consider the era in which he lived, when mental disorders were ill understood and often treated in barbaric ways. Even such luminaries as the Kennedys were not immune to the era's poorly conceived ideas of how to treat mental illness, lobotomizing Rosemary Kennedy, younger sister of President John F. Kennedy, and leaving her unable to speak intelligibly. Considering the ignorance of the time, any reticence by Hughes to seek treatment would be understandable.

Here we should pause for a moment to discuss OCD. It's an affliction many of us discuss casually, often as if it's just a humorous personality quirk: "I'm so OCD. I hate when my books aren't in alphabetical order." Actual OCD can be debilitating, however, resulting in intrusive thoughts, such physical compulsions as repeated hand washing or picking at one's skin, and illogical repeated behaviors. These behaviors are genuine compulsions that generally cannot be controlled and that often disrupt a person's life and health. Various forms of therapy and medication are required to help manage the symptoms. Without proper management, severe cases can all but cripple a person's ability to function.

Leonardo DiCaprio fully immersed himself in the role of Howard Hughes, which involved intense depictions of mental illness. *Miramax/Warner Bros./Photofest*

Hughes had no one to help him manage his symptoms, at least no one professionally qualified to do so. Early in his life, his OCD was undiagnosed and untreated. It built over the course of years. Scorsese depicts this by carefully introducing symptom after symptom and increasing their intensity as the film wears on. For example, in an early scene, after touching a chair in his screening room, Hughes reacts as if he has something stuck on his hand, though there is nothing there. It's minor but an early signal of what's to come. Later, he obsesses over a piece of fluff on someone's lapel, he gets caught in an uncontrollable cycle of asking for blueprints from a staff member, he washes his hands until he bleeds, and other symptoms that grow in severity as the movie progresses.

Too much sensory input and being surrounded by too many people at once triggers him, too. At the premier of *Hell's Angels*, flashbulbs become weapons, faces washed out in their bright lights. Having to tread over the broken bulbs overwhelms him so much that, when it comes time to do a preshow interview, he can only offer vague, nonspecific answers to questions that haven't been asked. (Hughes was partially deaf, which also contributed to the difficulty of navigating such a mob scene.)

Such frantic situations were often difficult for him to withstand. When first meeting Katharine Hepburn's family, the meal is a chaotic web of cross-talk and overlapping conversations, stitched together brilliantly by Scorsese and longtime editor Thelma Schoonmaker. At least four conversations are happening at once, often involving the same people bouncing back and forth between them. Even for viewers it becomes difficult to follow. For Hughes, it was maddening. He finally snaps when one of the Hepburns says the family does not care about money. "That's because you have it," Hughes says. "You don't care about money because you've always had it." The moment mortifies Katharine Hepburn, but it's an instructive part of his character, not just in showing his difficulty in such situations, but also in depicting how focused he was on working and accomplishing things.

Much of the film, most importantly those moments of fraying reality, hinges on Schoonmaker's talents as an editor. It's easy to see why she took home a statue for this picture, too. The sense of being unbalanced along with Hughes, of being fixated on an object or just feeling *off* from everyone else, comes as much from the cutting as it does from DiCaprio's performance.

The centerpiece for the trio of Schoonmaker's, DiCaprio's, and Scorsese's talents on this picture and of the narrative overall is Hughes's dramatic mental snap prior to his Senate hearings, when he locked himself in a room for months on end. This sequence showcases the flip side of the Hughes's coin, the mad contrast to his innovative magic. The picture builds one triumph atop another, from successful film to huge business ventures to record-breaking flights to bedding the most desirable actresses in the world. They are peppered with setbacks, yes—his clashes with Trippe and Brewster; OCD flare-ups; a couple of plane crashes, one nearly fatal—but largely his trajectory is (appropriately) upward. With Scorsese, however, a character's collapse is almost always inevitable. The hermit sequence is Hughes's collapse. It's a difficult scene, disturbing in a way outside the violence and vulgarity that usually provide the cringes in Scorsese pictures. Movie images flicker across Hughes's scarred skin. His brain is caught in repetitive thought loops. Milk bottles are emptied by the dozen and then filled with urine. Assistants arrive to aid him, but we're not even sure if they are real or hallucinations.

Most frightening of all is that this is based on truth and may even underplay what Hughes went through during his real-life isolation. He really did lock himself naked in a screening room. He lived there in pain and solitude for four months. He ate nothing but chocolate bars. His body was wracked with pain, even the touch of clothing causing him discomfort. His health fell apart. His hygiene was nonexistent. This was a man—a brilliant, adventurous man—disintegrating at the seams. And shockingly, the real Howard Hughes would only grow worse as the years went by. "By 1968 Hughes had become the ghoulish recluse that history would remember. He was only 63, but looked thirty years older. Emaciated, with freakishly long hair and nails," he went so far as to purchase a local TV station simply so he could dictate its programming, which usually involved playing the same movie over and over and over and over.[4] The breakdown is horrific to witness and is one of the most memorable of the director's career.

A common theme in Scorsese's work is one of collapse, yet for a few brief moments, it almost appears as if *The Aviator* will buck the trend. Hughes manages to break free of the snare his mind has set him in and attends a Senate hearing Brewster has staged to embarrass the mogul. Instead, the billionaire playboy lifts himself up and walks out of the hearings triumphant, then goes on to pilot his massive Hercules aircraft on its one and only flight. These are, by any measure, major victories.

Yet before he has even a few moments to bask in these glories, he sees men in white gloves seeming to surround him. Whether they are real or not, we don't know, but they terrify him. Something snaps. He sees great things ahead but cannot reconcile that with his fear of these men. He begins to repeat to himself, "The way of the future. The way of the future. The way of the future. The way of the future." His *real* collapse is yet to come, a terrible reminder that the most difficult battles we face are the ones waged inside us.

CONCLUSION AND IMPACT

The Aviator was a tremendous critical success, receiving eleven Academy Award nominations and winning five, including Best Supporting Actress for Cate Blanchett. It also won Best Film at the BAFTAs and Best Picture at the Golden Globes. For both Blanchett and DiCaprio, the film added credence to the argument that both are among the greatest performers of this generation. Schoonmaker was again awarded for her work as editor, a reminder of her importance in Scorsese's oeuvre. Finally, it allowed Scorsese to indulge in his love of old cinema, showcasing how Hughes made *Hell's Angels* as well as playing with color to emulate the two-strip and three-strip Technicolor of the period.

But more important than critical accolades is what *The Aviator* did for the director's working relationship with Leonardo DiCaprio. Following *Casino*, De Niro ceased to be Scorsese's go-to actor. This wasn't a conscious choice on the director's part; it was merely a combination of circumstance and age. De Niro was lined up to be in *Gangs of New York*, for example, but production delays caused scheduling conflicts that could not be worked out.[5] He was asked to take a lead role in *The Departed*, too, as either Frank Costello or police Captain

Queenan, but turned it down to direct his own film, *The Good Shepherd*.[6] He finally returned to Scorsese's work after a twenty-four-year absence with 2019's *The Irishman*.

With this picture, Scorsese found another performer willing to put in the work and reach the depths of emotional complexity he found in De Niro. He and DiCaprio would go on to make three more pictures together after this, each markedly different than the other, also much like his work with De Niro. But unlike the director's work with De Niro, the next collaboration between Scorsese and DiCaprio would finally net Martin Scorsese his elusive Academy Award for Best Director.

21

THE DEPARTED
(2006)

FILM DETAILS

RELEASE DATE: September 26, 2006
WRITTEN BY: William Monahan
STARRING: Leonardo DiCaprio, Matt Damon, Jack Nicholson, Mark Wahlberg, Martin Sheen, Vera Farmiga
RUNNING TIME: 151 minutes

ABOUT THE FILM

If it takes a star-studded cast and plot-heavy picture to finally get Martin Scorsese an Oscar for Best Director, so be it. Despite being another film with a focus on the criminal underworld, *The Departed* doesn't bear much resemblance to previous Scorsese crime pictures. It's a remake of the 2002 Hong Kong thriller *Infernal Affairs*, which won critical acclaim and a slew of Asian cinema awards upon release. It even spawned two sequels. Scorsese's version adheres closely to the original's tight plot, moving the setting to Boston and loosely basing the crime boss on real-life mobster Whitey Bulger but otherwise leaving the story beats intact. The result is a narrative-dense picture lighter on the deeper character exploration typical of the director's work.

In *The Departed*, police cadets Billy Costigan (Leonardo DiCaprio) and Colin Sullivan (Matt Damon) graduate the academy and enter the state police at roughly the same time. Costigan's unsavory family background prompts Captain Oliver Queenan (Martin Sheen) and Sergeant Sean Dignam (Mark Wahlberg) to put Costigan in deep undercover, stripping him of his identity so he can successfully infiltrate a gang led by Frank Costello (Jack Nicholson), *the* Boston crime boss. What they don't realize is that Sullivan has been working for Costello since he was a child, and with Sullivan quickly rising through the ranks, that gives Costello a huge edge over the police. Queenan, Dignam, and others know there is a mole in the state police; they just don't know who it is—and it's Sullivan who is tasked with finding him. In other words, his job is to root out himself. Meanwhile, both Sullivan and Costello know there is a police informant somewhere in the gang—Costigan—but no one knows *his* identity, either. Through an intricate chess match of deception, Costigan grows closer to Costello, Sullivan grows closer to discovering who Costigan is (and vice versa), and it all completely implodes when Costigan discovers that crime boss Costello had been an FBI informant all along. After a series of moves and countermoves, Costello's men kill Queenan; Sullivan shoots and kills Costello; Costigan discovers that Sullivan is the mole and attempts to take him in, only to be killed for his efforts; then Sullivan is hailed as a hero, only for *him* to be killed by Dignam. And that's only skimming the surface. Needless to say, there is a lot going on.

ANALYSIS

Are we defined by our deeds? Do our intentions matter, or does that only matter if someone else *knows* our intentions? And to what extent does someone else's view alter who we really are? *The Departed* is one of the most plot-heavy pictures of Scorsese's career. For a director whose work is often typified by narratives that are less driven by plot than they are by character exploration and episodic storytelling, this picture's narrative tapestry demands close attention throughout. You can't drop in in the middle. The story beats, complex character relationships, and twists and turns represent the kind of traditional story Scorsese normally eschews.

Gripping as the plot is, however, beneath its intrigue and suspense is a film concerned with examining the notions of trust; betrayal; truth; lies; and, most of all, identity. And while pure plot isn't in Scorsese's wheelhouse, those themes certainly are:

> The world I came from was very much based on loyalty and trust, and even beyond family ties; it comes from the old Sicilian world where godparents were as

important as blood relatives. And I think that's why so many of the stories I've done are rooted in a kind of tribal behavior that has to do with betrayal. When a person does "betray" the other—he or she—why does that happen? What puts that person very often in a place where they have no choice, they couldn't do otherwise—and where the decision is not good either way—that's very interesting to me.[1]

Both Costigan and Sullivan are central to these themes, though they permeate every other character, as well. Through its crime-driven thrills, *The Departed* explores the masks we wear, the different people we can be depending on circumstances and surroundings, and how that affects our relationships with others. One of the first ways it does this is through introducing the idea of code switching. The term itself is not used in the picture, but the concept is. Code switching is when someone moves effortlessly between two languages or ways of speaking, often dependent on context. The term is a linguistic one but in recent years has come to be part of discussions on culture and culture clashes, especially among those who float between differing social classes or ethnic groups. "Many of us subtly, reflexively change the way we express ourselves all the time. We're hop-scotching between different cultural and linguistic spaces and different parts of our own identities—sometimes within a single interaction," journalist Gene Demby observed.[2] Think of the person whose Southern drawl is more pronounced when home among family but that disappears in business contexts, or the person of color who speaks one way when among fellow people of color and another when with people of other ethnic groups (a practice so common, comedians Keegan-Michael Key and Jordan Peele made it a mainstay on their acclaimed sketch show *Key and Peele*). Code switching is especially common among those who have left deeply ethnic or cultural communities, often employed out of a desire to leave behind the past, out of shame, or simply to fit in with a new community.

When Costigan is first called into Queenan's office, Dignam drills him about his life and background. One of the things he zeroes in on is whether Costigan spoken differently when home with his father in South Boston when compared to when he spent time on the upper-class North Shore with his mother. And naturally, he did. From a plot perspective, this gives them a good reason to choose Costigan for their deep-undercover assignment. He's already adept at fitting in as a so-called Southie, or poor resident of South Boston. He can change his manner on the fly depending on who he's talking to, essential in what he's being asked to do. Beyond the plot, it's also instructive about who Costigan is and the neighborhood he comes from. He aspired to escape, to rise above the petty crooks and criminals that line his family tree. Still, he knows that to be accepted in that rough community means being one of them. It means putting on false faces and pretending he is something he is not in order to remain part of the group. It *also* means pretending he's not a Southie when among his higher-class kin, too, acting in a way that perhaps does not come naturally to him in order to successfully navigate a world he does not belong to. This is the complicated realm of code switching.

For Costigan, though it helps him in his undercover work, it also serves to confuse his sense of self. Who is he, really? Is he the working-class young man who escaped his poor neighborhood and became something more than a street thug? Is he a dedicated police officer playing a role? Or is he a fraud, someone pretending to be "better" than the place he was born but destined to remain what he's always been: an unimportant member of a lower rung of society? There are no answers to these questions, not even for Costigan himself. The deeper he gets into his assignment, the more uncertain he becomes about where he belongs. Maybe he's a great police officer waiting to rise above it all. Maybe what Dignam told him is correct: He's just a future thug from a family of thugs. Maybe he's all of it. Maybe he's none of it.

Sullivan's sense of self is clearer. Groomed as a young boy by the allure of Costello's power and influence, Sullivan doesn't appear to doubt who he is and why he is with the police. His role is to further Costello's interests. He came from the South Boston streets, yes, but like Costello, he believes he's smarter than those working-class shlubs. (Henry Hill expresses similar aloofness in *GoodFellas*.) And under Costello's tutelage, the lines aren't merely blurred between cop and criminal. There *are* no lines. "When you decide to be something, you can be it. That's what they don't tell you in the church," Costello tells him. "When I was your age, they'd say you could become cops or criminals. Today what I'm saying to you is this: When you're facing a loaded gun, what's the difference?"

Sullivan's choice of apartment plays into this idea. That his apartment has a clear view of the golden dome of the Massachusetts State House is important symbolism, both with relation to the film's themes of corruption and vice and for Sullivan himself. That gold dome is an aspiration for him, something that represents what he knows he can never be: legitimate, honorable, just. That's not to say the government is any of these things—much of *The Departed* makes clear it is anything but—but in Sullivan's eyes, having the dome at a distance but still visible is layered with meaning. It makes legitimacy and power seem attainable yet just out of reach. Living there is like hanging a favorite idol on your wall: "This is someone I aspire to be." For the audience, the suggestion is otherwise.

Having Sullivan looking over the State House instead brings to mind corruption and the corrosiveness of power and the reasons so many distrust government.

Part of this choice comes from the isolation inherent in poor urban communities, especially ethnic urban communities. The extent to which street toughs and organized crime can influence the character of a neighborhood is spelled out in the opening lines of narration, as Costello tells us, "I don't want to be a product of my environment. I want my environment to be a product of me." As he says this, we see footage of street fights (reminiscent of the opening scene of *Who's That Knocking at My Door?*), lines of police in the streets, civil unrest. South Boston is a character unto itself. The picture isn't focused on unpeeling what life is like there—there is no focus on everyday life as a Southie and little attention paid to regular people in the community—yet the influence of the neighborhood permeates everything. It's written onto the skin of the characters. It's etched into their bones. We see this throughout the director's work, especially in his crime pictures, though it's also present in movies like *After Hours*, in which Paul Hackett takes a short cab ride within his own city and yet ends up in a world that is all but alien to him, populated by a people and local culture he does not know how to navigate.

That's South Boston and the people who live there. It's a world unto itself. It's also why Sullivan plants himself within view of the State House rather than in his own neighborhood. It's an exercise in faking it until you make it. Costigan can only survive in the world of South Boston because he's not just a cop; he's *from* that world. He is uniquely qualified to fit in. And most important of all, he aspires to be better than his origins, which makes him easy to manipulate. When Sergeant Dignam reads him the riot act about his family's unsavory past, it feels relentless and unfair, as if Costigan is being held accountable for the actions of others. But it's *meant* to feel that way. We have to accept the idea that he would be willing to throw away respectability and stability in order to operate in deep undercover. He's told in no uncertain terms that he won't last in the police force—not because he's incapable but because a host of factors make him unsuitable for life in uniform. He'll be compromised. He'll be driven away. He'll never earn the respect of his peers. If he actually wants to do some good, Dignam convinces him, it will have to entail going back to his roots as a street kid. This means throwing away the idea of appearances and accepting the notion of looking like he never escaped his community.

Costigan is not driven by pride. He's pragmatic. He recognizes that identity is something malleable; it's not something we can necessarily control because so much of what we think of as our identity is based not on how we see ourselves but on how others see us. He really is just some kid from a South Boston family of criminals. Maybe Dignam is right. In the eyes of the world, maybe that's all he'll ever be. So he agrees to throw away his success in pursuit of the greater good.

Roger Ebert observed that, for both Costigan and Sullivan, their act is so thorough and so ingrained in their day-to-day life, it's difficult to excise it from what we see on-screen—to the credit of Leonardo DiCaprio and Matt Damon, who must provide layers of performance in order to present the honesty such compounded *dishonesty* demands in order to be convincing. "It is in the nature of the movies that we believe most characters are acting or speaking for themselves," Ebert wrote. "But in virtually every moment of this movie, except for a few key scenes, they are not. Both actors convey this agonizing inner conflict so that we can sense and feel it, but not see it; they're not waving flags to call attention to their deceptions."[3]

The layers of mistrust and the idea that no one is who they seem permeates everything, even one-off bit players. A priest, for example, appearing to sit in judgment of Costello and his crew, yet a priest who moments later is revealed to have been abusing young boys (a real-life scandal outlined in detail in the brilliant *Spotlight* in 2015). Or when Costigan and Dr. Madolyn Madden (Vera Farmiga), the psychiatrist treating Costigan and dating Sullivan, discuss the harm and value of lying, their conversation is as much a metacommentary on the film itself as it is an insight into the characters. "If you lie, you'll have an easier time getting what you want," Dr. Madden tells Costigan, and though she's talking about his request for Valium, the statement serves as a broader comment on the film's narrative. Everything in this movie is false. Everyone is playing multiple roles, to the point where some aren't sure of who they really are.

Costigan's ability to fake it, his natural code switching, is evident during his therapy session. As the pair talk about lying and truth, the scene crosscuts with Costigan acting as an accomplice to murder, meeting with Captain Queenan and Sergeant Dignam, and working through mental anguish at home as he confronts the things he has to do while undercover. It's a remarkable bit of out-of-continuity editing that goes a long way toward underscoring the degree to which he must walk between worlds.

Still, Costigan is smart. He understands how the neighborhood works. Getting close to Costello means getting on his radar without getting himself killed—and in the criminal underworld, getting noticed is a good way to get killed. But he stirs up just the right kind of trouble and lands himself in a room with Costello, which is just one passage in the larger maze he must navigate. Scorsese himself knows this well, having witnessed this kind of street politics from his apartment window in Little Italy. Swap New York for Boston, swap Italians for the Irish, and the gist is the same. Make too great a name for yourself on the street without the sanction of the local boss, and it's trouble.

Or better yet, make *no* name for yourself. Because that's the paradoxical thing about a picture so intent on the idea of identity: These characters are tearing their souls to pieces to shape how they are seen, yet the most important thing for *all* of them is to not be seen at all. Such is the nature of identity.

In the end, virtually all the main characters, save Dignam and Dr. Madden, are killed, some justifiably, some not. If there is a lesson here, perhaps it's less about truth, trust, and betrayal as it is about one simple idea: There is nothing more important than being true to who you really are. Anything else is a death sentence, figuratively or otherwise. For a director who has repeatedly struggled through box-office bombs and studio interference to stay true to who he is as a creator, surely that message resonated.

CONCLUSION AND IMPACT

The Departed is rarely listed among Scorsese's best works. It is as of this writing not considered a classic, modern or otherwise, and is never uttered in conversations of the best films of all time. Still, it got Martin Scorsese over the hump.

Prior to *The Departed*, Scorsese had been nominated for Best Director in the Academy Awards five times, including for two of the movies widely considered among the best of all time, *Raging Bull* and *GoodFellas*. For *Raging Bull*, he lost to Robert Redford's *Ordinary People*; for *GoodFellas*, to Kevin Costner's *Dances with Wolves*, widely considered one of the biggest snubs in Oscar history. He was also nominated for his work on *The Last Temptation of Christ*, *Gangs of New York*, and *The Aviator*. (Note that Best Director is not the same as Best Picture. *Taxi Driver*, for example, was nominated for Best Picture but not for Best Director.)

So when he finally won for *The Departed*, close to forty years after his debut, there was both a sigh of relief as well as some whispering that maybe the Academy was merely making up for previous slights. Graham King, producer on the picture, shot "lasers out of his eyes at the reporter who suggested backstage at the Academy Awards that the crime drama might have been a lesser work from its newly anointed Oscar-winning director."[4] In fact, after getting passed over several times, including exhaustive awards campaigns for *Gangs of New York* in 2002 and *The Aviator* in 2004, Scorsese "had come to terms with the fact that the Academy doesn't honor the kinds of films he makes, and his publicist Leslee

Scorsese's return to the world of organized crime not only featured a star-studded cast, but it also finally landed him his long-awaited Oscar for Best Director. *Warner Bros./Photofest*

Dart made it clear at the outset that he wouldn't be jumping through the usual hoops" lobbying for an award with *The Departed*.[5] Yet buzz preceded it, buzz that suggested regardless if *The Departed* was a classic, it was time to finally honor Martin Scorsese: "So obvious was this outcome that Scorsese's film-maker pals—Francis Ford Coppola, George Lucas and Steven Spielberg—were tapped to present the honor that night."[6]

So did he even deserve the Oscar for this picture? Of course he did. That *The Departed* does not sit with his very best does not matter. Comparing Martin Scorsese's work to *his own work* is almost unfair because by the time he did *The Departed* he had already done pictures like *Taxi Driver*, *Raging Bull*, and *GoodFellas*. Take any midtier picture by Alfred Hitchcock or Akira Kurosawa, and you still might have some of the most outstanding directing work of the year. Movies like *Suspicion* and *Dial M for Murder* are fantastic, but stacked next to the best by the same creator—*Rear Window*, *Psycho*, *The Birds*, *Vertigo*, and so on—they seem like lesser movies. Such is the case here. *The Departed* was going against *Babel*, *Letters from Iwo Jima* (directed by Clint Eastwood), *The Queen*, and *United 93*. All good movies, but the only other strong case for the award is for Eastwood's war movie. So Martin Scorsese won the award because he *earned* it. It took a while, sure, but he got there, and he deserved it. That he got there with a picture that *seemed* like a crime movie but that was actually a movie about being something we aren't ended up being a great setup for his next picture, too, a genre film that wound up being his most probing psych eval since *Bringing Out the Dead* and a picture very much about being something you're not.

22

SHUTTER ISLAND
(2010)

FILM DETAILS

RELEASE DATE: February 19, 2010
WRITTEN BY: Laeta Kalogridis
STARRING: Leonardo DiCaprio, Mark Ruffalo, Ben Kingsley, Michelle
Williams, Emily Mortimer
RUNNING TIME: 139 minutes

ABOUT THE FILM

For most directors, *Shutter Island* would be one of the better movies of their career, a well-crafted, gripping thriller with a shocking twist. For Martin Scorsese, it's a lesser film, only worth a cursory chapter in an otherwise lengthy summation of his career. I'm not doing that, mind you. *Shutter Island* is as worthy of dissection as any other Scorsese picture, one rich with layered characters and themes that run well beneath the movie's surface trappings. It's such a different kind of picture for him, however, that it's easy to overlook how it fits into the grand sweep of his work.

Based on the novel of the same name by Dennis Lehane (*Mystic River*), *Shutter Island* sinks viewers into the journey of supposed US marshal Edward "Teddy" Daniels (Leonardo DiCaprio) or, more accurately, Andrew Laeddis, a man who killed his mentally disturbed wife after she drowned their three children and who as a result also suffered a debilitating mental breakdown. Now he imagines himself as Teddy, paired up with Marshal Chuck Aule (Mark Ruffalo) to first find a missing patient at the Shutter Island facility for the criminally insane, then to root out a conspiracy involving government mind-control experiments. All of this is in his head, however, revealed to both Teddy and the audience in a twist ending worthy of M. Night Shyamalan. His partner is actually Dr. Sheehan, colleague of Dr. John Cawley (Ben Kingsley). The pair were making one last effort to free Teddy of his delusions; otherwise he would undergo a lobotomy. Their efforts briefly work, but in the end, Teddy lapses back into delusion—or does he? As with most of *Shutter Island*, the answer is not always clear upon first viewing.

(Note that, due to the nature of this film, most characters have two names. For the purposes of this chapter, I generally refer to them by the name Laeddis [a.k.a., Edward "Teddy" Daniels] *perceives* them to have because those are the names the characters are referred to throughout most of the movie. This includes his own name.)

ANALYSIS

A man is his experiences. There is no running from them. There is no shutting them away. We can only face them or go mad trying to hide from them. But often, the guilt of trying to hide from them can be so overpowering it can break us. In many ways, *Shutter Island* is a bog standard "twist" thriller, the sort of pure genre picture Martin Scorsese tends to avoid unless business arrangements or an impending career crisis forces his hand toward the mainstream (e.g., *The Color of Money* and *Cape Fear*). What boils beneath the surface is the real draw, however, because it not only lets Scorsese tinker with a modern take on classic noir and gothic thriller, but it also allows him to delve into character exploration in a way he'd never done before.

Shutter Island is a rare Scorsese film where the idea of spoilers actually matters. Similar to such pictures as *The Sixth Sense*, an integral part of the experience is not knowing what is coming and then, on second viewing, seeing the picture with new eyes. Many (if not most) Scorsese works are more concerned with the journey than any particular destination. We're not on the edge of our seats wondering if LaMotta will win his next fight or if Hughes will get his "Spruce Goose" to fly. It's the character study that is important in these works, the life experiences they explore, the worlds and people they help us understand.

Here, because the picture is told from Teddy's perspective, a character study is inherently flawed, coming as it does through an unreliable narrator. At the very least it requires repeated viewings to get to the core of what drives him—and what drives him is the classic Scorsese anguish: guilt. Driven by mental illness, Teddy's wife set fire to their apartment. Rather than seek help for her, they moved to a lakeside cottage to seek peace. There, she drowned their three children. In his grief, he shot and killed her. These compounded layers of tragedy drive him so mad that he becomes disconnected from reality. At the start of the picture, however, we know none of this. Like Teddy, we believe he is a federal investigator searching for a missing woman who (of course) drowned her children.

The very first lines of the picture ring differently once you know the truth: "Pull yourself together, Teddy. It's just water. It's a *lot* of water." Initially, this just appears to be seasickness, not an uncommon trait to give a character. When he arrives at the docks of Shutter Island, the guards are strapping weapons and looking ready for trouble, despite no evident danger—because the real danger is Teddy himself, though he doesn't know it yet. When he mentions to Deputy Warden McPherson (John Carroll Lynch) that his boys seem on edge, the Deputy Warden says, "Right now, we all are." It's the truth, too, but not for the reasons Teddy thinks. *He* is the one they fear. He's the reason they are ready for trouble.

This entire song and dance is an elaborate ruse, an experiment to snap Teddy out of his psychosis and return him to reality. How much we see on-screen is real and how much is imaginary is never quite clear. In some instances, we're seeing Teddy interact with real people playing roles for the benefit of the experiment. In others, the people we see do not exist. He and his "partner," Chuck Aule (who is actually Teddy's psychiatrist, Dr. Sheehan) are taken to see Dr. John Cawley, the head psychiatrist at the facility. A dangerous patient has escaped, he tells them, and the pair are tasked with tracking her down. The patient, Rachel Solando (Emily Mortimer), allegedly drowned her own children. It's as if Dr. Cawley is planting seeds in Teddy's head, hoping to get him to recognize himself in the story. Somehow, this woman disappeared from her cell. The doctor says it's like Rachel "evaporated," an appropriate descriptor, given the nature of Teddy's wife's crimes. He also explains to Teddy that Rachel has created a fictional reality around herself, believing the doctors and nurses and staff around her are actually cops and delivery people and others. Teddy asks, "How is it possible the truth never gets through to her?" He doesn't realize he's asking about himself.

The answer to his question, of course, is that feeling guilt over tragic failures can be the unseen hand guiding a person's thoughts and actions. Despite the theme being so prevalent in the director's work, rarely is it as *direct* as this. Scorsese characters are wracked with guilt but often don't know why. They sense that they are sinful in some way but either cannot face it directly (Charlie in *Mean Streets*), shift blame onto others (Jake in *Raging Bull*), or feel guilt for things they did not do (Paul in *After Hours*). Frank Pierce's guilt in *Bringing Out the Dead* is the closest to that experienced by Teddy, rooted in a failure on his part to save someone who could have been saved. Teddy's is further compounded not only by the fact that it was his *children* he lost—three of them, all young—and that he could have prevented it had he gotten the help his wife needed but also by the fact that he took his wife's life as a result. It was more a mercy killing than one stemming from hurt and anger, but to perceive so much blood on your hands? "Out, damn'd spot! Out, I say!"[1]

Everything he sees and experiences over the course of the picture is a manifestation of this crushing burden. When a storm hits while Teddy and Chuck are exploring a graveyard, the storm is Teddy's subconscious screaming at him, imploring him to either snap back to reality or run further from it. He's inundated with images of water, images of the sea, of crashing waves and the quiet violence of nature. These are contrasted with visions of fire and ash, of clouds of cigarette smoke that seem to have lives of their own, of matches that act as daggers in the dark. Even in his fantasy world, he cannot escape the tragedy that transformed him. Hints of it appear repeatedly, symbolism woven into the seemingly ordinary. Even the skies pour down the very thing used to kill his children. Curious, then, that Dr. Cawley and Dr. Sheehan (as Chuck) seem to encourage him to plunge further into his fantasy. That's the one thing Teddy is right about: They *are* conducting experiments on the mind—on *his* mind. "Crazy people are the perfect subjects," he says. "They talk; no one listens." But here, people are listening intently.

While in a mausoleum, Chuck seems to urge on Teddy's delusions. "Everything about this place stinks," he says, offering a laundry list of suspicious activities that seem to point to the island being some grand government experiment. He all but urges him to question everything he sees. This would seem to push him further into madness rather than draw him out of it. He does it again later, after the storm (if there ever actually was a storm), when he urges Teddy to go to ward C. He pushes Teddy further into the fictional world he's created for himself, presumably in the hope of making him *see* that it's fictional. That appears to be his entire MO. When he offers Teddy a copy of the intake form for Andrew Laeddis, the imagined arsonist who set the nonexistent fire that Teddy believes killed his wife, the papers are actually Teddy's. Chuck is attempting to trigger a break from the fantasy.

This happens again when Teddy confronts Rachel Solando, who has supposedly reappeared after being missing for a day. She's actually a nurse playing a role, but Teddy doesn't realize that. Instead, he believes she is a deranged patient who has mistaken him for her dead husband. "My Jim is dead, so who the fuck are you?" she demands. It's a layered question. To Teddy, it appears to be part of the trauma Rachel is experiencing. Once you know Rachel is just playing a role, it seems to just be part of her act. In reality, it's both of these things, but most important of all, it's an honest question. It's an attempt to force Teddy to think about who he really is. It's a push toward the truth. Who *is* he?

As Teddy searches ward C for the truth behind Shutter Island, he encounters a patient in solitary, George Noyce (Jackie Earle Haley). This prompts a discussion about truth and deception. "This isn't about the truth," Noyce tells him. "It's about you." Noyce questions him about Chuck, suggesting his partner is not all that he seems. "I trust this man," Teddy insists. But Noyce knows what's really happening and says, "Then they've already won."

Teddy already mistrusts the caretakers of the island, deeply so, but for the wrong reasons. The audience can't trust them, either, in no small part because the reality we're offered is often twisted and difficult to believe. Teddy's curious ride with the warden late in the picture, for example: The warden seems to try to open Teddy's mind to violence, suggesting it's a basic part of human nature and trying to tease out his capacity for horrific acts. If Teddy is in truth a deranged man disconnected from reality, then why take this approach? Or was most of this conversation in his mind? We know some of the things he does and endures are real. He really does beat up a fellow patient; he blows up Dr. Cawley's car; he assaults a guard. These things really happen. But he also has phantom conversations. We know the warden is real, but perhaps that conversation wasn't. After all, a lengthy conversation with the "real" Rachel Solando (this time played by Patricia Clarkson) never actually took place because the person doesn't exist. And he sees phantom versions of his deceased wife (Michelle Williams) again and again. Truth and fiction are tightly wound together because they are also wound together in his mind: the fire caused by his wife, the false story of an arsonist, the drowning, the imaginary patient, and on and on. It's all layered together into a tangled knot, with every action, every memory, every conversation having several meanings. The use of multiple meanings cascades over the picture until even for the viewer true thoughts and fiction become a difficult-to-decipher blend. When Teddy confronts Dr. Cawley about the Shutter Island operation—experimenting with the human mind as part of a government operation, or so Teddy believes—Cawley responds indignantly, "I've built something valuable here, and valuable things have a way of being misunderstood in their own time. Everyone wants a quick fix; they always have. I'm trying to do something people, yourself included, don't understand, and I'm not going to give up without a fight."

This response is perfectly in keeping with what Teddy is accusing the doctor of doing, but upon second and third viewing, it's clear that Cawley is actually speaking about his attempts to treat Teddy and that his comments are intended for his fellow doctors, not Teddy himself. His work really *is* misunderstood, as the other doctors don't believe in what he's doing. He really is trying to avoid a quick fix (i.e., medication). This is all a grand experiment, one last chance at shaking Teddy from his delusions. And it works, at least momentarily. Once pushed beyond the limits of credulity, Teddy comes to his senses and realizes he's actually Andrew Laeddis, a man whose wife murdered their children and a man who in turn killed her.

In the picture's final moments, however, it appears that the effect was only temporary. Andrew again begins speaking to Dr. Sheehan as if he's Teddy and the doctor is Chuck, hinting at the same conspiracy that had already consumed him. Dr. Sheehan is heartbroken at the relapse. But as with all in *Shutter Island*, things are not as they seem. Teddy drops a clue with his final words to Sheehan: "Which would be worse: To live as a monster or to die as a good man?" As soon as he asks the question and begins to walk away, Dr. Sheehan stands and calls for him, "Teddy?" But Andrew doesn't respond to the name Teddy. He just walks on because in that moment he is Andrew, his real self. He gives one last look to Dr. Cawley. His eyes are clear. He is not seeing anything that isn't there. This sudden regression was an act. He's made a choice. He's going to die as a good man rather than live as a monster: lobotomized, empty, a shell of who he was, but a good man, nonetheless.

In Scorsese pictures, escaping one's past is a trick few can manage. The past is defined by past deeds, misdeeds, and ill-made decisions, and it hangs over Scorsese protagonists like a vulture. Even as far back as *Who's That Knocking at My Door?* the Girl finds that a past for which she bears no blame still affects her life in a negative way. In a very Catholic way, the only way to purge these past sins, real or imagined, is through sacrifice. That's how you absolve yourself. Paul Hackett is entombed as a statue (*After Hours*). Sam Bowden's family is torn apart before he can move past his sins (*Cape Fear*). Henry Hill gives up having all his desires fulfilled just to cut ties from his past (*GoodFellas*). Paradoxically, Frank Pierce has to let someone die in order to lift his guilt (*Bringing Out the Dead*). And of course, the ultimate sacrifice is Jesus Christ's in *The Last*

Temptation of Christ, one made not for himself but for all of mankind. Teddy's decision is not so broad and sweeping, but it comes from a similar place. "He was literally taking the weight of the cross, that character, the guilt that he had, what he did, what he experienced in his life," Scorsese said. "That guilt was real, and that is interesting to me."[2]

That *Shutter Island* gave the director an opportunity to explore a character's debilitating guilt through the lens of classic film genres—noir, gothic horror, procedural thriller—was in some ways just a bonus. Few directors are as steeped in film history as Scorsese. He is a walking, talking list of obscure references to little-seen pictures. A chance to dabble with some of those techniques and to give nods to those older films, especially in a genre he doesn't usually work in, is an appealing one.

But ultimately, for Scorsese it always comes down to character and theme. He may not typically make this kind of thriller, but if the theme is there, it becomes a Scorsese picture. *Shutter Island* is a picture steeped in Catholic imagery. It's less overt here than in other pictures. There are no crosses, no crucifixes, no rosary beads, but the bloody search for redemption is. "The most important legacy of my Catholicism is guilt," the director once said. "A major helping of guilt, like garlic."[3] Andrew Laeddis (a.k.a., US marshal Edward "Teddy" Daniels) can probably say the same.

CONCLUSION AND IMPACT

Despite *Shutter Island* being a picture seemingly well out of Scorsese's wheelhouse, or at least what most people would consider his wheelhouse, it ended up being a major financial success, netting nearly $295 million worldwide on its $80 million budget. Only the *Wolf of Wall Street* would earn more money (*not* adjusted for inflation). It was a hit with international audiences. Critically it was more of a mixed bag, but genre pictures had never been his forte, no matter how well crafted. As good as pictures like *The Color of Money* and *Cape Fear* are, they don't *bleed* Scorsese. He made them his, yes, but they aren't representative of what he does best. His next film wouldn't be, either, yet it would still manage to turn a shockingly unexpected genre from him—a family-friendly adventure—into a colorful, dynamic window into his soul.

23

HUGO
(2011)

FILM DETAILS

RELEASE DATE: October 10, 2011 (New York Film Festival), November
23, 2011 (wide release)
WRITTEN BY: John Logan
STARRING: Asa Butterfield, Chloë Grace Moretz, Ben Kingsley, Sacha
Baron Cohen
RUNNING TIME: 126 minutes

ABOUT THE FILM

A PG-rated family adventure that leans heavily on special effects, children with parent issues, and a slightly otherworldly sense of wonder, *Hugo* may as well be a Steven Spielberg film. It certainly has all the surface trappings of one. Yet dig deeper, and this unlikely entry into the Scorsese catalog suddenly seems tailor-made for the director, who was in his late sixties when it was made.

Adapted from the book *The Invention of Hugo Cabret* by Brian Selznick (who is distantly related to legendary producer David O. Selznick), both tell the story of Hugo Cabret (Asa Butterfield), an orphan living in the walls of a French train station. Hugo has no home and no family, but what he does have is a broken mechanical man, an automaton that is his last link to his deceased father. A cranky old toy shopkeeper (Ben Kingsley) catches him stealing parts, which the boy uses to repair the automaton, and insists he work to atone for his theft. Hugo befriends the man's goddaughter Isabelle (Chloë Grace Moretz), and together the pair uncover the mystery of the automaton only to reveal another mystery: how the mechanical man is linked to Isabelle's godfather. They discover that he is Georges Méliès, a real-life, celebrated film pioneer who created hundreds of groundbreaking early films, including *A Trip to the Moon* (1902) and *A Fantastic Voyage* (1904). Once beloved but now forgotten by the public, Méliès lives in obscurity, thinking his art is forgotten—but thanks to Hugo and Isabelle, he is rediscovered, and his work is finally given the honor it deserves. Though Hugo and his adventures are fictional, Méliès's story is very real, including his collapse into anonymity and subsequent rediscovery. Appropriate, then, that a student of film history like Martin Scorsese should direct a picture that is as much a love letter to early cinema as it is a family-friendly adventure story.

ANALYSIS

There comes a point in a person's life when they begin thinking about their legacy, about what they will leave behind, about the things that will define them after they are gone. This is especially true of creative people, who live and breathe and exist through their creations. *Hugo* is a picture about many things— loss, isolation, family—but most of all, it's a film about legacy.

That Martin Scorsese would explore this subject matter in the latter stages of his career is hardly surprising. His first feature had been released forty-five years prior. At the time he made *Hugo*, he was quickly approaching his seventies. Scorsese is not the type to stop looking ahead to new projects; his ceaseless work since *Hugo* is proof enough of that. Even as this is written, the director has several productions under way. However, he has always looked to the past, as well. No one has scrutinized Martin Scorsese's work as thoroughly as Martin Scorsese himself. Further, few in the industry have as much love, admiration, and knowledge of cinema history as he does. Combine that with our natural tendency to begin looking back as we get older and to start thinking about what we're going to leave behind, and the appeal of this PG-rated, family-friendly, Spielbergian adventure movie—perhaps the most un-Scorsese picture of his career—becomes apparent.

The primary legacy that takes center stage is that of Georges Méliès, an early pioneer of filmmaking who helped propel the new art form from a novelty into a true exploration of dreams and fantasies. When we first meet Kingsley's character, he appears to be nothing more than a bitter, old man to provide a foil for our plucky, young protagonist, a cliché from a thousand children's fables. He shows a strange interest in Hugo's notebook, but the interest could be anything. We've seen enough fables of this sort to guess it's probably something related to greed: a link to hidden wealth, perhaps, or maybe just the general disdain for children, a trait typical in stories such as this. But it doesn't take long for it to become apparent that Kingsley is not the standard cliché. His interest in Hugo—or more precisely, his interest in making Hugo go away—is rooted in a deep, unseen pain.

As Hugo and Isabelle probe further into mysteries Méliès does not wish them to discover, we learn why he feels such pain: The things he poured his soul into appear lost to time, destined to be forgotten. It's not merely that he was a success who has since been cast aside by the public, a once-renowned man now working in anonymity. That alone might be cause for bitterness. No, his pain runs much deeper than that. Méliès believes his life's work has been *destroyed*. Imagine such a shadow hanging over you. Imagine the makings of your very being wiped away without a trace. He would feel a shell of who he was, as if a piece of himself was missing, maybe the most vital piece. And indeed, that is how the Méliès of *Hugo* feels.

All this begins, however, with Hugo exploring his own legacy and that of his father (Jude Law, in a brief cameo). All he has left of his father is an automaton, a kind of clockwork figure that can draw pictures when it's working. These were (and remain) real creations dating back to ancient times. From the medieval era forward, the craft that went into these automatons took dramatic leaps forward, with some able to play musical instruments, write or draw, dance, and more. The real-life history of these devices is remarkable, and in the real world, Méliès really was an aficionado. In this fictional world, Hugo seeks to repair the automaton, hoping it will give him one last message from his father. They used to repair it together, so it symbolizes a shared creation, a legacy the two of them share. He wants to preserve a part of the past that represents an important aspect of his life.

Scorsese is no stranger to such efforts to preserve the past. He is the founder of the Film Foundation, a nonprofit devoted to film preservation and restoration. "Of all the arts, [film is] the most fragile," Scorsese said. "Very often we do find ourselves having to make the case for it—make the case that film is art, make the case to preserve the past and support the artists of the present."[1] The restoration and preservation of a beloved film by an influential director, the restoration and preservation of a beloved relic left behind by your father—these ideas each spring from the same place.

The past Hugo wishes to preserve isn't about physical objects, of course. Though he's adept with his hands, clockworks and automatons are not his real concern. The physical object is merely his last remaining connection to his father, the one touchstone he still has to the normal life of his youth, when he still had a parent who loved him, before being taken in and forced to work for an alcoholic uncle and before he then became a homeless boy living in the walls of a train station. The automaton is the last vestige of their relationship. Much as film made Scorsese who he is, this mechanical man made Hugo who he is. The boy's efforts may be personal, but they lead him down a path that intersects directly with Scorsese's real-world concerns about honoring and preserving the rich history of cinema. The automaton represents one thing for Hugo but something quite different to Isabelle's Papa Georges, the bitter, old toy stand proprietor. When he and Isabelle discover who Isabelle's godfather really is, they are astonished: not necessarily because they know his work—they don't—but because they had no idea he was a creative genius.

The pair learn that Papa Georges (a.k.a., Méliès) began doing stage magic but became enamored with the potential of film in 1895 after seeing a private showing of the Lumière brothers' cinematograph, an early camera and projector. He went on to create his own, and in 1896 he began making films—*hundreds* of them between then and 1913, films of wild imagination and increasing complexity, pioneering special effects and in-camera tricks and gaining international renown for the flights of fancy he put on-screen. But financial troubles eventually consumed him, he burned his sets and costumes, and his films were melted down to make shoe heels. Indeed, most of the facts of Méliès's life as depicted in *Hugo* are true. Some small details were changed—he was not found by a boy named Hugo, and he did not marry the actress Jehanne d'Alcy (Helen McCrory) until 1925, after he had stopped making movies—but the essentials are factual.

In the real world, it was in 1924, after writer Georges-Michel Coissac interviewed him for a book on French cinema, that his name was dragged back out of obscurity. That book was the first time the filmmaker's importance began to be recognized and his work rediscovered. The next few years were a time of renewal for Méliès, a time when newspapers and magazines began to profile the old master, and in 1929 a grand gala was held to celebrate his work, just as seen in *Hugo*. He spent the last eight years of his life beloved and honored for his art, which was very nearly forgotten.

So consider a man like Martin Scorsese being confronted by such a story. Set aside Scorsese's desire to preserve film history. Instead, look at him as a creator, as a man who expresses who he is through his art. How tragic must it be to consider your life's work being forgotten. How crushing an idea that must be. Until 2006, Scorsese's legacy appeared to be on course to be "The Best Director

Not Named Alfred Hitchcock or Stanley Kubrick Never to Win a Best Director Oscar." *The Departed* rectified that oversight. With that monkey off his back and the latter years of his career looming before him, it's little surprise that matters of legacy became important to him, even if only subconsciously. While the director was in the midst of filming *Hugo*, film critic Richard Schickel observed that Scorsese "says that at his age (sixty-eight during this flurry of activity), he more and more feels the pressure of time and his own mortality. So much to do, possibly so little time" and also noted that the director "worries about leaving enough money to ensure his children's future" because so much of his money is directed right back into his films or toward film preservation.[2]

There were times in Scorsese's career when he worried he'd never make a film again. The dark days of the late 1970s, when drugs fueled him, his health declined, and *New York, New York* was a box-office and critical bomb. Or most of the 1980s, when he struggled to get dream projects funded and relied on small scripts (*After Hours*) and commercial cash grabs (*The Color of Money*) to stay relevant. The fear of fading away from the work he loved so much had to have been a spiritual burden on the middle portion of his career. So *Hugo* is about not wanting to be forgotten. It's about the importance of that which we leave behind and of being recognized for it. It's about the parts of our soul we give to the world.

In *Hugo*, Méliès all but gives up after his muse—film—is taken from him. His days are modest drudgery at a train station. Simply evoking the memory of what he used to do is painful to him. When Hugo and Isabelle accidentally get into a chest containing many of his old drawings, he breaks down, calling Hugo cruel. Hugo does not understand why. He only knows he has somehow hurt the man. But for Méliès, seeing those old images is a painful reminder of a part of himself he believed was lost.

Creative people want to create. They *need* to create. They also wish for their creations to be recognized, even if they were created primarily for themselves. So when Hugo and Isabelle first show interest in Méliès' life work, he cannot embrace their interest because, as far as he knows, his life's work is gone. Without it, he is no longer the man he was. It's only when author René Tabard (Michael Stuhlbarg) enters the scene that things change. Tabard is not only a great student and fan of Méliès's, but he also actually owns a reel of *A Trip to the Moon*. He screens a copy for the children and d'Alcy. Méliès discovers that a piece of his legacy still remains. That alone is enough to awaken him.

And in those final moments of the picture, when it's revealed that after an exhaustive search, more than eighty of his films have been found (as of this writing, more than two hundred Méliès pictures have been discovered), Georges

Méliès is *himself* again, a purveyor of fantasy, a master of magic, a weaver of dreams—a man who has recaptured his legacy and who knows his place in the world is secure.

CONCLUSION AND IMPACT

Hugo was a first for Scorsese in many ways and not merely for being a family-friendly children's adventure. The CGI-heavy picture was also a 3-D production, a technique at the time often slammed as a trendy gimmick but that Scorsese embraced to beautiful result. "No one had ever shot like this in 3D before," producer Graham King told the *Hollywood Reporter*. "A small part of what's great about how Scorsese tells you a story is the way he moves those cameras, right? The tracking shot in *Goodfellas*, for example. I thought, if he does those kinds of tracking shots in 3D—wow. It'll be fantastic."[3]

The movie is peppered with the kind of small stories Scorsese delights in, too, including a whimsical romance between a pair of endearing regulars at the station (Frances de la Tour and Richard Griffiths), which is often played like a silent film, and the almost-tragic sadness of Sacha Baron Cohen's Inspector Gustave Dasté character, who pines for a florist (Emily Mortimer) and who masks the shame he feels for his war-crippled leg through authoritarian malice, though his heart isn't truly in it.

Critically, the picture was a hit, seen as a delightful surprise from a director generally associated with darker fare. *Hugo* earned eleven Academy Award nominations, including Best Picture and Best Director, winning five (mostly in technical categories), and also landed on a slew of critics' top-ten lists. Yet at the box office, Hugo bombed. On a budget exceeding $150 million, it barely scraped its way to a $185 million international take. After marketing costs and other factors, it was a net loss for the studio. "Let's just say that it hasn't been an easy few months for me," King said at the time. "There's been a lot of Ambien involved."[4]

In some ways *Hugo* marks the start of the final phase of Scorsese's career—and given the subject matter, that's appropriate. This is a director with nothing left to prove. All that's left is for him to tie a bow on his legacy before he shouts his final "Action!" Perhaps that's why his next picture would be one of his wildest and most carefree yet: a biopic on a scummy stock scammer that ended up being one of the biggest hits of his career.

THE WOLF OF WALL STREET (2013)

FILM DETAILS

RELEASE DATE: December 17, 2013
WRITTEN BY: Terence Winter
STARRING: Leonardo DiCaprio, Jonah Hill, Margot Robbie
RUNNING TIME: 180 minutes

ABOUT THE FILM

For all his pictures featuring unsavory characters operating on the wrong side of the law, depictions of pure, unadulterated, gleefully malicious greed are surprisingly rare in the Scorsese filmography. There is a light kiss of it in *GoodFellas*, but Henry is motivated more by the high of being a mobster than he is by the money. Greed is written all over *Casino*, yet Robert De Niro's character, "Ace," is more concerned with running a tight operation than he is squeezing dollars out of it for himself. The power is the draw, not the money. The scammers of *The Color of Money* do it for the hustle, not the cash. Even billionaire Howard Hughes in *The Aviator* was motivated more by a sense of adventure and accomplishment than he was by accumulating more wealth. Then along comes *The Wolf of Wall Street*, which dives headlong into a subject that had previously only been on the periphery of Scorsese's most common themes.

Based on the real-life story of stock scammer Jordan Belfort, who chronicled his rise and fall in an autobiography of the same name, *The Wolf of Wall Street* follows Belfort (Leonardo DiCaprio) as he and his cohorts at disgraced firm Stratton Oakmont—right-hand man Donnie Azoff (Jonah Hill) chief among them—rip off investors, take copious amounts of drugs, sleep with prostitutes, and generally engage in every form of debauchery imaginable before their white-collar crimes eventually catch up with them. After ripping off countless millions from investors on penny stocks, FBI investigator Patrick Denham (Kyle Chandler) takes Belfort down, shattering the young con man's marriage to Naomi Lapaglia (Margot Robbie) and toppling a firm that in just a few short years had earned one of the seediest reputations in an industry already known for immoral levels of greed.

Much like *The Aviator*, *The Wolf of Wall Street* was a pet project brought to Scorsese by DiCaprio, who won a bidding war against Brad Pitt for the rights to the story.[1] The film kicked around Hollywood for a few years, attached to several other directors (including Ridley Scott) before finally coming back to DiCaprio's first choice.

Ironically, given the subject matter of the movie, production company Red Granite was caught in a financial fraud scandal, allegedly moving around billions illegally. The story is still unfolding as of this writing and threatens to implicate a number of global high rollers. In addition to producers Joey Mc-Farland, Riza Aziz, and Jho Low, the "globe-spanning investigation also has implicated a former Malaysian prime minister, employees of a prestigious Wall Street investment bank, a member of the Fugees rap group and a top Republican fundraiser."[2] Though DiCaprio was gifted a Picasso painting by Low, which he has since returned, "It is believed DiCaprio, Scorsese and others involved in the film did not know the source of Red Granite's money."[3] And for their part, in 2017, Red Granite representatives insisted none of the funding for the film "was in any way illegitimate."[4] Still, when life imitates art . . .

ANALYSIS

Is it possible to sympathize with the unsympathetic? And is there anything to be learned from someone as deeply selfish as Jordan Belfort? "Greed, for the lack of a better word, is good. Greed is right, greed works. Greed clarifies, cuts through, and captures the essence of the evolutionary spirit. Greed, in all of its forms; greed for life, for money, for love, knowledge has marked the upward surge of mankind," said Gordon Gekko (Michael Douglas) in *Wall Street* (1987), Oliver

Stone's morally gray examination of 1980s' Wall Street culture that inspired just as many people to pursue a career in finance as it did repulse them.

There is not much gray in *The Wolf of Wall Street*, which examines some of the same ideas but in a much different way. Jordan Belfort makes little effort to justify or explain his pursuit of wealth and the voracious appetites it feeds. The film is presented in the same whirlwind, episodic, narration-driven style of *GoodFellas* and *Casino* but without the moral complexities of either. Belfort is, for lack of a better term, a dirtbag. Whereas Henry Hill is put off by the violent depths his colleagues will sink to and Sam "Ace" Rothstein struggles to maintain an air of respectability in his operations, Belfort cares for nothing beyond his next Quaalude or sexual encounter. Hill has little remorse in ripping people off, but he doesn't appear to take much joy in it, either. Rothstein knows he's manipulating high rollers in his casino, but that's the cost of doing business in an industry where both sides are knowingly playing one another. Belfort, on the other hand, knowingly targets vulnerable people down on their luck, gleefully takes their money, and flips them off as he does it. He seems to *enjoy* running people into the ground. He measures his value as a human being by his wealth. "Money doesn't just buy you a better life, better food, better cars, better pussy," he says. "It also makes you a better person."

Belfort gets his start under the tutelage of Mark Hanna (Matthew McConaughey), an eccentric Wall Street broker who waves away the idea that it's mutually beneficial for broker and client alike to make money on their investments. The only goal, he says, is to move money from your client's pocket into your own. Belfort takes this notion to heart. When he learns about the huge commissions generated by selling penny stocks—high-risk, low-cost stocks often associated with unproven new companies—he begins to build a firm focused entirely on pushing these highly profitable (for him) investments. Initially, he's not bilking the rich with these deals. The focus is on working-class people who can't afford to lose money on a bad investment. His first wife, Teresa Petrillo Belfort (Cristin Milioti), calls him out on it:

> "Wouldn't you feel better if you sold that stuff to rich people who could, like, afford to lose all that money?"
> "Of course, but rich people don't buy penny stocks. They just don't."
> "Why not?"
> (*in narration*) "Because they're too smart, that's why not."

This utter lack of respect for the people who provide a living for Belfort is evident from the start of the picture to the end. He pumps his fist when he hears a potential client's spouse has passed away, knowing that vulnerability makes them a good mark. He flips people off or feigns sexual assault while on the phone with them. The suicide of former employees gets but a casual, dismissive mention. When he breaks the fourth wall to explain to the audience how an IPO (initial public offering) works, he interrupts himself and says the details don't matter; all that matters is that they were making money hand over fist. He later interrupts another fourth-wall-breaking explanation when telling the audience how his scams worked. The clear message—and it's one that doesn't change throughout the picture—is that Belfort doesn't care about anything other than getting his. "There is no nobility in poverty," he tells his employees. "I have been a rich man, and I have been a poor man, and I'll choose rich every fucking time."

Typically, Scorsese films contain some kind of insight into the people on-screen, an examination of the human condition. Even if seen through the lives of deplorable people, he depicts themes that apply to all of us in some way. He has a talent for making us empathize with horrid people. *The Wolf of Wall Street* contains none of that. Belfort (or at least the Belfort we see on-screen) has no layers. His inner life is as shallow as his public persona. Debauchery is certainly nothing new in the Scorsese catalog—drinking, violence, sex, drugs, and rock and roll are as essential to his work as trees are to Christmas—but rarely are these traits presented as being so much *fun*. Typically, such lifestyles come laden with their own problems. In *Mean Streets*, Charlie's street life leaves him wracked with unfocused guilt. The weight of impending violence weighs on Henry Hill's soul. Drug use in *Bringing Out the Dead* leaves people empty shells of what they once were. Jake LaMotta's attraction to violence comes in part through a deep sense of self-loathing and insecurity. And so on.

So what does *Wolf* tell us about Belfort? What *drives* his greed-over-all philosophy? Is there a more complex morality underlying his actions or an inner turmoil or conflict that leads him down this ugly road? Not really. He's a shallow man focused on shallow pursuits. And while it would be unfair to suggest that his pursuits are depicted as being without consequence—he does lose it all in the end, after all, and along the way he ruins his family, crashes cars, and has embarrassing drug overdoses—the presentation is that these events are zany and hilarious. Belfort pops Quaaludes while his luxurious yacht sinks. He overdoses and only manages to save Donnie from choking to death thanks to a dose of cocaine (and taking it is likened to Popeye eating spinach), the punch line of the entire sequence being that Belfort crashed on his way home after driving in a drug-induced stupor. And on and on. Scorsese pictures don't *judge* their characters. His focus has always been to depict unsavory people in ways that allow us to see them as human beings rather than clichéd crooks and criminals

Scorsese's filmography is filled with depictions of sleazy characters, but perhaps none is as sleazy as Leonardo DiCaprio's take on stock scammer Jordan Belfort. *Paramount Pictures/Photofest*

and scumbags, to understand that these are people as layered and complex and nuanced as the rest of us.

But there is no nuance in Jordan Belfort. This is a picture that probably wouldn't work without DiCaprio's charm. As sleazy as the character is, there are moments when he's undeniably entertaining. When FBI agent Patrick Denham interviews Belfort on Belfort's yacht, for example, their cat-and-mouse verbal sparring is pointed and funny. His frustration at being cut off from sex by Naomi is also humorous, as is the moment when he turns it around on her thanks to a hidden camera. And when he decides to renege on his deal with the FBI and stick with his company, it's difficult to avoid feeling some degree of pity for him. That's all thanks to DiCaprio.

There is a glee to the proceedings that makes *Wolf* a black comedy rather than a character profile or drama. It may use many of the same techniques and approaches Scorsese perfected in *GoodFellas*, but unlike that film, *Wolf* doesn't ask to be taken seriously—quite the opposite. Even if the stories in it are true— Belfort is hardly the most credible of sources, after all—they are often so preposterous that it's hard to believe they reflect reality. Though many of the techniques are familiar, Scorsese does try a few new things. In several scenes, rather than narration we hear the characters' thoughts, listening as they say one thing and think another. There is also a surprising amount of CGI enhancement in the picture. Fresh off the production of *Hugo*, Scorsese abandoned the tangible, tactile approach to set construction he took in *Gangs of New York* and instead relied heavily on digital set extensions. These effects are largely seamless, so invisible that, even when you know where they are used, they're difficult to spot.

After three hours of sex, drugs, and ripping people off, Belfort's schemes finally collapse underneath him. His tiny empire crumbles. He is shamed, loses it all, and ends up in prison. The picture asks no sympathy for Belfort from the audience, nor would he get any if asked. Here, Scorsese's often-nonjudgmental approach to depicting heels means this is all presented matter-of-factly. There is no condemnation, nor is there sadness in his downfall. It just *is*.

In the film's final moments, the real Jordan Belfort makes an appearance to introduce his fictional version, who now gives presentations on sales techniques. For a brief moment, the aspect ratio of the picture changes, subtly suggesting that Belfort is lesser than he was: smaller, shrunken, less significant. He has been diminished. Then, in a callback to an earlier scene, Belfort—DiCaprio's Belfort, not the real one—begins asking attendees to sell him a pen. There, in his element and talking about selling, the aspect ratio opens up again. These shifting aspect ratios tell us something important about him: Jordan Belfort isn't really alive unless he's selling someone something they don't need. So in a way, there is pity for Belfort after all: pity that he had such an empty inner life; pity that such unfocused greed drove him; pity for him, but no sympathy. Not even Martin Scorsese could manage that trick.

CONCLUSION AND IMPACT

Today, the real-life Jordan Belfort is still paying restitution to his many victims. He pushes a sales training program online and gives motivational speeches. Leonardo DiCaprio even endorsed his program, saying, "Jordan stands as a shining example of the transformative qualities of ambition and hard work."[5] And unsurprisingly, he continues to be a lightning rod for controversy.

As for the movie, *The Wolf of Wall Street* ended up being a huge success, raking in close to $400 million worldwide, making it Scorsese's highest-grossing film to date (not adjusted for inflation). It received largely positive reviews from critics, too, who likened it to *GoodFellas* on Wall Street. It received five Academy Award nominations, including yet another nod for Best Picture and Best Director, as well as acting nominations for DiCaprio and Hill.

Wolf received its fair share of criticism, too, however, especially for its un-critical portrayal of Belfort. In an open letter to Scorsese and DiCaprio, Chris-tina McDowell, daughter of Belfort associate Tom Prousalis, said the movie celebrated "our national obsession with wealth and status and glorifying greed and psychopathic behavior" and that the pair of moviemakers "successfully aligned yourself with an accomplished criminal, a guy [Belfort] who still hasn't made full restitution to his victims."[6] The *Wall Street Journal* called it a "hol-low spectacle," among many similar criticisms in other outlets.[7] For his part, DiCaprio said, "I hope people understand we're not condoning this behavior, that we're indicting it. The book was a cautionary tale and if you sit through the end of the film, you'll realize what we're saying about these people and this world, because it's an intoxicating one."[8]

In some ways, *The Wolf of Wall Street* was Scorsese doing what he's often had to do in his career: making something familiar in order to earn him the luxury of pursuing a more personal project next. And that's exactly what hap-pened here. Following the huge financial success of this picture, the director finally settled in to make a picture he'd been trying to get made for decades, a slow, meditative examination of faith set on the island of Japan. Like his previ-ous two films focused on faith, it would be a financial failure, but at this juncture of his career, how much does that really matter?

㉕

SILENCE
(2016)

FILM DETAILS

RELEASE DATE: December 23, 2016
WRITTEN BY: Jay Cocks, Martin Scorsese
STARRING: Andrew Garfield, Adam Driver, Tadanobu Asano, Ciarán
  Hinds, Liam Neeson
RUNNING TIME: 161 minutes

ABOUT THE FILM

Silence has been called the third in an unofficial trilogy focused on exploring men of faith, a film that follows in the footsteps of *The Last Temptation of Christ* and *Kundun* in examining just how deeply faith can mold us, shape us, challenge us, and drive us. It's also the third in a series of pictures Scorsese struggled for years to get made, joining *Temptation* and *Gangs of New York* as personal projects that for a time seemed as if they'd never materialize.

But on the heels of the massive success that was *The Wolf of Wall Street*, *Silence* finally came together after twenty-six years of gestation. The movie is based on a 1966 book of the same name by Shūsaku Endō. The novel chronicles the Shimabara rebellion, an Edo-period uprising in 1637 and 1638 that led to strict enforcement of Japan's laws of the time against Christianity, and more specifically examines the experience of Christian missionaries in the region who struggled with holding fast to their beliefs or renouncing them in order to end the suffering of others.

When Jesuit priest Cristóvão Ferreira (Liam Neeson) writes of the brutal torture of Christians he witnesses in Japan, two priests he mentored, Sebastião Rodrigues (Andrew Garfield) and Francisco Garupe (Adam Driver), are shocked—but they are even more stunned by the news that Ferreira allegedly renounced his faith. Seeking the truth, the pair journey to Japan with fisherman Kichijirō (Yōsuke Kubozuka), hoping to save Ferreira's soul. There, they encounter villagers who live in fear of their faith being discovered. They remain in hiding for a time, administering to the villagers and taking their confessions, but they are discovered after Kichijirō betrays them to Governor Inoue Masashige (Issey Ogata). Garupe is drowned while trying to save a group of unrepentant Christians from being murdered by Masashige's men. Rodrigues remains in their custody. Rodrigues finally reunites with Ferreira, who says he renounced his faith years ago under the belief that Christianity could not survive in Japan. After struggling with the decision, Rodrigues finally relents and commits apostasy, renouncing his faith, marrying a Buddhist woman, and living out his days in peace. But after his death, as his body is being burned, we see a crucifix in his hands, telling us that, for long years, he silently clung to his beliefs.

ANALYSIS

There is nothing unusual about questioning your faith. For some, this kind of self-reflection will strengthen their faith. For others, it will cause them to abandon it. Regardless of the outcome, questioning is human. We're hard-wired for it.

Far more unusual is unwavering faith even in the face of torture and death. Martin Scorsese has examined this idea several times in his career, most prominently in his three movies focused on the subject. *Silence* is the third of those movies, and it may be the most difficult of the three both in terms of entertainment value—the pacing is glacial—and when it comes to the questions it poses about the nature of belief. In *Last Temptation* and *Kundun*, the main characters are not merely men of faith; they are divine beings in human form, aspects of God and Buddha, respectively, who walk the earth as mortals. By contrast, in *Silence* the men Scorsese focuses on are mortals through and through. There is nothing divine or supernatural about them. All that sets them apart from others is the strength of their faith.

And the conditions under which their faith is challenged are horrifying. The very first shot of the film depicts decapitated heads. We then see people being tortured at natural hot springs, scalding water slowly dripped on them. These

Martin Scorsese's third film on the nature of faith and spirituality took more than two decades to go from idea to finished film. *Paramount Pictures/Photofest*

men "asked to be tortured so they could demonstrate the strength of their faith and the presence of God within them." This sets the tone early and establishes a potent message for the picture to explore: Faith is so powerful that people are willing to suffer and die rather than turn away from it.

For Sebastião Rodrigues and Francisco Garupe, their journey to Japan is not merely to administer to the Christians there, who once numbered 300,000 strong. It's not to find out the truth about whether Cristóvão Ferreira truly renounced his faith, either. It's to save Ferreira's soul. If he is hiding his faith, then his eternal soul is in danger, and because he mentored them, they feel a personal debt to him.

Once there, they find that Christians must live in secret, hiding their beliefs for fear of being tortured or killed. Anthony Lane describes the scene in the *New Yorker*:

There are pageants of cruelty on view, as the faithful are hung on crosses and planted at the sea's brink, so that the tide will rise and lash them into submission and a drenching death; others, while still alive, are bundled in straw and either incinerated or casually tipped overboard; nastiest of all is the plight of those who are shrouded and suspended upside down, with a careful nick in their necks, so that the blood will not go to their heads but drip downward. Thus, they are kept unfainting and awake. What binds the scenes together is Rodrigues, bearing witness and—so he hopes and prays—sharing in the anguish of his flock.[1]

"To hide like this must be a terrible burden," Rodrigues says in narration. "I was overwhelmed by the love I felt from these people even though their faces couldn't show it. Long years of secrecy had made their faces into masks. Why do they have to suffer so much? Why did God pick them to bear such a burden?" The dilemma faced time and again by characters in the film, the main characters and supporting cast alike, is in being asked to renounce their faith or face terror and death. Many do, stepping on sacred images to display their (often-feigned) willingness to walk away from their beliefs. Kichijirō, the fisherman who brought Rodrigues and Garupe to the country, does this so effortlessly that one begins to wonder just how devout he really is. Yet the things he has faced have been horrific. He has seen friends and family burned alive for refusing to deny their Christianity. "Wherever I go," he says, "I see the fire and smell the flesh." So he casually defiles sacred icons so that he might live, then, when in safety and privacy, begs to be given a chance to make confession. For him, what is in his heart is more important than what he outwardly displays.

This is not so easy for Rodrigues. It's not about desecrating iconography. Caesar A. Montevecchio observes, "as Rodrigues distributes various trinkets of Christianity to the villagers, even undoing his rosary and giving out individual beads, he notes with an air of disapproval that he thinks the people value signs of faith more than faith itself."[2] His focus is instead on their hearts and souls. Initially, he believes his purpose in life is to spread his spiritual beliefs to others, no matter where he is. It is why he walks the earth. When in hiding from the inquisitors, he sees his own reflection in a body of water, and in it he sees Christ's face. This is not hubris on his part, at least not overtly. Rather, it's a sincere belief that he shares a similar purpose. It is his role to bring people into God's love, and if he must suffer to reach this end, as Christ did, then so be it. That is his fate. And much like Jesus Christ, Rodrigues is betrayed by someone close to him, in this case Kichijirō, who turns him in to the inquisitors for a handful of coins. Later, while in a cell, Kichijirō asks to be forgiven. Rodrigues agrees. He does not sense malice in him; in fact, he only thinks of him as worthy of pity, a wretched and sad man. Scorsese called Kichijirō a "character (Rodrigues) can't stand who keeps running around asking for confession, and keeps ratting on all the Christians. It turns out that's Jesus. Jesus is the man you can't stand. He's the one you've got to forgive. He's the one you've got to love."[3]

When first set before the inquisitors, Rodrigues is defiant. Slaughter will not suppress a people's true belief, he says. It will do the opposite. "The blood of martyrs is the seed of the church," he tells them. Truth is universal, and God's word is truth no matter where you are in the world. Yet Governor Inoue Masashige, who heads the inquisition, sees it differently. He says that Christianity cannot thrive in Japan; it does not belong there: "Everyone knows a tree which flowers in one kind of Earth may decay and die in another. It is the same with the tree of Christianity. The leaves decay here."

This is not a battle Rodrigues can win, and that is what so thoroughly tests his faith. He watches his friend Garupe die trying to save villagers from being drowned by inquisitors. He sees innocent people tortured and killed. He sees people of faith renounce their beliefs. Masashige tells him their blood is on his hands: "Think of the suffering you have inflicted upon these people just for your selfish dream of a Christian Japan." All he has to do is renounce his faith, and their suffering will end. He saw Christ's image in his own reflection, but his task is the *opposite* of Christ's. In order to bring healing, he must turn away from God's word, not embrace it; "*Silence* takes the trajectories of Jesus and the Dalai Lama, who must learn to accept their immense, sacred responsibilities, and reverses them in the story of Rodrigues, the priest who embarks on a holy mission and is ultimately stripped of everything he values."[4]

When Rodrigues is finally reunited with Ferreira, he finds a man who will not acknowledge the faith he once devoted his life to spreading. Ferreira gave up. "There is a saying here: Mountains and rivers can be moved, but man's nature cannot be moved," he tells his former student. Now, rather than spread the Gospel, Ferreira teaches people about medicine and astronomy, spreading scientific knowledge rather than the word of God. Unspoken in this is that Ferreira is clearly worn down and terrified. It's not that he lacks faith; it's that his mental and spiritual endurance has been spent. He knows he was fighting a battle that he could not win, so he capitulated. Ferreira insists that the Japanese do not truly believe in the Christian God, anyway; their belief is based on a misunderstanding, a twisted and incorrect view of what God is. Those who have died in God's name, he says, did not die for the Christian God.

Seeing his old mentor thinking this way devastates Rodrigues. He thinks it is "worse than any torture to twist a man's soul in this way." He believes love—human love, God's love, *all* love—can overcome any trial. And indeed, for Scorsese, that is one of the central themes of the film: "It's about love itself. And pushing the ego away, pushing the pride away. It's about the essential nature of Christianity itself."[5]

Masashige thinks otherwise, challenging the most deeply held reasons Rodrigues has to live. People suffer and die in the name of Jesus, but, Masashige says with a stab, Rodrigues is not Jesus: "You see Jesus . . . and believe your trial is just like his. Those five in the pit are suffering too, just like Jesus, but they don't have your pride. They would never compare themselves to Jesus. Do you have the right to make them suffer?"

For Ferreira, there is a degree of pragmatism in the renunciation of his faith. God is silent, he says, but Rodrigues doesn't have to be. Apostatizing himself, renouncing God in order to end the suffering of these people, would be the "most painful act of love that has ever been performed." Finally, when challenged again to turn his back on Christianity, Rodrigues sees the image of Christ before him, and Christ speaks, telling him it's okay, go ahead, take the step. Desecrate Christ's image and renounce his faith. Rodrigues does. The moment is depicted in near silence.

Rodrigues later marries a Japanese woman and adopts a Buddhist lifestyle. He appears to have fully renounced his beliefs, just as Ferreira did, but Ferreira makes a telling comment when he says, "Only our Lord can judge your heart." *Our* lord. Ferreira still believes, but he believes in silence. And though he gives no sign of it through many long years, Rodrigues does, too. Our final image of him is his body in a cremation basket, burning. Nestled in his hand is a hidden crucifix. He died with his family, in silence, his faith with him until the very end.

Several decades prior, Scorsese's Jesus Christ questioned his own divinity and was plagued with doubts about his purpose in the world, only at the end, when tempted by Satan, embracing his role as the savior of mankind. As an older, more mature filmmaker, *Silence* tells a much different story of faith. Rodrigues sees Christ in himself, and he never wavers; he never doubts; he never buckles. But he also does not outwardly embrace his role, for to do so would mean doing harm to others. His decision to embrace his faith in silence is a pragmatic one, one born from his desire to end the suffering of those around him.

Faith is not a display. It's not a show. It's not an icon or symbol or speech. It is something inside us, something personal, something intertwined with who we are. No amount of torture could take that from Rodrigues. Even in his long years of outwardly walking away from the tenets of Christianity, he still held them inside himself.

CONCLUSION AND IMPACT

Martin Scorsese spent nearly thirty years trying to get this movie made, facing a series of ups and downs that repeatedly pushed the project further and further into the future. It was a passion project. But perhaps unsurprisingly, given its plodding pace and heady subject matter during a time when the box office is dominated by gigantic CGI action, *Silence* was also a huge financial flop, unable to scrape together even half of its production budget.

Critics loved it, however, and while it didn't get the sea of Academy Award nominations that have almost become traditional for Scorsese movies, it landed on a slew of lists of the best films of the year and won strong critical accolades. Perhaps more importantly, it provided Scorsese closure on a project that had consumed years of his life—an important accomplishment for a director entering his twilight years.

Not that there is any sign of him slowing down. His next picture would be a nearly $200 million crime epic using cutting-edge CGI technology and featuring an array of acting luminaries, including Al Pacino, Harvey Keitel, Joe Pesci, and a name intimately familiar to Martin Scorsese fans: Robert De Niro, in his first role for the director in twenty-four years. It would be another mob picture, but it would be unlike any he had done before.

26

THE IRISHMAN (2019)

FILM DETAILS

RELEASE DATE: September 27, 2019 (New York Film Festival), November 1, 2019 (theaters), November 27, 2019 (Netflix)
WRITTEN BY: Steven Zaillian
STARRING: Robert De Niro, Al Pacino, Joe Pesci
RUNNING TIME: 209 minutes

ABOUT THE FILM

They say you can't go home again. But no one told Martin Scorsese that. *The Irishman* is a sprawling crime epic starring Scorsese mainstays Robert De Niro, Joe Pesci, and Harvey Keitel, as well as actors like Al Pacino, Anna Paquin, Ray Romano, and others. The picture is an amalgam of Scorsese old and new, a period piece focused on gangsters and featuring many of his old players but one relying heavily on cutting-edge technology and, far more importantly, a story focused on the idea of looking back on one's life.

The road to *The Irishman* was a long (and expensive) one. The film is based on the book *I Heard You Paint Houses*, a biography of mob hitman Frank Sheeran, who told his story to Charles Brandt while on his deathbed. Though his claims are unproven and controversial—former FBI agent John Tamm and others say Sheeran's tale is "baloney, beyond belief"—Sheeran confessed to knowing the truth behind one of the enduring mysteries of the twentieth century: who was behind the disappearance of Teamsters leader Jimmy Hoffa.[1] Sheeran claims he murdered the infamous union leader.

Much like the extended gestation of *Gangs of New York*, *Silence*, and *The Last Temptation of Christ*, *The Irishman* took a long time to get off the ground—twelve years, according to De Niro, who, much as he did with *Raging Bull*, introduced the director to the book upon which it's based. "I read it and I said, 'Marty, you should read this book because I think maybe this is what we should try and [do],'" De Niro said. "We started this whole process in 2007, so it's been a long time coming."[2]

Though the Hoffa narrative dominates the film, *The Irishman* is about the full scope of Sheeran's adult life. The story spans roughly sixty years, and with the emergence of digital "de-aging" technology that allows decades to be digitally painted off an actor, it became possible to tell Sheeran's story without having to use multiple actors portraying him and his cohorts at different periods of their lives. Doing an entire film with that tech, however, would prove to be an expensive proposition.

At one point, Paramount was behind the production, but as costs rose and rose and rose—reports peg the budget at upward of $160 million, making it

Joe Pesci and Robert De Niro had one last hurrah with Martin Scorsese in *The Irishman*, and thanks to digital technology, they played younger versions of themselves. *Netflix/Photofest*

Scorsese's most expensive picture to date—the studio got cold feet and bailed out.[3] It took Netflix to step in and rescue the production, an unusual arrangement given Scorsese's deep belief in the purity of the theater experience. It takes big money to make a big picture, though, and the director said, for a picture like this, he needed corporate backing that was willing to roll the dice on his grand vision: "People such as Netflix are taking risks. *The Irishman* is a risky film. No one else wanted to fund the pic for five to seven years. And of course we're all getting older. Netflix took the risk."[4]

The picture filled gossip columns for two years. Writers speculated about theatrical releases, financing, the ballooning budget, and more. It stirred up controversy, too, thanks to Netflix's reticence to give it a proper theater release. "Netflix is facing pressure from other industry groups to conform to Hollywood norms," the *Hollywood Reporter* observed months prior to release.[5] The movie was released in theaters on November 1, 2019, and onto Netflix's streaming service just weeks later, on November 27, but the theatrical release was limited to a scant few independent theaters scattered across the country.

Prior to release, president of the National Association of Theater Owners John Fithian was dismayed not only that the picture would be in the theater for just a few short weeks but also that the number of theaters showing it would be numbered in the dozens rather than in the thousands: "This is a major director, a cinephile, who has made all kinds of important movies for our industry. And *The Irishman* is going to play on one-tenth of the screens it should have played on, had Netflix been willing to come to an understanding with our members."[6] (By contrast, a heavily Scorsese-inspired movie released around the same time, *Joker*, debuted on more than four thousand screens.)

But the times, as Scorsese documentary-subject Bob Dylan once sang, are a-changin', and not even Martin Scorsese is immune. Movies are a big business, and despite decades of critical acclaim and having already earned his place among the all-time greatest directors, even Scorsese is subject to Hollywood's focus on the bottom line. He had to go where the money was. Because of that, potentially the last great mob movie by one of the twentieth century's greatest directors was seen by most on home television screens rather than in theaters.

Just as unusual for him was the extent to which technology dictated how the finished product appeared. Though in many ways an old-school director who prefers traditional filmmaking techniques, Scorsese is no Luddite. Pictures like *The Aviator* and *Hugo* lean heavily on contemporary digital special effects. So does *The Wolf of Wall Street*, though in that case most effects are invisible, made up largely of digital compositing to create locations that don't actually exist. None of this is remarkable. Tools are tools. The extent to which *The*

Irishman would use digital technology would prove to be groundbreaking, though, especially for a movie that has more in common with *The Godfather* than it does *Star Wars*. Technical wizardry was used throughout the entire three hours and thirty minutes to make De Niro, Pesci, and others appear younger than they actually were, often by decades. The results are nearly seamless, though early in the process the question of whether it would work worried even Scorsese. "Why I'm concerned, we're all concerned is that we're so used to watching them as the older faces," Scorsese said. "Now, certain shots need more work on the eyes. . . . Does it change the eyes at all? If that's the case, what was in the eyes that I liked? Was it intensity? Was it gravitas? Was it threat?"[7] He needn't have worried. If *The Irishman* accomplished anything, it was to prove that de-aging technology is no longer just for action tentpoles. It is ready for mainstream dramas.

For a time, it appeared that Scorsese was done with mob movies. He told film critic Richard Schickel that "*Casino* was the final one." He went on to make *The Departed*, but that was a much different kind of crime picture than what had come before. Still, even all those years ago, he dropped a tantalizing hint at what was to come. Schickel asked if the director would ever again be drawn toward doing another mob picture. Scorsese told him, "No. If anything, it would be something that would be from a perspective of someone who's in their 70s, looking back."[8] A decade later, that's exactly what *The Irishman* ended up being.

In *The Irishman*, Frank Sheeran (De Niro) is a World War II veteran working as a delivery truck driver after the war. After getting caught running scams on the side, he is recruited into the Bufalino crime family by Russell Bufalino (Pesci), a quietly menacing mob boss who sees potential in Sheeran's sociopathic brand of muscle. Russell introduces Frank to union leader Jimmy Hoffa (Pacino), and Frank begins to work for him as a bodyguard. The arrangement is a productive one, until Hoffa does a brief stint in prison for fraud and loses control of the union. Once released, he seeks to again be elected president of the Teamsters. Eager to reclaim the top spot in "his" union, Hoffa's campaign promise to stop loaning money to mob-connected entities proves a bridge too far for Bufalino and his associates. Hoffa is told he must back down. He refuses. That seals his fate. Frank is ordered to kill the man who was once a friend of his family, and as he always had, he does his grisly duty. After Hoffa's murder, Frank's family grows distant, and one of his daughters, Peggy (Paquin), stops speaking to him altogether. He spends his final years first in prison and then alone in a nursing home, every person he was ever close to now cut out of his life or dead. And that is where he dies, alone and unloved.

ANALYSIS

"You don't know how quickly time goes by until you get there." It's fitting that Frank Sheeran delivers this, the film's thesis, to an anonymous nurse with just ten minutes left in the movie rather than to a loved one or someone close to him. In all his seventy-plus years, Frank was never truly close to anyone. To Jimmy Hoffa, for a time, until he put a bullet in his friend's head. To Russell Bufalino, though only to the extent that he was Russell's muscle. But not to his wives. Not to his daughters. Frank was little more than an empty shell, a sociopath dutifully trudging his way through a life of theft, murder, and betrayal.

Though the excitement built around *The Irishman* centered on the idea of Scorsese doing one last mob movie with the likes of De Niro, Pesci, and Keitel, along with his first work with Pacino, the picture is less about the mob than it is about memory and legacy, about the way we fall into relationships with people and fall out of them again, and about how little agency we often have in our own lives. The mob narrative provides the surface-level excitement, but the real meat is underneath.

For all the wild things he gets involved in, Frank Sheeran has little agency. Throughout the picture's three-and-a-half hour running time, he is rarely an active participant in the decisions that guide the course of his life. Near the start of his criminal endeavors, he offers to sell sides of stolen beef to a connected man. This gets his foot in the door. Following that one decision, all else is largely out of his hands. He's pulled into the wider world of organized crime by Russell Bufalino. It's Russ who effectively gives him to Hoffa, for whom he acts as muscle. It's also Russ who pushes him to kill the same man. Between that introduction and murder, he spends most of his time doing Hoffa's bidding. For someone as imposing as Frank Sheeran, he's not a man who takes control of his own life, but the significance of this is not clear to either the audience or to Frank himself until he is in his twilight years. By then, it's too late.

Frank's relationships form the core of the narrative—his ties to Hoffa, his work with Russell, his ever-decaying closeness (or lack thereof) to his daughters—and they tend to be relationships of habit or convenience. Russell serves as a mentor to him, quietly molding him into the ruthless killer he'd become, but if there is true affection there it's tainted by the realities of their mob relationship. Russell admires Frank's skills, but one gets the sense that it's the same sort of admiration he'd give a brawny workhorse plowing the fields. Frank, meanwhile, is just along for the ride—*literally*, in the case of the narrative framing of the picture, which depicts the pair and their wives driving toward Detroit for the inevitable end of the Hoffa story. Frank drives. Russell directs him. So it goes.

With his family, there is mere emptiness. He provides for them but doesn't *love* them. His first wife is cast aside as soon as he meets a woman he finds more desirable. His second wife is relegated to chattering in the back seat of the car. And his four daughters, though he says he loves them, are kept at arm's length, living in fear of his ease with violence, intimidated by his imposing presence, and left wanting a true father figure, which Peggy ends up finding in Hoffa. It's not that Scorsese ignores the Sheeran family life—in fact, numerous scenes depict them picnicking together, out bowling, and acting as families do—it's that Frank's family life largely involves going through the motions. He never truly knows how to love them and is only able to confront this reality at the end of his days.

The one true display of love and joy we see in all this comes not between Frank and his daughters but between Hoffa and Peggy (played by Paquin as an adult and by Lucy Gallina as a child). She adores him, and he her, while her own father is kept at a distance. In fact, Peggy goes the entire film with only two lines. Most of her screen time is spent staring silently at her father with disappointment and loathing. This has been a point of criticism for some— "(Scorsese) doesn't particularly understand women, nor has he sought to," one critic wrote—though her seemingly slight role belies the importance of her presence in the film.[9] It's true that the director's pictures are virtually always focused on the male experience, with most female characters barely even reaching "supporting" status. A strong case can be made that Scorsese's filmography has a dearth of strong female characters (though it's worth noting that a whopping nine women have received Academy Award nominations for roles in Scorsese films, two of them winning). And indeed, this appears to be the case with Peggy, too, a surprising choice given that she's portrayed by an Oscar-winning actress. Peggy's case can be deceiving, however. Her dialogue is scant, amounting to about six or seven words in the entire picture, but her presence is a potent one. She is both a personification of Frank's guilt and a representation of his detachment from anything that can be seen as humanity or love. Indeed, she is the moral conscience of the narrative, the one who forces us to look past the intrigue and conflicts and drama and see Frank's life for what it truly is. She represents how the audience *should* react to the kind of life led by people like Frank Sheeran.

If in *GoodFellas* and *Casino* we take a perverse kind of joy in seeing bad people do bad things, then here our reaction is different. The emptiness of Frank's existence is stark. He coasts through his days, killing as ordered and finding no joy in anything: not in his job, not in his family, and not even a sick kind of joy in the brutality he engages in. He just *is*. So when he trudges through his final days alone in a nursing home, he has nothing left to look back on, save bloodied hands and an empty legacy. The one light he might have had, his daughters, is closed to him. One daughter admits they were always frightened of him, that they couldn't go to him with their problems because they feared what he might do—an early scene depicts him brutalizing a shopkeeper who shoved Peggy— and that, despite his claims to have done the things he did to protect them, they never felt safe in his presence. And as for Peggy, she won't even speak to him, turning her back on him from the moment of Hoffa's disappearance to Frank's eventual death. More than anyone else in the movie, she sees him for what he truly is, and her judgment is unwavering.

Hers is a small role on the surface, yet in many ways it's one of the film's most important. Paquin may lack lines to deliver, but Peggy's silence is potent and a major part of what makes her such an effective character. She carries a heavy load with her silence, and that silence has a lot to say about who and what Frank Sheeran is. The picture would be weaker without her presence.

Indeed, that the movie opens and closes on a Frank Sheeran who has no one is no accident. The opening shot pushes through the corridors of a nondescript nursing home and lands on an elderly Sheeran in a wheelchair, beginning to tell the story he'll continue to tell as narration throughout the film. He is not surrounded by loved ones. He appears to have no friends in the nursing home. All he has are his memories of a life ill led.

This makes Scorsese's (likely) final gangster epic quite different from what came before. Despite criticism to the contrary, fan favorites like *GoodFellas* never truly *glorify* the lifestyle they depict. The fall, after all, is the most essential ingredient of these rise-and-fall stories. They were *exciting*, though, and for brief moments it was easy to see how intoxicating the mob life could be. Not in *The Irishman*. Frank's hits aren't adrenaline-filled rushes of violence. They're so matter-of-fact that even a flashy hit like his murder of rising star Joseph "Crazy Joe" Gallo (Sebastian Maniscalco) is just another job to be done, little different than a blue-collar worker loading another box on the truck. The work isn't thrilling or alluring; it's cold and empty.

If *The Irishman* is a victory lap for Scorsese and his collaborators, something many commentators characterized it as in the days leading to its release, then no one told him that. There is no victory here, no glory, no basking in the glow of a life well led. *The Irishman* is filled with regret at having let the days slip by and at having failed to nurture the relationships that should have been most important.

Wedged in the middle of the story of Frank Sheeran's life is the Jimmy Hoffa story, or at least the latter portion of it, making *The Irishman* something of a

Frankenstein's monster. Picking up after Hoffa had already risen to one of the most powerful people in the country, the infamous labor leader is depicted by Pacino as a hot-headed, stubborn mule of a man, beloved by his legions of union members but a terror behind closed doors when he doesn't get what he wants. Here Pacino doesn't merely steal scenes (and indeed, he steals every scene he's in). The entire *narrative* is snatched up from Sheeran, with Hoffa's story becoming the fulcrum upon which it pivots. Sheeran's lack of agency is clearest here. Anyone who gets caught up in Hoffa's orbit is quickly in deep. Hoffa clashes with industry leaders, with other unions, and especially with the new American royalty of the period, the Kennedys. For an hour or more, they are a looming presence that casts a shadow over all Hoffa does, appearing on-screen only via news clips but influencing his every decision. Much as he does with Peggy's character, Scorsese plays with implication here, too. Phrases, gestures, glares—they all speak volumes. When news of the assassination of John F. Kennedy appears on television, Hoffa doesn't say anything. Instead, his face reads quiet relief—and perhaps of something more, some unspoken knowledge that is outside this film's reach. It's as if Hoffa knew the president was killed by the same people he was financially tied to. (The strong implication that Kennedy was killed at the behest of the mafia, which lost access to countless millions thanks to Kennedy's Cuba policies, is reaffirmed later, too.)

It's a curious choice, this decision to veer into Hoffa's life for the middle chunk of the picture. A creative editor could probably lift two hours out of the middle of *The Irishman* and present it as its own distinct movie. These are the only stretches when the film is concerned with anyone but Frank. We need these scenes, though. We need the life and vigor Hoffa brings to the narrative because they serve as a reminder that Frank Sheeran wasn't just some street thug. He was surrounded by some highly influential people, people who could shape the fabric of American life at a whim. Yet despite this proximity to power, Frank himself died a nobody. We only know his name because he (claims to have) killed his friend. Otherwise, the world would have no memory of him.

And this is a picture *framed* by memory. The opening scene is Frank telling his story to an off-screen observer. We then move back decades, to Frank and Russ on their long drive to go kill Hoffa, a memory that itself fades into yet another layer of memory as they recall the first time they met decades before *that*. And so it goes throughout, memories nested within memories, all told by a lonely old man in a nursing home.

The Irishman would have been a much different picture had it been made by a younger Scorsese. This is a picture concerned with looking backward, with assessing one's life, with taking stock of your legacy. These are themes that pepper each of his last several movies, with both *Silence* and *Hugo* examining the importance of leaving something behind, the things that give light to our souls, and our reasons to continue on each day. Yet Sheeran left nothing behind, save fractured relationships and bloody corpses.

CONCLUSION AND IMPACT

As of this writing, it's too soon to say what kind of impact *The Irishman* will have on Martin Scorsese's legacy, not to mention the legacies of De Niro, Pesci, and Pacino. As this is written, the film is enjoying time as a critical darling. How that will translate to financial success and awards recognition and whether it will continue to be highly regarded in the years to come remains to be seen.

Some things are clear, however. This may be the last great picture made via one of the most remarkable collaborations in film history. Scorsese and De Niro join Kurosawa and Mifune, Hitchcock and Stewart, Hitchcock and Grant, and a scant handful of others as pairings who repeatedly created indelible landmarks in cinema. As this book goes to print, Scorsese is in preproduction on *Killers of the Flower Moon*, a picture that, if it sees the light of day, will star both De Niro and the director's second great acting collaborator, Leonardo DiCaprio. Perhaps that will be his last hurrah. Perhaps *The Irishman* is, and we just don't realize it yet.

No matter how that theoretical picture pans out, *The Irishman* serves to remind the viewing public of the genius in our midst. The legacy Martin Scorsese leaves behind is enormous. Though pigeonholed by mainstream viewers as a mob-movie director, his body of work is vast and varied, and his devotion to the purity of the cinematic experience borders on the religious.

It's often hard to tell when you are living in the midst of important artistic history. A director like, say, Alfred Hitchcock, was tremendously popular in his day, and in his later years, he earned the respect of his peers, but fully grasping the scale of his artistic achievements took the benefit of hindsight. Such is the case with Martin Scorsese. Anyone reading this knows his work is great. It has been decades since Roger Ebert declared him our greatest living director. Yet it will take some time before those of us who watched Scorsese's career unfold can truly understand the significance of his impact on cinema.

If *The Irishman* is the director taking stock of his life and work, then it's a bleaker picture than his career warrants. That much is certain. Through rich character studies, black comedies, lush period pieces, meditative explorations of faith, bold biopics, and—yes—hyperviolent mob movies, Martin Scorsese has created a body of work that will still be influencing moviemakers for decades to come. It seems like only yesterday that we were shocked by *Taxi Driver* or thrilled by *GoodFellas*, and now he's nearing eighty and, presumably, the end of his career. But perhaps Frank Sheeran said it best: "You don't know how quickly time goes by until you get there."

NOTES

INTRODUCTION

1. Gavin Smith, "The Art of Vision: Martin Scorsese's Kundun," *Film Comment*, January/February 1998.
2. Gabrielle Donnelly, "Martin Scorsese Interview: 'Catholicism Is Always in You,'" *Catholic Herald*, December 22, 2016.
3. Anthony DeCurtis, "What the Streets Mean," *South Atlantic Quarterly*, Spring 1992.
4. Mary Pat Kelly, "Director Martin Scorsese Blends Improvisation with Discipline in Making His Movies," *Washington Post*, February 24, 2012.
5. Sam Ashurst, "Thelma Schoonmaker: Martin Scorsese's 'The Irishman' Is 'Not Goodfellas' (Exclusive)," Yahoo Movies UK, February 8, 2019, https://www.yahoo .com/entertainment/scorseses-netflix-movie-irishman-not-goodfellas-says-thelma -schoonmaker-200309938.html.
6. Ian Christie, "Martin Scorsese's Testament," *Sight and Sound*, January 1996.
7. Peter Biskind, "Slouching toward Hollywood," *Premiere*, November 1991.

CHAPTER 1: *WHO'S THAT KNOCKING AT MY DOOR?* (1967)

1. Richard Schickel, *Conversations with Scorsese* (New York: Alfred A. Knopf, 2011), 72.
2. Schickel, *Conversations with Scorsese*, 70.
3. Anthony DeCurtis, "What the Streets Mean," *South Atlantic Quarterly*, Spring 1992.
4. Roger Ebert, "Scorsese's Last Temptation," *Chicago Sun Times*, July 24, 1988.

5. DeCurtis, "What the Streets Mean."
6. Roger Ebert, "I Call First," *Chicago Sun Times*, November 17, 1967.

CHAPTER 2: *BOXCAR BERTHA* (1972)

1. Karen G. Jackovich, "Barbara Hershey Drops Her Hippie Past and a Name, Seagull, and Her Career Finds Wings," *People*, May 28, 1979.
2. Richard Schickel, *Conversations with Scorsese* (New York: Alfred A. Knopf, 2011), 90.
3. Schickel, *Conversations with Scorsese*, 91.
4. Martin Scorsese, commentary, *Mean Streets*, directed by Martin Scorsese (Warner Home Video, 2004), DVD.
5. Vincent LoBrutto, *Martin Scorsese: A Biography* (Westport, CT: Praeger, 2007), 129.

CHAPTER 3: *MEAN STREETS* (1973)

1. Martin Scorsese, commentary, *Mean Streets*, directed by Martin Scorsese (Warner Home Video, 2004), DVD.
2. Tonelli, Bill, "Arrivederci, Little Italy," *New York Magazine*, September 16, 2004.
3. Jen Chung, "Neighborhood Wants San Gennaro to Sleep with the Fishes," Gothamist, March 26, 2007, https://gothamist.com/news/neighborhood-wants-san -gennaro-to-sleep-with-fishes.
4. Chuck Willis, *Destination America* (New York: DK, 2005).
5. Stefano Luconi, "Forging an Ethnic Identity: The Case of Italian Americans," *Revue française d'études américaines*, no. 96 (2003): 89–101.
6. Roger Ebert, "Martin Scorsese and His New York Story," *Chicago Sun-Times*, March 5, 1989.
7. Scorsese, commentary.
8. Pauline Kael, *5001 Nights at the Movies* (New York: Henry Holt, 1982), 473.

CHAPTER 4: *ALICE DOESN'T LIVE HERE ANYMORE* (1974)

1. Leighton Grist, *The Films of Martin Scorsese, 1963–77: Authorship and Context* (New York: St. Martin's Press, 2000), 98.
2. "Second Chances," *Alice Doesn't Live Here Anymore*, directed by Martin Scorsese (Warner Home Video, 2004), DVD.
3. Peter Biskind, "Slouching toward Hollywood," *Premiere*, November 1991.

4. Diane Jacobs, *Hollywood Renaissance* (Lancaster, UK: Gazelle Book Services, 1977), 141.

5. Ellen Burstyn, commentary, *Alice Doesn't Live Here Anymore* (Warner Home Video, 2004), DVD.

6. Spencer Rich, "Single-Parent Families Rise Dramatically," *Washington Post*, May 3, 1982.

7. Alison Burke, "10 Facts about American Women in the Workforce," Brookings, December 5, 2017, https://www.brookings.edu/blog/brookings-now/2017/12/05/10 -facts-about-american-women-in-the-workforce/.

8. Laura M. Holson, "Murders by Intimate Partners Are on the Rise, Study Finds," *New York Times*, April 12, 2019.

CHAPTER 5: *TAXI DRIVER* (1976)

1. Anthony DeCurtis, "What the Streets Mean," *South Atlantic Quarterly*, Spring 1992.

2. Chris Mitchell, "The Killing of Murder," *New York Magazine*, January 7, 2008.

3. Thomas Tracey, "2017 Was Record-Low for Homicides in New York City, with NYPD Logging Lowest Number in Nearly 70 Years," *New York Daily News*, December 31, 2017.

4. Roger Ebert, *The Great Movies* (New York: Broadway Books, 2002), 451.

5. CNN Staff, "Transcript of Video Linked to Santa Barbara Mass Shooting," CNN, May 27, 2014, https://www.cnn.com/2014/05/24/us/elliot-rodger-video-transcript/index.html.

6. BBC News Staff, "Elliot Rodger: How Misogynist Killer Became 'Incel Hero,'" BBC, April 26, 2018, https://www.bbc.com/news/world-us-canada-43892189.

7. Mark Hay, "The Strange, Centuries-Long History of Satanic Pedophile Panics," Vice, November 15, 2018, https://www.vice.com/en_us/article/59vgwa/the-strange -centuries-long-history-of-satanic-pedophile-panics.

8. Richard Ruelas, "2 Arizona Arrests Have Ties to QAnon Conspiracy Theory Movement," *Arizona Republic*, August 7, 2018.

9. Amanda Robb, "Anatomy of a Fake News Scandal," *Rolling Stone*, November 16, 2017.

10. Stephen Puddicombe, "*Taxi Driver* and the Frightening Truth about Our Current Political Climate," Little White Lies, February 19, 2017, https://lwlies.com/articles/taxi-driver-travis-bickle-alt-right-politics/.

11. Thompson, Richard, "Interview: Paul Schrader," *Film Comment*, March–April 1976.

12. Lori Mattix and Michael Kaplan, "I Lost My Virginity to David Bowie," Thrillist, November 3, 2015, https://www.thrillist.com/entertainment/nation/i-lost-my -virginity-to-david-bowie; Stereo Williams, "David Bowie and Rock 'n' Roll's Statutory

Rape Problem," Daily Beast, January 17, 2016, https://www.thedailybeast.com/david
-bowie-and-rock-n-rolls-statutory-rape-problem; Christopher Turner, "Sugar and Spice
and All Things Not So Nice," Guardian, October 2, 2009, https://www.theguardian
.com/theguardian/2009/oct/03/brooke-shields-nude-child-photograph.

13. The Graham Norton Show, season 19, episode 9, aired May 20, 2016, on BBC
One.

14. Sigmund Freud, Case Histories II (London: Penguin, 1988), 132.

15. Alan Moore and Dave Gibbons, Watchmen, no. 1, DC Comics, September 1986.

16. Hugh Hart, "Watchmen's World Draws Directly from Strangelove, Taxi
Driver," Wired, March 4, 2009.

17. John Hinckley Jr., letter to Jodie Foster, March 30, 1981.

18. Doug Stanglin, "Federal Judge Allows Would-Be Reagan Assassin John Hinckley to Live by Himself," USA Today, November 17, 2018.

CHAPTER 6: *NEW YORK, NEW YORK* (1977)

1. Anthony DeCurtis, "What the Streets Mean," South Atlantic Quarterly, Spring
1992.

2. Martin Scorsese, commentary, New York, New York, directed by Martin Scorsese
(Warner Home Video, 2004), DVD.

3. Chris Hodenfield, "You've Got to Love Something Enough to Kill It," American
Film, March 1989.

4. Martin Scorsese, American Film Institute interview, seminar hosted by James
Powers, 1975.

5. Scorsese, commentary.

6. Vincent Canby, "Film: 'New York' in a Tuneful Era," New York Times, June 23,
1977.

7. Chris Nashawaty, "How 'Rocky' Nabbed Best Picture," Entertainment Weekly,
February 19, 2002.

8. Peter Biskind, Easy Riders, Raging Bulls: How the Sex-Drugs-and-Rock-'n'-Roll
Generation Saved Hollywood (New York: Simon and Schuster, 1998), 378–79.

CHAPTER 7: *RAGING BULL* (1980)

1. Stephen Galloway, "Martin Scorsese's Journey from Near-Death Drug Addict to
'Silence,'" Hollywood Reporter, December 8, 2016.

2. Peter Biskind, Easy Riders, Raging Bulls: How the Sex-Drugs-and-Rock-'n'-Roll
Generation Saved Hollywood (New York: Simon and Schuster, 1998), 386–87.

3. Martin Scorsese, "*Raging Bull*: Before the Fight," *Raging Bull*, directed by Martin Scorsese (MGM, 2006), DVD.

4. Martin Scorsese, *Scorsese on Scorsese*, rev. ed. (London: Faber and Faber, 2003), 113–14.

5. Vincent LoBrutto, *Sound-on-film: Interviews with Creators of Film Sound* (Westport, CT: Praeger, 1994), 36.

6. Joe Pesci, "The Bronx Bull," *Raging Bull*, directed by Martin Scorsese (MGM, 2006), DVD.

7. Anthony DeCurtis, "What the Streets Mean," *South Atlantic Quarterly*, Spring 1992.

8. Yohana Desta, "'This Is Overwhelming': Why Martin Scorsese Almost Didn't Make *Raging Bull*," *Vanity Fair*, April 28, 2019.

9. Richard Schickel, "Brutal Attraction: The Making of *Raging Bull*," *Vanity Fair*, March 2010.

10. DeCurtis, "What the Streets Mean."

11. Scorsese, "*Raging Bull*: Before the Fight."

CHAPTER 8: *THE KING OF COMEDY* (1982)

1. Mike Evans, *The Making of* Raging Bull (Phoenix, AZ: 101 Distribution, 2009), 124–29.

2. Simon Abrams, "Martin Scorsese on *The King of Comedy*'s Modern Relevance: 'There Are So Many Ruperts around Us,'" *Vanity Fair*, June 27, 2016.

3. Martin Scorsese, "*The King of Comedy*: A Reconsideration," in *Scorsese by Ebert*, by Roger Ebert (Chicago: University of Chicago Press, 2008), 78.

4. Jane E. Brody, "Personal Health: Do's and Don'ts for Thwarting Stalkers," *New York Times*, August 25, 1998.

5. Tim Grierson, "How 'The King of Comedy' Proved Jerry Lewis Was a Great Actor," *Rolling Stone*, August 20, 2017.

6. Abrams, "Martin Scorsese."

7. Scott Macaulay, "Scorsese, De Niro, Lewis and Bernhard Recall *The King of Comedy*," *Filmmaker*, May 1, 2013.

CHAPTER 9: *AFTER HOURS* (1985)

1. Martin Scorsese, commentary, *After Hours*, directed by Martin Scorsese (Warner Home Video, 2004), DVD.

2. Martin Scorsese, *Filming for Your Life: Making* After Hours (Warner Home Video, 2004).

3. Sam Ashurst, "Thelma Schoonmaker: Martin Scorsese's 'The Irishman' Is 'Not Goodfellas' (Exclusive)," Yahoo Movies UK, February 8, 2019, https://www.yahoo .com/entertainment/scorseses-netflix-movie-irishman-not-goodfellas-says-thelma -schoonmaker-200309938.html.

4. Scorsese, *Filming for Your Life.*

5. Scorsese, *Filming for Your Life.*

6. Scorsese, *Filming for Your Life.*

7. Roger Ebert, *Scorsese by Ebert* (Chicago: University of Chicago Press, 2008), 87.

CHAPTER 10: *THE COLOR OF MONEY* (1986)

1. Richard Schickel, *Conversations with Scorsese* (New York: Alfred A. Knopf, 2011), 161.

2. Chris Hodenfield, "You've Got to Love Something Enough to Kill It," *American Film*, March 1989.

3. Richard Corliss, "Remembering Paul Newman, Humanitarian and Actor," *Time*, September 27, 2008.

4. Richard Corliss, "Midsection: Cross Purposes," *Film Comment*, September/ October 1988.

5. Schickel, *Conversations with Scorsese*, 165.

6. Peter Biskind and Susan Linfield, "Chalk Talk," *American Film*, November 1986.

7. Hodenfield, "You've Got to Love."

CHAPTER 11: *THE LAST TEMPTATION OF CHRIST* (1988)

1. Martin Scorsese, *Scorsese on Scorsese*, rev. ed. (Faber and Faber, 2003), 124.

2. Allan Parachini and Dennis McDougal, "Art in the Eighties: Censorship: A Decade of Tighter Control of the Arts," *Los Angeles Times*, December 25, 1989.

3. Richard Corliss, "Midsection: Cross Purposes," *Film Comment*, September/ October 1988.

4. Richard Schickel, *Conversations with Scorsese* (New York: Alfred A. Knopf, 2011), 168–69.

5. Richard Alleva, "On Screen: *The Last Temptation of Christ*," *Crisis Magazine*, October 1, 1988.

6. Scorsese, *Scorsese on Scorsese*, 118.

7. John Dart, "Church Declares 'Last Temptation' Morally Offensive," *Los Angeles Times*, August 10, 1988.

8. Corliss, "Midsection."

9. Dart, "Church Declares."

10. Schickel, *Conversations with Scorsese*, 174–75.

11. Aljean Harmetz, "Ministers Vow Boycott over Scorsese Film on Jesus," *New York Times*, July 13, 1988.

12. James D. Davis, "Christians Up in Arms over Movie," *South Florida Sun Sentinel*, July 30, 1988.

13. Anthony DeCurtis, "What the Streets Mean," *South Atlantic Quarterly*, Spring 1992.

14. Roger Ebert, "*The Last Temptation of Christ*: A Reconsideration," in *Scorsese by Ebert* (Chicago: University of Chicago Press, 2008), 104.

CHAPTER 13: *GOODFELLAS* (1990)

1. Vincent Patrick, "Not-So-Organized Crime," *New York Times*, January 26, 1986.

2. Martin Scorsese, commentary, *GoodFellas*, directed by Martin Scorsese (Warner Home Video, 2004), DVD.

3. George Anastasia, "Five Myths about the Mafia," *Washington Post*, May 5, 2017.

4. Anastasia, "Five Myths."

5. Gavin Smith, "Martin Scorsese Interviewed," *Film Comment*, September/October 1990.

6. Amy Taubin, "Martin Scorsese's Cinema of Obsessions," *Village Voice*, September 18, 1990.

7. Legs McNeil and Gillian McCain, eds., *Please Kill Me: The Uncensored Oral History of Punk* (New York: Grove Press, 1996), 358–59.

8. Christopher Hooton, "*The Sopranos* and *GoodFellas* Shared 27 Actors," *Independent*, January 29, 2016.

9. Jim Hemphill, "Of Tarantino and TV: The Legacy of *GoodFellas*," *Filmmaker*, April 22, 2015.

10. Sam Ashurst, "Thelma Schoonmaker: Martin Scorsese's 'The Irishman' Is 'Not Goodfellas' (Exclusive)," Yahoo Movies UK, February 8, 2019, https://www.yahoo.com/entertainment/scorseses-netflix-movie-irishman-not-goodfellas-says-thelma-schoonmaker-200309938.html.

CHAPTER 14: *CAPE FEAR* (1991)

1. Janet Maslin, "Film: Martin Scorsese Ventures Back to 'Cape Fear,'" *New York Times*, November 10, 1991.

2. Maslin, "Film."

3. Peter Biskind, "Slouching toward Hollywood," *Premiere*, November 1991.

4. Biskind, "Slouching."

5. Daniel Cerone, "Playing the End of Innocence: Movies: Juliette Lewis Surprises Critics with a Strong Performance as the Teen-aged Daughter in 'Cape Fear.'" *Los Angeles Times*, November 20, 1991.

CHAPTER 15: *THE AGE OF INNOCENCE* (1993)

1. Gavin Smith, "Martin Scorsese Interviewed," *Film Comment*, November/December 1993.

CHAPTER 16: *CASINO* (1995)

1. J. Patrick Coolican, "Was Life Really Better When the Mob Ruled Las Vegas?" *Las Vegas Sun*, February 20, 2012.
2. Ian Christie, "Martin Scorsese's Testament," *Sight and Sound*, January 1996.
3. Thessaly La Force, "I Can't Stop Watching 'Casino' and Thinking about Its Clothes," Vice, June 17, 2014, https://www.vice.com/en_us/article/xd54xd/i-cant-stop-watching-casino-and-thinking-about-its-clothes.
4. Cathy Scott, "Does the Mob Still Exist in Las Vegas? Good Question," *Psychology Today*, December 31, 2014.
5. La Force, "I Can't Stop."
6. Christie, "Martin Scorsese's Testament."
7. David G. Schwartz, "In Las Vegas, One of the Mob's Biggest Money Earners Tells All," *Forbes*, November 5, 2018.
8. Natasha Vargas-Copper, "Canon Fodder: Martin Scorsese's Casino," *GQ*, November 10, 2011.

CHAPTER 17: *KUNDUN* (1997)

1. Martin Scorsese, *Scorsese on Scorsese*, rev. ed. (London: Faber and Faber, 2003), 225.
2. Ian Christie, "Martin Scorsese's Testament," *Sight and Sound*, January 1996.
3. Amy Taubin, "Everything Is Form," *Sight and Sound*, February 1998.
4. Ben Blanchard, "China Tells Dalai Lama Again to Respect Reincarnation," Reuters, September 10, 2014, https://www.reuters.com/article/us-china-tibet/china-tells-dalai-lama-again-to-respect-reincarnation-idUSKBN0H50ST20140910.
5. Jake Swearingen, "China Will Make the Dalai Lama Reincarnate Whether He Likes It or Not," *Atlantic*, September 10, 2014.

6. Patrick Brzeski, "Martin Scorsese's 'The Irishman' Lands Distributor in China," *Hollywood Reporter*, August 16, 2016.

7. Michael Wilmington, "Heaven Sent," *Chicago Tribune*, January 16, 1998.

CHAPTER 18: *BRINGING OUT THE DEAD* (1999)

1. Richard Schickel, *Conversations with Scorsese* (New York: Alfred A. Knopf, 2011), 219.

CHAPTER 19: *GANGS OF NEW YORK* (2002)

1. Richard Schickel, *Conversations with Scorsese* (New York: Alfred A. Knopf, 2011), 226.

2. Laura M. Holson, "2 Hollywood Titans Brawl over a Gang Epic," *New York Times*, April 7, 2002.

3. Kevin Baker, "The First Slum in America," *New York Times*, September 30, 2001.

4. Leslie M. Harris, *In the Shadow of Slavery: African Americans in New York City, 1626–1863* (Chicago: Chicago University Press, 2003), 279.

CHAPTER 20: *THE AVIATOR* (2004)

1. Dr. Dean Keith Simonton, "Are Genius and Madness Related? Contemporary Answers to an Ancient Question," *Psychiatric Times*, May 31, 2005.

2. Erin Hill, "Martin Scorsese on Leo DiCaprio: 'We Speak the Same Language,'" *Parade*, June 12, 2012.

3. Richard Schickel, *Conversations with Scorsese* (New York: Alfred A. Knopf, 2011), 243.

4. Rene Chun, "How to Recreate Howard Hughes' Legendary Screening Room," *Wired*, December 17, 2015.

5. Laura M. Holson, "2 Hollywood Titans Brawl over a Gang Epic," *New York Times*, April 7, 2002.

6. Scott Feinberg, "'Awards Chatter' Podcast—Robert De Niro ('The Comedian')," *Hollywood Reporter*, November 27, 2016.

CHAPTER 21: *THE DEPARTED* (2006)

1. Mick Brown, "Martin Scorsese Interview for *Shutter Island*," *Telegraph*, March 7, 2010.
2. Gene Demby, "How Code-Switching Explains the World," NPR, April 8, 2013, https://www.npr.org/sections/codeswitch/2013/04/08/176064688/how-code-switching -explains-the-world.
3. Roger Ebert, "*The Departed*," *Chicago Sun Times*, July 6, 2007.
4. "'Departed' Producer Defends Scorsese at Oscars," Reuters, February 26, 2007, https://www.reuters.com/article/us-oscars-king/departed-producer-defends-scorsese -at-oscars-idUSN2626323420070226.
5. Kristopher Tapley, "10 Years Later: 'The Departed,' the Oscars, and the Non-Campaign Campaign," *Variety*, October 4, 2016.
6. Tapley, "10 Years Later."

CHAPTER 22: *SHUTTER ISLAND* (2010)

1. William Shakespeare, *Macbeth*, act V, scene 1.
2. Kaleem Aftab, "Martin Scorsese in Conversation: Guilt Trips of the Great Director," *Independent*, December 13, 2013.
3. Arturo Serrano, "The Spectacle of Redemption: Guilt and Violence in Martin Scorsese's *Raging Bull*," *Studia Gilsoniana*, April–June 2015, 131.

CHAPTER 23: *HUGO* (2011)

1. Adam Yuster, "Robert De Niro, Leonardo DiCaprio, Jonah Hill Honor Martin Scorsese at MoMA Film Benefit," *Hollywood Reporter*, November 21, 2017.
2. Richard Schickel, *Conversations with Scorsese* (New York: Alfred A. Knopf, 2011), 383.
3. Jay A. Fernandez and Carolyn Giardina, "Making of *Hugo*," *Hollywood Reporter*, November 15, 2011.
4. Patrick Goldstein, "Graham King on 'Hugo's' Box-Office Woes: 'It's Been Painful,'" *Los Angeles Times*, February 6, 2012.

CHAPTER 24: *THE WOLF OF WALL STREET* (2013)

1. Pamela McClintock, "Scorsese, DiCaprio Cry 'Wolf,'" *Variety*, March 25, 2007.
2. Shashank Bengali, "The Global Financial Scandal That Has Spread from Malaysia to Hollywood," *Los Angeles Times*, July 10, 2019.

3. Bengali, "Global Financial Scandal."

4. Alex Ritman, "Jordan Belfort Says He Knew 'Wolf of Wall Street' Producers Were 'F—ing Criminals,'" *Hollywood Reporter*, January 30, 2017.

5. Leonardo DiCaprio, endorsement video, Jordan Belfort, thewolfnetwork.com.

6. Ben Child, "The Wolf of Wall Street Criticised for 'Glorifying Psychopathic Behaviour,'" *Guardian*, December 30, 2013.

7. Joe Morgenstern, "'Wolf of Wall Street' Skims the Surface of Sin," *Wall Street Journal*, December 24, 2013.

8. John Hiscock, "Martin Scorsese Faces Mounting Criticism over *The Wolf of Wall Street*," *Telegraph*, January 3, 2014.

CHAPTER 25: *SILENCE* (2016)

1. Anthony Lane, "Martin Scorsese's Strained Silence," *New Yorker*, December 22, 2016.

2. Caesar A. Montevecchio, "Silence," *Journal of Religion and Film* 21, no. 1 (April 2017).

3. Richard Schickel, *Conversations with Scorsese* (New York: Alfred A. Knopf, 2011), 367.

4. Bilge Ebiri, "Scorsese, 'Silence,' and the Mystery of Faith," *Village Voice*, February 22, 2017.

5. Schickel, *Conversations with Scorsese*.

CHAPTER 26: *THE IRISHMAN* (2019)

1. Bill Tonelli, "The Lies of the Irishman," Slate, August 7, 2019, https://slate.com/culture/2019/08/the-irishman-scorsese-netflix-movie-true-story-lies.html.

2. Evan Real, "Robert De Niro on Making 'The Irishman' with Martin Scorsese: 'It's Been a Long Time Coming,'" *Hollywood Reporter*, April 23, 2019.

3. Ben Mendelson, "Inside the Debate between Netflix and Big Theater Chains over 'The Irishman,'" *Forbes*, July 31, 2019.

4. Jacob Stolworthy, "The Irishman: Martin Scorsese's 'Risky' Netflix Film to Be Released in Cinemas," *Independent*, December 3, 2018.

5. Rebecca Keegan, "Oscars 2020: How Netflix Plans to Win Best Picture with Scorsese's Mob Drama," *Hollywood Reporter*, February 27, 2019.

6. Nicole Sperling, "Inside the Debate between Netflix and Big Theater Chains over 'The Irishman,'" *New York Times*, November 1, 2019.

7. Stephen Sorace, "Scorsese says De Niro, Pacino's CGI Use in 'The Irishman' Left Him 'Concerned,'" Fox News, May 30, 2019, https://www.foxnews.com/entertainment/martin-scorsese-de-niro-pacino-the-irishman-de-aging.

8. Richard Schickel, *Conversations with Scorsese* (New York: Alfred A. Knopf, 2011), 210.

9. Anne Cohen, "Does *The Irishman* Have a Woman Problem?" Refinery29, November 1, 2019, https://www.refinery29.com/en-gb/2019/11/8670267/the-irishman-anna-paquin-lines-women-dialogue?utm_source=feed&utm_medium=rss.

BIBLIOGRAPHY

Abrams, Simon. "Martin Scorsese on *The King of Comedy*'s Modern Relevance: 'There Are So Many Ruperts around Us.'" *Vanity Fair*, June 27, 2016.

Aftab, Kaleem. "Martin Scorsese in Conversation: Guilt Trips of the Great Director." *Independent*, December 13, 2013.

Alleva, Richard. "On Screen: *The Last Temptation of Christ*." *Crisis Magazine*, October 1, 1988.

Anastasia, George. "Five Myths about the Mafia." *Washington Post*, May 5, 2017.

Ashurst, Sam. "Thelma Schoonmaker: Martin Scorsese's 'The Irishman' Is 'Not Goodfellas' (Exclusive)." Yahoo Movies UK. February 8, 2019. https://www.yahoo.com/entertainment/scorseses-netflix-movie-irishman-not-goodfellas-says-thelma-schoonmaker-200309938.html.

Baker, Kevin. "The First Slum in America." *New York Times*, September 30, 2001.

BBC News Staff. "Elliot Rodger: How Misogynist Killer Became Incel Hero." BBC. April 26, 2018. https://www.bbc.com/news/world-us-canada-43892189.

Bengali, Shashank. "The Global Financial Scandal That Has Spread from Malaysia to Hollywood." *Los Angeles Times*, July 10, 2019.

Biskind, Peter. *Easy Riders, Raging Bulls: How the Sex-Drugs-and-Rock-'n'-Roll Generation Saved Hollywood*. New York: Simon and Schuster, 1998.

———. "Slouching toward Hollywood." *Premiere*, November 1991.

Biskind, Peter, and Susan Linfield. "Chalk Talk." *American Film*, November 1986.

Blanchard, Ben. "China Tells Dalai Lama Again to Respect Reincarnation." Reuters. September 10, 2014. https://www.reuters.com/article/us-china-tibet/china-tells-dalai-lama-again-to-respect-reincarnation-idUSKBN0H50ST20140910.

Brody, Jane E. "Personal Health: Do's and Don'ts for Thwarting Stalkers." *New York Times*, August 25, 1998.

Brown, Mick. "Martin Scorsese Interview for *Shutter Island*." *Telegraph*, March 7, 2010.

Brzeski, Patrick. "Martin Scorsese's 'The Irishman' Lands Distributor in China." *Hollywood Reporter*, August 16, 2016.

Burke, Alison. "10 Facts about American Women in the Workforce." Brookings. December 5, 2017. https://www.brookings.edu/blog/brookings-now/2017/12/05/10-facts-about-american-women-in-the-workforce/.

Burstyn, Ellen. Commentary. *Alice Doesn't Live Here Anymore*. DVD. Directed by Martin Scorsese. Warner Home Video, 2004.

Canby, Vincent. "Film: 'New York' in a Tuneful Era." *New York Times*, June 23, 1977.

Cerone, Daniel. "Playing the End of Innocence: Movies: Juliette Lewis Surprises Critics with a Strong Performance as the Teen-aged Daughter in 'Cape Fear.'" *Los Angeles Times*, November 20, 1991.

Child, Ben. "*The Wolf of Wall Street* Criticised for 'Glorifying Psychopathic Behaviour.'" *Guardian*, December 30, 2013.

Christie, Ian. "Martin Scorsese's Testament." *Sight and Sound*, January 1996.

Chun, Rene. "How to Recreate Howard Hughes' Legendary Screening Room." *Wired*, December 17, 2015.

Chung, Jen. "Neighborhood Wants San Gennaro to Sleep with the Fishes." Gothamist. March 26, 2007. https://gothamist.com/news/neighborhood-wants-san-gennaro-to-sleep-with-fishes.

CNN Staff. "Transcript of Video Linked to Santa Barbara Mass Shooting." CNN. May 27, 2014. https://www.cnn.com/2014/05/24/us/elliot-rodger-video-transcript/index.html.

Cohen, Anne. "Does *The Irishman* Have a Woman Problem?" Refinery29. November 1, 2019. https://www.refinery29.com/en-gb/2019/11/8670267/the-irishman-anna-paquin-lines-women-dialogue?utm_source=feed&utm_medium=rss.

Coolican, J. Patrick. "Was Life Really Better When the Mob Ruled Las Vegas?" *Las Vegas Sun*, February 20, 2012.

Corliss, Richard. "Midsection: Cross Purposes." *Film Comment*, September/October 1988.

——. "Remembering Paul Newman, Humanitarian and Actor." *Time*, September 27, 2008.

Dart, John. "Church Declares 'Last Temptation' Morally Offensive." *Los Angeles Times*, August 10, 1988.

Davis, James D. "Christians Up in Arms over Movie." *South Florida Sun Sentinel*, July 30, 1988.

DeCurtis, Anthony. "What the Streets Mean." *South Atlantic Quarterly*, Spring 1992.

Demby, Gene. "How Code-Switching Explains the World." NPR. April 8, 2013. https://www.npr.org/sections/codeswitch/2013/04/08/176064688/how-code-switching-explains-the-world.

"'Departed' Producer Defends Scorsese at Oscars." Reuters. February 26, 2007. https://www.reuters.com/article/us-oscars-king/departed-producer-defends-scorsese-at-oscars-idUSN2626323420070226.

Desta, Yohana. "'This Is Overwhelming': Why Martin Scorsese Almost Didn't Make *Raging Bull.*" *Vanity Fair*, April 28, 2019.

DiCaprio, Leonardo. Endorsement video. Jordan Belfort. thewolfnetwork.com.

Donnelly, Gabrielle. "Martin Scorsese Interview: 'Catholicism Is Always in You.'" *Catholic Herald*, December 22, 2016.

Ebert, Roger. "*The Departed.*" *Chicago Sun Times*, July 6, 2007.

———. *The Great Movies*. New York: Broadway Books, 2002.

———. "I Call First." *Chicago Sun Times*, November 17, 1967.

———. "Martin Scorsese and His New York Story." *Chicago Sun-Times*, March 5, 1989.

———. *Scorsese by Ebert*. Chicago: University of Chicago Press, 2008.

———. "Scorsese's Last Temptation." *Chicago Sun Times*, July 24, 1988.

Ebiri, Bilge. "Scorsese, 'Silence,' and the Mystery of Faith." *Village Voice*, February 22, 2017.

Evans, Mike. *The Making of* Raging Bull. Phoenix, AZ: 101 Distribution, 2009.

Feinberg, Scott. "'Awards Chatter' Podcast—Robert De Niro ('The Comedian')." *Hollywood Reporter*, November 27, 2016.

Fernandez, Jay A., and Carolyn Giardina. "Making of *Hugo.*" *Hollywood Reporter*, November 15, 2011.

Freud, Sigmund. *Case Histories II*. London: Penguin Freud Library, 1988.

Galloway, Stephen. "Martin Scorsese's Journey from Near-Death Drug Addict to 'Silence.'" *Hollywood Reporter*, December 8, 2016.

Goldstein, Patrick. "Graham King on 'Hugo's' Box-Office Woes: 'It's Been Painful.'" *Los Angeles Times*, February 6, 2012.

The Graham Norton Show. Season 19, episode 9. Aired May 20, 2016, on BBC One.

Grierson, Tim. "How 'The King of Comedy' Proved Jerry Lewis Was a Great Actor." *Rolling Stone*, August 20, 2017.

Grist, Leighton. *The Films of Martin Scorsese, 1963–77: Authorship and Context*. New York: St. Martin's Press, 2000.

Harmetz, Aljean. "Ministers Vow Boycott over Scorsese Film on Jesus." *New York Times*, July 13, 1988.

Harris, Leslie M. *In the Shadow of Slavery: African Americans in New York City, 1626–1863*. Chicago: Chicago University Press, 2003.

Hart, Hugh. "*Watchmen*'s World Draws Directly from Strangelove, *Taxi Driver.*" *Wired*, March 4, 2009.

Hay, Mark. "The Strange, Centuries-Long History of Satanic Pedophile Panics." Vice. November 15, 2018. https://www.vice.com/en_us/article/59vgwa/the-strange-centuries-long-history-of-satanic-pedophile-panics.

Hemphill, Jim. "Of Tarantino and TV: The Legacy of *Goodfellas*." *Filmmaker*, April 22, 2015.

Hill, Erin. "Martin Scorsese on Leo DiCaprio: 'We Speak the Same Language.'" *Parade*, June 12, 2012.

Hinckley Jr., John. Letter to Jodie Foster. March 30, 1981.

Hiscock, John. "Martin Scorsese Faces Mounting Criticism over *The Wolf of Wall Street*." *Telegraph*, January 3, 2014.

Hodenfield, Chris. "You've Got to Love Something Enough to Kill It." *American Film*, March 1989.

Holson, Laura M. "2 Hollywood Titans Brawl over a Gang Epic." *New York Times*, April 7, 2002.

———. "Murders by Intimate Partners Are on the Rise, Study Finds." *New York Times*, April 12, 2019.

Hooton, Christopher. "*The Sopranos* and *GoodFellas* Shared 27 Actors." *Independent*, January 29, 2016.

Jackovich, Karen G. "Barbara Hershey Drops Her Hippie Past and a Name, Seagull, and Her Career Finds Wings." *People*, May 28, 1979.

Jacobs, Diane. *Hollywood Renaissance*. Lancaster, UK: Gazelle Book Services, 1977.

Kael, Pauline. *5001 Nights at the Movies*. New York: Henry Holt, 1982.

Keegan, Rebecca. "Oscars 2020: How Netflix Plans to Win Best Picture with Scorsese's Mob Drama." *Hollywood Reporter*, February 27, 2019.

Kelly, Mary Pat. "Director Martin Scorsese Blends Improvisation with Discipline in Making His Movies." *Washington Post*, February 24, 2012.

La Force, Thessaly. "I Can't Stop Watching 'Casino' and Thinking about Its Clothes." Vice. June 17, 2014. https://www.vice.com/en_us/article/xd54xd/i-cant -stop-watching-casino-and-thinking-about-its-clothes.

Lane, Anthony. "Martin Scorsese's Strained Silence." *New Yorker*, December 22, 2016.

LoBrutto, Vincent. *Martin Scorsese: A Biography*. Westport, CT: Praeger, 2007.

———. *Sound-on-Film: Interviews with Creators of Film Sound*. Westport, CT: Praeger, 1994.

Luconi, Stefano. "Forging an Ethnic Identity: The Case of Italian Americans." *Revue française d'études américaines*, no. 96 (2003): 89–101.

Macaulay, Scott. "Scorsese, De Niro, Lewis and Bernhard Recall *The King of Comedy*." *Filmmaker*, May 1, 2013.

Maslin, Janet. "Film: Martin Scorsese Ventures Back to 'Cape Fear.'" *New York Times*, November 10, 1991.

Mattix, Lori, and Michael Kaplan. "I Lost My Virginity to David Bowie." Thrillist. November 3, 2015. https://www.thrillist.com/entertainment/nation/i-lost-my-virginity -to-david-bowie.

McClintock, Pamela. "Scorsese, DiCaprio Cry 'Wolf.'" *Variety*, March 25, 2007.

McNeil, Legs, and Gillian McCain, eds. *Please Kill Me: The Uncensored Oral History of Punk*. New York: Grove Press, 1996.

Mendelson, Ben. "Inside the Debate between Netflix and Big Theater Chains over 'The Irishman.'" *Forbes*, July 31, 2019.

Mitchell, Chris. "The Killing of Murder." *New York Magazine*, January 7, 2008.

Montevecchio, Caesar A. "Silence." *Journal of Religion and Film* 21, no. 1 (April 2017).

Moore, Alan, and Dave Gibbons. *Watchmen*, no. 1. DC Comics, September 1986.

Morgenstern, Joe. "'Wolf of Wall Street' Skims the Surface of Sin." *Wall Street Journal*, December 24, 2013.

Nashawaty, Chris. "How 'Rocky' Nabbed Best Picture." *Entertainment Weekly*, February 19, 2002.

Parachini, Allan, and Dennis McDougal. "Art in the Eighties: Censorship: A Decade of Tighter Control of the Arts." *Los Angeles Times*, December 25, 1989.

Patrick, Vincent. "Not-So-Organized Crime." *New York Times*, January 26, 1986.

Pesci, Joe. "The Bronx Bull." *Raging Bull*. DVD. Directed by Martin Scorsese. MGM, 2006.

Puddicombe, Stephen. "*Taxi Driver* and the Frightening Truth about Our Current Political Climate." Little White Lies. February 19, 2017. https://lwlies.com/articles/taxi-driver-travis-bickle-alt-right-politics/.

Real, Evan. "Robert De Niro on Making 'The Irishman' with Martin Scorsese: 'It's Been a Long Time Coming.'" *Hollywood Reporter*, April 23, 2019.

Rich, Spencer. "Single-Parent Families Rise Dramatically." *Washington Post*, May 3, 1982.

Righelato, Rowan. "*Taxi Driver*: The Awkward Teen of US Cinema." *Guardian*, January 20, 2017. https://www.theguardian.com/film/filmblog/2017/jan/20/taxi-driver-america-scorsese-schrader-de-niro.

Ritman, Alex. "Jordan Belfort Says He Knew 'Wolf of Wall Street' Producers Were 'F—ing Criminals.'" *Hollywood Reporter*, January 30, 2017.

Robb, Amanda. "Anatomy of a Fake News Scandal." *Rolling Stone*, November 16, 2017.

Ruelas, Richard. "2 Arizona Arrests Have Ties to QAnon Conspiracy Theory Movement." *Arizona Republic*, August 7, 2018.

Schickel, Richard. "Brutal Attraction: The Making of *Raging Bull*." *Vanity Fair*, March 2010.

———. *Conversations with Scorsese*. New York: Alfred A. Knopf, 2011.

Schwartz, David G. "In Las Vegas, One of the Mob's Biggest Money Earners Tells All." *Forbes*, November 5, 2018.

Scorsese, Martin. American Film Institute interview. Seminar hosted by James Powers, 1975.

———. Commentary. *After Hours*. DVD. Directed by Martin Scorsese. Warner Home Video, 2004.

———. Commentary. *GoodFellas*. DVD. Directed by Martin Scorsese. Warner Home Video, 2004.

———. Commentary. *Mean Streets*. DVD. Directed by Martin Scorsese. Warner Home Video, 2004.

———. Commentary. *New York, New York*. DVD. Directed by Martin Scorsese. Warner Home Video, 2004.

———. *Filming for Your Life: Making* After Hours. Warner Home Video, 2004.

———. "*Raging Bull*: Before the Fight." *Raging Bull*. DVD. Directed by Martin Scorsese. MGM, 2006.

———. *Scorsese on Scorsese*. Revised edition. London: Faber and Faber, 2003.

Scott, Cathy. "Does the Mob Still Exist in Las Vegas? Good Question." *Psychology Today*, December 31, 2014.

"Second Chances." *Alice Doesn't Live Here Anymore*. DVD. Directed by Martin Scorsese. Warner Home Video, 2004.

Serrano, Arturo. "The Spectacle of Redemption: Guilt and Violence in Martin Scorsese's *Raging Bull*." *Studia Gilsoniana*, April–June 2015.

Shakespeare, William. *Macbeth*.

Simonton, Dr. Dean Keith. "Are Genius and Madness Related? Contemporary Answers to an Ancient Question." *Psychiatric Times*, May 31, 2005.

Smith, Gavin. "The Art of Vision: Martin Scorsese's *Kundun*." *Film Comment*, January/February 1998.

———. "Martin Scorsese Interviewed." *Film Comment*, September/October 1990.

———. "Martin Scorsese Interviewed." *Film Comment*, November/December 1993.

Sorace, Stephen. "Scorsese Says De Niro, Pacino's CGI Use in 'The Irishman' Left Him 'Concerned.'" Fox News. May 30, 2019. https://www.foxnews.com/entertainment/martin-scorsese-de-niro-pacino-the-irishman-de-aging.

Sperling, Nicole, "Inside the Debate between Netflix and Big Theater Chains over 'The Irishman.'" *New York Times*, November 1, 2019.

Stanglin, Doug. "Federal Judge Allows Would-Be Reagan Assassin John Hinckley to Live by Himself." *USA Today*, November 17, 2018.

Stolworthy, Jacob. "*The Irishman*: Martin Scorsese's 'Risky' Netflix Film to Be Released in Cinemas." *Independent*, December 3, 2018.

Swearingen, Jake. "China Will Make the Dalai Lama Reincarnate Whether He Likes It or Not." *Atlantic*, September 10, 2014.

Tapley, Kristopher. "10 Years Later: 'The Departed,' the Oscars, and the Non-Campaign Campaign." *Variety*, October 4, 2016.

Taubin, Amy. "Everything Is Form." *Sight and Sound*, February 1998.

———. "Martin Scorsese's Cinema of Obsessions." *Village Voice*, September 18, 1990.

Tonelli, Bill. "Arrivederci, Little Italy." *New York Magazine*, September 16, 2004.

———. "The Lies of the Irishman." Slate. August 7, 2019. https://slate.com/culture/2019/08/the-irishman-scorsese-netflix-movie-true-story-lies.html.

Tracey, Thomas. "2017 Was Record-Low for Homicides in New York City, with NYPD Logging Lowest Number in Nearly 70 Years." *New York Daily News*, December 31, 2017.

Turner, Christopher. "Sugar and Spice and All Things Not So Nice." *Guardian*, October 2, 2009. https://www.theguardian.com/theguardian/2009/oct/03/brooke -shields-nude-child-photograph.

Vargas-Copper, Natasha. "Canon Fodder: Martin Scorsese's *Casino*." *GQ*, November 10, 2011.

Williams, Stereo. "David Bowie and Rock 'n' Roll's Statutory Rape Problem." Daily Beast. January 17, 2016. https://www.thedailybeast.com/david-bowie-and-rock-n -rolls-statutory-rape-problem.

Willis, Chuck. *Destination America*. New York: DK, 2005.

Wilmington, Michael. "Heaven Sent." *Chicago Tribune*, January 16, 1998.

Yuster, Adam. "Robert De Niro, Leonardo DiCaprio, Jonah Hill Honor Martin Scorsese at MoMA Film Benefit." *Hollywood Reporter*, November 21, 2017.

INDEX

ABOUT THE AUTHOR

Eric San Juan has authored or coauthored twelve books and counting, including several works of film and television criticism. He examines the cinema of Alfred Hitchcock in both *A Year of Hitchcock: 52 Weeks with the Master of Suspense* and *Hitchcock's Villains: Murderers, Maniacs and Mother Issues* (Scarecrow Press, 2009 and 2013, respectively), with author Jim McDevitt, and explores the films of Akira Kurosawa with *Akira Kurosawa: A Viewer's Guide* (Rowman & Littlefield, 2018). He contributed to the pop culture philosophy of *Geek Wisdom: The Sacred Teachings of Nerd Culture* (2011) and authored both *Stuff Every Husband Should Know* and *Stuff Every Groom Should Know* (2011 and 2013, respectively). He has also independently published works of criticism on *Breaking Bad*, *Mad Men*, and *The Walking Dead* and has written two books on local history.

Following a thirteen-year career as a full-time editor and journalist, he now works as a freelance writer. In 2014, his *Philadelphia Weekly* feature "After Sandy: The Jersey Shore Two Months Later" was recognized by the Keystone Press Awards, and his work on politics, craft beer, and other wide-ranging topics has appeared in dozens of newspapers, magazines, and web publications. When he's not in his ever-growing vegetable garden, you can find him online at ericsanjuan.com, as well as on Facebook, Twitter, and other social media platforms.

Lightning Source UK Ltd.
Milton Keynes UK
UKHW011144111220
374916UK00001B/28

9 781538 127650